8/21

1

midwest

MEN, MONSTERS AND THE MODERN UNIVERSE

George Lovi and Wil Tirion's

MEN, MONSTERS AND THE MODERN UNIVERSE

Willmann–Bell, Inc.

P.O. Box 35025
Richmond, Virginia 23235
United States of America

Publishers and Booksellers

Serving Astronomers Worldwide
Since 1973

Published by Willmann-Bell, Inc.
P.O. Box 35025, Richmond, Virginia 23235

First published 1989

Printed in the United States of America

Library of Congress Cataloging-in-Publication Data

Lovi, George.
    Men, monsters, and the modern universe / George Lovi and Wil
  Tirion
       p.   cm.
    ISBN 0-943396-24-7 :
    1. Stars,–Atlases,–Amateur's manuals. 2. Constellations–Atlases-
-Amateurs' manuals. I. Tirion, Wil. II. Title.
  QB63.L68 1989
  523.8'022'3- -dc20   89-14621
                                           CIP

Preface

In even a casual review of today's popular astronomy literature you will frequently find pictures from old-time star atlases to illustrate a point. But if you want to see one of these atlases in its entirety you will have to look far and wide and even then you might not find a truly representative example.

This book began with the chance encounter of Alexander Jamieson's *Celestial Atlas* at the U.S. Naval Observatory library. Published in 1822 it appeared near the end of the $2\frac{1}{2}$ century era of old-time pictorial atlases. In addition to the maps with their mythological figures, there were tables and narratives that attempted to blend the old with the newest discoveries which were then coming at an ever accelerating rate. Most appealing was the way the atlas was produced: in convenient book form with maps designed to easily fit on a book-sized page. Other pictorial atlases of the period tended to be relatively large and unwieldy, whether bound or unbound. Additionally, the Jamieson work appeared just at the time that the sky contained the greatest number of constellations, both the traditional ancient ones recognized by Western peoples as well as a number of post-classical "modern" ones of which quite a few are no longer recognized.

Copies of Jamieson's maps were made and filed away until, again by chance, they were compared and contrasted with a modern set of charts by Wil Tirion. While the mythology of the night sky is not part of astronomy, *per se*, it remains a significant part of ancient culture, lore, and beliefs which has enjoyed a growing vogue in recent years. Also it remains with us in the way we divide up the sky into more manageable parts—today these divisions number 88. Learning 88 of anything can be a formidable undertaking and with the constellations even more so because the names themselves are not a part of everyday language. Fortunately, most of the constellations have a story of which we include samplings of the leading ones; some are among the most famous examples of ancient mythology. Remember the story and you will more easily know the constellation. Know the constellations and soon you will start to place objects within these celestial subdivisions, and the nighttime sky will come alive with a blend of our ancient past and our most up-to-date discoveries.

Therefore, the main objective of this book is to introduce you the constellations in a memorable way and to start you looking at the sky's most easily observable objects with nothing more than your eyes and possibly a pair of binoculars or a small telescope. By placing the Jamieson charts on left-hand pages and the Tirions on right-hand ones, the two sets can be compared side-by-side by lifting the intervening pages.

Since the night sky moves through a yearly cycle this book also contains a set of six seasonal star charts that are useful throughout virtually the entire populated world.

Opposite each of the Tirion *Bright Star Atlas 2000.0* charts you will find a set of tables. These list objects that are representative and, like the stars, are the more prominent examples of their particular type—many are visible with a good pair of binoculars, typical exceptions being some of the deep-sky objects and the fainter variable stars. The final tables were developed by Brian Skiff of Lowell Observatory. He is an active observer and author and his firsthand familiarity with the sky has brought that "something extra" to these listings, particularly in the selection of appropriate objects in a way cold data never can. Skiff is particularly interested in double stars and you will find them well represented in his tables. It does not take an observer long to realize that there are many ways to classify the brightness or magnitude of a non-stellar object and that a low magnitude number may not be indicative of the visibility of the object; here is where that firsthand familiarity is invaluable. To minimize this problem the list has been weighted toward those objects which are most conspicuous. The criteria used to select the objects are covered in the section immediately preceding *The Bright Star Atlas 2000.0*.

The Tirion atlas charts have straight right ascension lines which make it easy for the user to measure the positions of included objects or plot additional ones, as described at the end of page 70. This is not that simple with some atlases.

We would like to thank Brenda Corbin, Librarian of the U.S. Naval Observatory, for her help during our research at this truly priceless national treasure house, as well as Sandra Kitt, Librarian at the Richard S. Perkin Memorial Library at New York's American Museum–Hayden Planetarium, who also made her facility available and offered assistance in the preparation of this work. Additionally, we wish to express our appreciation to Steven L. Beyer, an instructor in constellation lore at the Hayden Planetarium, who read the manuscript and offered valuable comments, as did Brian Skiff. Conversations with David Fox, an active observer with the Richmond Astronomical Society, started us thinking seriously about what to include in the data tables and for this we are grateful.

Finally, we would like to acknowledge Dorrit Hoffleit who has been the principle cataloguer of the 9,096 stars that comprise the Yale *Bright Star Catalog, Fourth Edition* and is the stellar data base for *The Bright Star Atlas 2000.0*.

For Further Reading

This book concerns itself with but a relatively limited aspect of astronomy, basically the constellations as seen by both early and modern eyes. However, it is the objective of this book to entice you into further pursuit of both the lore and science of astronomy.

For information on the sometimes knotty subject of star names, the *Short Guide to Modern Star Names and Their Derivation* by Paul Kunitzsch and Tim Smart (Otto Harrassowitz, 1986) is the best currently available work; its senior author is perhaps today's leading authority on the subject. Also available is a Dover Publications reprint of the classic 19th-century work by R. H. Allen, *Star Names: Their Lore and Meaning.*

For those who wish to delve deeper into the celestial canopy than covered by the Tirion maps in this book, there is Tirion's *Sky Atlas 2000.0* (Sky Publishing Corp., 1981) which goes down to magnitude 8.0, and Tirion, Rappaport, and Lovi's *Uranometria 2000.0*, Vol. I and II (Willmann-Bell, Inc., 1987, 1988) which goes to magnitude 9.5. For detailed tabular listings of the constituents of the atlas contained in this book and *Sky Atlas 2000.0*, there is Dorrit Hoffleit's *Bright Star Catalog* (Yale University Observatory, 1982) to magnitude 6.5 and the more comprehensive *Sky Catalogue 2000.0*, Vol. 1 and 2, (Sky Publishing Corp., 1982, 1985) respectively, stars to magnitude 8.0 and double stars, variable stars, and nonstellar objects. A stellar catalogue by Barry N. Rappaport and Wayne H. Warren, Jr. is in preparation for *Uranometria 2000.0* and will contain much useful data for stars down to magnitude 9.5.

Terence Dickinson's *Nightwatch* (Camden House, 1983) is a truly unique introduction to observing the sky with and without a telescope which also offers much theoretical astronomical information. The book has lavish full-color photographs, artwork, and maps, but equally significant is the way it helps the beginner get started on the right foot. Dickinson's *The Universe... And Beyond* (Camden House, 1986) is another lavishly illustrated, although theoretical, work by this gifted Canadian author.

The three-volume *Burnham's Celestial Handbook* by Robert Burnham, Jr. (Dover Publications, 1978) is a virtual constellation-by-constellation encyclopedia of the deep sky which no serious observer should be without. Although it contains no constellation maps, the author clearly states that this work is intended as a companion for a star atlas (such as those we listed). Shorter single-volume sky guides by constellation are Menzel and Pasachoff's *A Field Guide to the Stars and Planets* (Houghton Mifflin Co., 1983), as well as Ridpath and Tirion's *Universe Guide to the Stars and Planets* (Universe Books, 1984); both contain constellation charts.

For detailed information about double and variable star observing, which this book only touches upon, there is Couteau's *Observing Visual Double Stars* (The MIT Press, 1982) and David Levy's *Observing Variable Stars: A Guide for the Beginner* (Cambridge University Press, 1989).

There is a bewildering variety of introductions to astronomy available nowadays, including a number of textbooks which treat the subject in a formal organized manner. In this category Jay Pasachoff's *Contemporary Astronomy* (Saunders College Publishing, 1989), *Exploration of the Universe* by Abell, Morrison and Wolff (Saunders College Publishing, 1987), and William Hartmann's *Astronomy: The Cosmic Journey* (Wadsworth Publishing Co., 1987) are approachable works by professional astronomers with a flair for communicating with laypeople. Hartmann, incidentally, is also an accomplished space artist who with space artist Ron Miller authored *Cycles of Fire* (Workman Publishing, 1987) another superb introduction to the cosmos with lavish color illustrations.

Steven L. Beyer's *The Star Guide* (Little Brown and Co., 1986), or Lloyd Motz and Carol Nathanson's *The Constellations* (Doubleday, 1989), present modern information in an appealing manner.

The two leading astronomy magazines are *Astronomy* and *Sky & Telescope*, the first being more layperson oriented, while the second (in which this book's co-author has a monthly "Rambling Through the Skies" column) is aimed at the more serious astronomy aficionado, observer, student, and professional; it is issued by Sky Publishing Corp. Astro-Media, the publisher of *Astronomy*, also issues three other astronomy related magazines: *Telescope Making* for the amateur telescope maker, *Deep Sky* for the serious observer and *Odyssey* for young people.

Both *Astronomy* and *Sky & Telescope*—available at many libraries and at well-stocked newsstands—include annual astronomy guides which list astronomy clubs, planetariums, museums, and other institutions and organizations where people can go to get more involved in cosmic pursuits.

Table of Contents

Introduction—The Heavenly Picture Book

The sight of a star-spangled sky on a perfectly clear moonless night is a stunning, overwhelming sight. This was especially so in earlier eras before some of the "progress" that gave rise to today's rampant atmospheric and light pollution. A common initial reaction of laypeople fortunate enough to get to see such a sky is that it's well-nigh impossible to tell one star from another. This is far from so.

Anyone—past or present—who has ever looked at the starry scene sooner or later notices that the stars' locations relative to each other do not change and, as a result, they form fixed patterns which rise, move across the sky, and set intact as if in some huge, perfectly synchronized parade.

We know today that the stars are enormously distant suns which, like our own Sun and its accompanying planets (one of which we live on), are in incessant motion. But because of their vast distances from us, these stellar movements can ordinarily be detected only by astronomers using delicate measuring procedures; the casual skywatcher would have to live many centuries—even millenia—to be able to notice changes in the patterns the stars form.

It is rather remarkable that since earliest times almost all peoples who observed the sky formed various sorts of imaginary pictures and patterns out of the unchanging stellar arrangements to help them recognize and identify the stars. These became known as *constellations* from the Latin "together" and "stars." (It is amazing how many people even today, even those informed in the sciences, confuse constellations with star clusters, which in the sky are far smaller physically related stellar gatherings.)

In the great majority of cases constellation patterns are but accidental apparent groupings of stars widely separated in space which happen to fall along a similar line of sight, just as three widely separated street lights down the block might appear to form a triangle when viewed from one's doorstep.

Forming pictures out of apparent stellar arrangements has always required a vivid imagination, not unlike the way children might perceive pictures being formed by fluffy clouds ("Say, Sis, doesn't that cloud look like a dog?"). This is because neither stars nor clouds contrive often enough to form more-or-less obvious likenesses. And here we have a fundamental truth about constellations: namely, that relatively few of them look anything like an obvious star picture. This is one of the reasons old star charts—such as those in the Jamieson *Celestial Atlas* here featured—had these fanciful pictorial outlines of people, animals, or objects around the stars of a particular constellation.

They were, in a sense, a prod to the imagination, and it may very well be that constellations are the earliest examples of what today we call "modern" art in which the viewer's imagination and mental imaging powers are called into play to perceive a picture or reality not immediately obvious.

This is a portion from one of the six charts found in Elijah H. Burritt's Geography of the Heavens *atlas printed in 1835. It is one of the few American astronomical works of the period. While the accuracy of Burritt's star positions leaves something to be desired, this work was a major influence in popularizing astronomy at the time, particularly in the United States.*

In this work we will look at the constellations through both ancient and modern eyes; in the first case with the help of the Jamieson renditions, then further on with the aid of modern star maps produced by today's master stellar cartographer, Wil Tirion. In the latter instance we see the constellations as they are regarded by today's astronomer: not as fanciful star pictures, but as definite sky areas that facilitate referring to particular locations, just as countries, states,

1

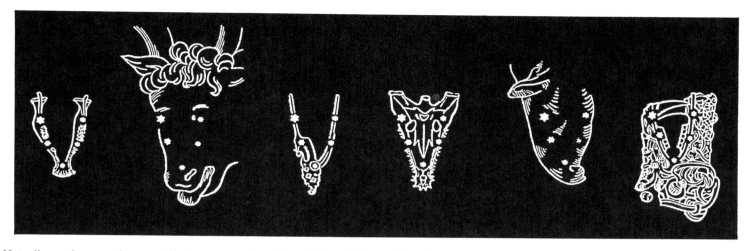

Not all peoples saw the constellations as we do. The striking V-shaped Hyades stars with Aldebaran was made into a wide variety of different constellations. Here is a sampling taken from the work From the Aratus Globe to the Zeiss Planetarium *by Helmut Werner. From left to right: a bull's mandible to the ancient Babylonians and even some present-day Borneo natives; the head of our classical Taurus; nut crackers for certain Celebes tribes; a crocodile skull for New Guineans; a tapir's head for the Aruaks in South America; and, finally, a wolf's jaw for ancient Germanic tribes in Europe.*

provinces, and other arbitrary political subdivisions on Earth help us refer to places on our planet.

In fact, since 1930 the constellations have had definite boundaries, not unlike the political ones on Earth, which were created by the International Astronomical Union (IAU) and appear on modern star maps such as Tirion's. These are lines of short dashes that run north-south and east-west which suggest those of some of the western states in the United States. However, a very common way of tracing out constellations on popular star maps is with the aid of lines connecting their principal stars to form some sort of pattern which, again, not too often suggests an obvious star picture. On the six Index-Locator charts preceding the more detailed Tirion maps (see page 74), the more prominent and better known constellations are delineated in this manner. Unlike the constellation boundaries, these stellar connecting lines are in no way "official," and they sometimes vary quite a bit from one map to another.

Today the IAU officially recognizes 88 constellations, which are listed on page 71. Yet in addition to these, there are also a number of unofficial star patterns called asterisms. Perhaps the best-known of these is the Big Dipper, whose prominent seven stars are located in the rear portion of Ursa Major, the Great Bear. In other cultures our Dipper has been regarded as some sort of wagon, carriage, chariot, or other type of vehicle; in England it has traditionally been called the Plough. Among some of the other currently popular asterisms are the "Great Square" in Pegasus, "Sickle" in Leo, "Teapot" in Sagittarius, and the prominent "Summer Triangle" formed by the bright stars Vega, Deneb, and Altair, each of which are in a separate constellation (Lyra, Cygnus, and Aquila, respectively).

The constellations we recognize today—the official 88—comprise two broad groups. Slightly over half (48) date back to ancient times and the rest are post-Renaissance creations. Among the oldest star patterns are groups such as Leo, the Lion; Hercules, the Strong Man; Orion, the Hunter-Warrior, and others. These trace back to some of the earliest

Mesopotamian civilizations in the Middle East that flourished some 5000 or more years ago. Some of these very old star pictures are even referred to in the Bible, whose "theater" was that same Middle East part of the world. For example, In Job 38:31 we read, "Canst thou bind the sweet influence of Pleiades, or loose the bands of Orion?" It refers to the famous star cluster in Taurus and the prominent three-star belt of Orion.

Regarding the perennial question as to why a certain star group was made into a particular constellation, there is good evidence that the ancients had certain master plans (or what we might today call a "systems approach") with respect to the placement of their star figures. To begin with, a pictorial resemblance was not necessarily a primary consideration; rather, these people decided that these stars here are to be a ram, those over there are an eagle. The locations in the sky of the stars in question was the main thing in a number of cases.

For example, when the Lion (later called Leo) was created five millenia ago in early Mesopotamia, its stars were situated at the Sun's location at the beginning of summer. That part of the sky is where the Sun reaches its maximum altitude, appropriate to a creature long regarded as the King of Beasts. Moreover, this time of year was associated with the fierce heat of summer. The Lion is one of those 12 special constellations of the zodiac, that band around the sky along which the Sun, Moon, and planets move and which we will discuss in greater detail further on.

There is also a rich lore associated with these ancient patterns, including a number of stories and legends of which some of the best-known ones come from ancient Greece; a sampling of these, as well as a few from other cultures, are mentioned in the commentary accompanying the Jamieson charts.

A significant milestone in the so-called "officializing" of the early Western constellations was the epic poem *Phaenomena* by Aratus of Soli, a Greek author who lived from about 314 to 245 B.C. This work is a description of the constella-

Aratus of Soli (ca. 310–245 B.C.), a Greek author and poet whose Phaenomena was one of the major influences in preserving the ancient Western constellations for posterity. This likeness, from a Soli copper coin, is perhaps the only one of Aratus in existence.

Constellation of the Big Bear

The star at the tip of the muzzle	Twins 25⅓°	N39⅚°	4
The western star of those in the two eyes	Twins 25⅚°	N43°	5
The eastern one of these	Twins 26⅓°	N43°	5
The western star of the two in the forehead	Twins 26⅙°	N47⅙°	5
The eastern one of these	Twins 26⅔°	N47°	5
The star at the end of the western ear	Twins 28⅙°	N50½°	5
The western star of the 2 in the neck	Crab ½°	N43⅚°	4
The eastern one of these	Crab 2½°	N44⅓°	4
The northern star of the 2 in the breast	Crab 9°	N42°	4
The southern one of these	Crab 11°	N44°	4–
The star in the left knee	Crab 10⅔°	N35°	3
The northern star at the end of the left forefoot	Crab 5½°	N29⅓°	3
The southern one of these	Crab 6⅓°	N28⅓°	3
The star above the right knee	Crab 5⅔°	N36°	4
The star below the right knee	Crab 5⅚°	N33°	4
Of those in the quadrilateral, the star on the back	Crab 17⅔°	N49°	2
Of these, the star on the flank	Crab 22⅙°	N44½°	2
The star at the beginning of the tail	Lion 3⅙°	N51°	3
The remaining star in the left thigh	Lion 3°	N46½°	2
The western star of those at the end of the left hind-foot	Crab 22⅔°	N29⅓°	3
The star east of this one	Crab 24⅙°	N28¼°	3
The star in the left ham	Lion 1⅔°	N35¼°	4–
The northern star of those at the end of the right hindfoot	Lion 9⅚°	N25⅚°	3
The southern star of these	Lion 10⅓°	N25°	3
The first star of the 3 in the tail after the beginning	Lion 12⅙°	N53½°	2
The middle one of these	Lion 18°	N55⅔°	2
The third one at the end of the tail	Lion 29⅚°	N25°	3
In all, 27 stars of which 6 are of 2nd magnitude, 8 of 3rd, 8 of 4th, 5 of 5th.			

This is an excerpt from Ptolemy's star catalogue in the Almagest. *Notice how the positions are keyed to the anatomy of the mythological character. From the* Great Books of the Western World. *Copyright 1952 by Encyclopaedia Britannica, Inc.*

tions then recognized, and its influence was such that the star groups he mentioned have basically survived to the present day. Aratus' epic is sort of an enlarged poetic version of a descriptive account of the constellations of a century earlier, also called *Phaenomena*, by Eudoxus of Cnidus, a Greek scientist.

It remained for the noted Alexandrian astronomer Claudius Ptolemy, who flourished in the second century, A.D., to "cast in concrete" the classic 48 constellations for the next 1½ millenia. His massive 13-volume *Almagest*, which is best known for its incorrect Earth-centered cosmos, not only touched upon just about every aspect of the heavenly scene as Ptolemy saw it, but also included a detailed star-by-star listing of those ancient 48 constellations. This compilation, translated into English along with the rest of *Almagest*, can be found in Volume 16 of *Great Books of the Western World*, published by the Encyclopaedia Britannica.

Looking at this list we see a major reason pictorial constellation outlines were necessary on old star maps; stars were largely identified by their location in the imaginary figure— "in the bear's nose," or "lady's ankle," and so on. The second, and much more practical system, was to specify a star's location with the use of celestial coordinates similar to latitude and longitude on Earth. This was also included in the Ptolemy listings.

A whole new era of constellation creation began when Western society ended its millenium-long mental siesta (known to historians as the Middle or Dark Ages) with the coming of the Renaissance. With the beginning of that period—in the late 16th century—the Danish astronomer Ty-

cho Brahe achieved unprecedented accuracy in observing the positions of heavenly bodies, and right after the beginning of the next century, in 1603, the Bavarian astronomy aficionado Johann Bayer—a lawyer by profession—produced that all-time classic, his *Uranometria*, the patriarch and most famous of the old pictorial star atlases. Largely utilizing Tycho's precise (for its era) star positions, Bayer was also able to achieve unprecedented accuracy for most of his star charts; indeed, his degree of precision equals or exceeds that of many present-day popular sky maps!

In addition to charting each of the classic 48 groups on a plate of its own, the *Uranometria* introduced a dozen new constellations in the far-southerly heavens, created in 1596 by the Dutch explorer Pieter Dirckszoon Keyser. Bayer also originated the star-labeling system, still used today, of assigning lower-case Greek letters to the principal stars of a constellation, with Roman letters also used here and there when the Greek alphabet was exhausted in a star-rich constellation. Yet on the back of each chart folio, Bayer lists a group's individual stars not only with its Greek label and position, but also its "astronomical anatomy"—its location in the fanciful figure.

Bayer's *Uranometria* inaugurated the nearly 2½-century-long era in which pictorial star charts flourished. In the course of this period, a number of additional post-classical new constellations were introduced, largely involving relatively faint stars left over after the classical groups were created. The 17th century German-Polish astronomer Johannes Hevelius and the 18th century Frenchman Nicolas Louis de Lacaille were together responsible for most of the new groups

This fine engraving of Auriga appeared in the famous Uranometria star atlas by Johann Bayer in 1603. While not the first printed star atlas, it was the first one to use the much improved star positions from Tycho Brahe's star catalog. The dark area at the bottom is part of the zodiacal band, within which the Sun, Moon, and planets appear to wander. U.S. Naval Observatory, Washington, D.C.

that still exist today, with the latter's contribution being a number of patterns around the south celestial pole representing inanimate objects, largely scientific objects and tools.

By the beginning of the 19th century, the sky was saturated with an all-but-unbelievable aggregation of uranographical[1] debris that were called constellations, some of them made up of some of the faintest leftover stars. There was a Printing Press, Electrical Machine, Hot-Air Balloon, and more, created as a celestial celebration of the technological wonders that were appearing in ever-increasing abundance. (Prussia's enigmatic intellectual tyrant, Frederick the Great, even stated before his death in 1786 that man has discovered just about everything in science and technology!)

Jamieson's *Celestial Atlas* appeared when the sky had this maximum profusion of constellations. Yet as the 19th century approached its midpoint, the pictorial star chart began being phased out, with the Jamieson work being one of the last such efforts—another reason we chose to reproduce it.

Perhaps one of the undertakers of the pictorial star map was the famous English astronomer John Herschel (son of the illustrious William Herschel, who, among the things, discovered the planet Uranus). He had this to say in his popular, widely-read 19th century book *Outlines of Astronomy* in discussing constellations:

> Of course we do not here speak of those uncouth figures and outlines of men and monsters, which are usually scribbled over celestial globes and maps, and serve, in a rude and barbarous way, to enable us to talk of groups of stars, or districts in the heavens, by names which, though absurd or puerile in their origin, have obtained a currency from which it would be difficult to dislodge them.

Although this classic comment helped provide the title for this book, today there is considerably greater cultural tolerance for the artistic efforts of earlier eras than in Herschel's more rigid times; witness, for example, the current proliferation of all types of museums, collections, even architectural landmark-preservation laws.

So, let us in this spirit enjoy the skies as our ancestors pictured it, then proceed to look at it through the eyes of modern astronomy through the agency of Wil Tirion's superb cartography.

Happy stargazing!

---

[1] The word "uranography" refers to celestial cartography.

An Overview of the Sky

We live in a universe of staggering size—one so immense that distances within it are typically stated in units such as *light years*, which indicates how far light travels in one year. Moving at some 186,000 miles per second, it covers some 5.9 trillion miles—that's 5,900,000,000,000—each year. And today's largest and most sophisticated telescopes can peer some 20,000,000,000 (20 billion) light-years into the cosmic void. Space is indeed the final frontier!

When each day our turning Earth carries us into its shadow, the light of our dazzling daytime star—the Sun—is blocked; we experience night, and, assuming the sky is clear, we can look out at this universe. The immense distances of the stars and other bodies gives us sort of a feeling that they are all attached to the inside surface of an enormous globe, half of which is visible, or above the horizon, at any given time and place when we're on the surface of the Earth. (This, of course, assumes a perfectly flat "sea type" horizon.) Therefore the visible celestial hemisphere seems to be a dome over our heads. Indeed, in a planetarium the heavenly bodies as seen with the unaided eye are projected onto just such a hemispherical dome which forms the ceiling of this "star theater"; the projection apparatus can show you the sky as seen from anywhere on Earth at any hour of the day or night at any date of the year. Therefore, for anyone interested in the sky, a planetarium is well worth visiting.

In order to map the positions against the sky of the myriads of heavenly bodies, astronomers actually do make use of just such an imaginary *celestial sphere*, which is but a mathematical entity. It's an infinitely huge globe larger than the entire physical universe. When we thus speak of a body's "position" in the sky (which enables us to plot it on star maps such as those in this book), we are actually referring to its *direction* from us on Earth. In effect, a line-of-sight is drawn from Earth to the body and continued infinitely outward until it touches the inside of the celestial sphere. This defines its position. Indeed, there are commercially available physical models (globes) of the celestial sphere.

The visible hemisphere above our horizon depends on our location on Earth as well as the date and time. Directly at its center is the overhead, or *zenith*, point, and 90° away from it all around us is the horizon. Regarding the observer's location on Earth, the major factor is the latitude, or distance north or south of the equator. In fact, as long as you're on the same parallel of latitude anywhere on Earth, you will see the same stars and constellations at the same positions in the sky relative to the horizon (compass direction and altitude) at the same local time on the same date. That is to say, that if, for example, you're in Denver, Philadelphia, Ankara (Turkey), or Beijing (China), if you look at the sky on January 15 around 10 p.m. local time, you will see the brilliant constellation Orion directly in the south a little more than

A modern "see-through" celestial globe called Starship Earth[T.M.] With an Earth globe and horizon ring inside, this device greatly facilitates understanding and visualizing Earth-sky relationships. (Globe cartography by George Lovi.)

halfway between horizon and zenith. All these cities are at about 40° north latitude. (However, the locations relative to the remote starry background of nearby solar system bodies such as the Sun, Moon, and planets will vary slightly for those cities at a particular time on a particular date because of their orbital motions, most noticeably for the nearby Moon.)

Because the Earth orbits the Sun in the course of a year, its night side faces different directions on different dates. This is the basic reason the appearance of the night sky changes as the year progresses. As seen at a particular hour each night, the stars drift in a westward direction from one night to the next. To facilitate locating the main stars and constellations during the year, we have provided a set of six general evening sky maps starting on page 74. Each chart covers two months according to the time schedules accompanying them. There are also horizon scales along the margins indicating where these lines fall over a great range of latitudes when you face in a northerly or southerly direction. This set of charts also serves as an overall guide on where to look for the most prominent stars and constellations stars, whereas the Jamieson and Tirion atlas charts cover smaller areas of the sky in greater detail.

Celestial Coordinates

Our celestial sphere—or sky—contains a network of grid lines similar to longitude and latitude on Earth which are called, respectively, right ascension and declination. They can be seen on both the Jamieson and Tirion charts as solid lines crisscrossing the maps; the former contains a secondary system, shown with dashed lines, which will be described presently.

We wish to emphasize at the outset that familiarity with these lines is *not* a prerequisite for the layperson to be able to locate stars and constellations, despite what certain other books imply, any more than the ability to read printed scores is necessary to enjoy hearing musical works. Like music, art, or virtually any other area of knowledge, astronomy can be approached on a number of levels. This is one reason our six general sky charts omit these grid lines. However, for those who are interested, we offer here a basic description of celestial coordinates.

If we extend the Earth's axis in either direction out to the celestial sphere, the points where it touches the inside of this globe form the north and south celestial poles. If you were to stand at the Earth's north pole, for example, the north celestial pole is at your zenith. By similarly extending the Earth's equator outward we define the *celestial equator* of the sky. It can be found on Tirion Charts 3 to 8 as a horizontal line marked 0° crossing the center of the map. And if you were located at the Earth's equator, its celestial counterpart would also pass directly overhead while reaching down to the east and west points on the horizon. In fact, regardless of your latitude, the equator always meets the horizon exactly east and west even though it makes different angles with the horizon at different latitudes. At the poles, however, it coincides with the horizon.

Just as there is a celestial equator, there are also corresponding celestial "latitude" circles representing *declination* running parallel to it, and numbered the same way as its terrestrial counterparts: 0° to 90° north and south of the equator. Just as for an observer on the equator the celestial equator passes directly overhead, so elsewhere do declination circles of the same numerical value as your latitude. If, for example, you're at 40° north, then the +40° declination circle passes through your zenith, along with any star or other object that happens to have a declination of +40°.

The celestial equivalent of longitude, right ascension, is not that simple. Terrestrial longitude is measured in degrees east and west of an arbitrary prime meridian (0°) which runs through Greenwich, England, and is numbered to 180° directly opposite in the Pacific Ocean. Right ascension, on the other hand, is numbered in hours and minutes of time eastward from the point where the Sun crosses the celestial equator at the beginning of northern spring. This point is called the March equinox, and can be found where the 0^h right ascension circle crosses the celestial equator (0°) on Tirion Charts 3 and 8. Also passing through this intersection is the slanting dashed line called the *ecliptic*, which represents the Sun's path against the sky during the year.

These right ascension hour values are based on *sidereal*, or star time, which is slightly different from that on your wrist; it runs four minutes faster per day than the solar-based civil

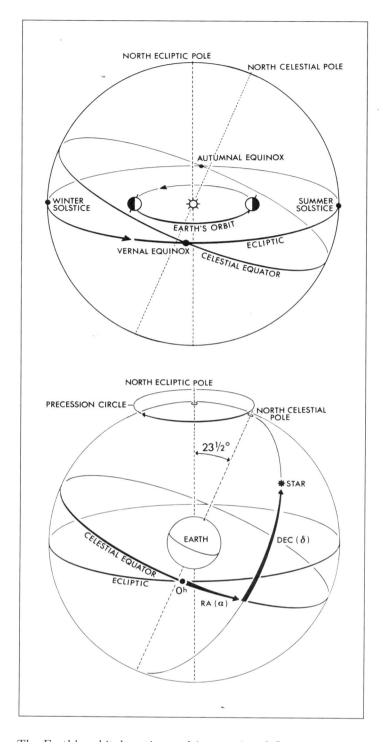

The Earth's orbital motion and its rotation define, respectively, the ecliptic and equatorial coordinate systems. The celestial sphere upon which these coordinates are projected is infinitely large, so the Earth is in effect always in its center. The bottom diagram shows that the celestial equivalent of longitude is right ascension (RA or α), which is measured eastward from the March or vernal equinox (0^h) along the celestial equator. The equivalent of latitude is declination (Dec. or δ) which, just as on Earth, is reckoned north and south of the equator. However, unlike the longitude and latitude on Earth which remains fixed over time, the entire coordinate grid of hour and declination circles precess generally westward around the sky over a period of about 25,800 years. Accordingly, a particular celestial coordinate location is also time dependent. (Diagrams by Wil Tirion).

time we live by. In fact, when the Earth exactly completes one rotation on its axis, it represents the passage of one sidereal day, which is 23 hours and 56 minutes by our watches. However, since in that period the Earth has been traveling in its curved orbit, the Sun's position against the sky has shifted slightly eastward (nearly one degree), so the Earth must rotate a bit more—the equivalent of four minutes—to present the same face to the Sun again.

In any case, these hour circles of sidereal time serve as the celestial equivalent of longitude and are used, along with declination, to specify a celestial body's position against the sky. For example, the brightest star in our sky, Sirius, is located at $6^h45^m09^s$, declination $-16°42'58''$. Please note: with right ascension the secondary and tertiary units represent minutes and seconds of *time*; with declination they are minutes and seconds of *arc* (they're not the same). Sirius can be found on the Tirion Chart 4, and both its position, as well as that of any other star or object on the map, can be read by lining up the object with the margin calibrations using a straightedge. However, on such small-scale charts positions cannot be read to anywhere near the accuracy with which object's positions are listed, as we just cited with Sirius.

One more thing: The latitude and longitude of a city on Earth is virtually fixed over periods of time. Not so with the stars. The Earth's axis wobbles like a slowing-down top once every 25,800 years in a motion called *precession*, which causes the entire coordinate grid of hour and declination circles to creep generally westward year after year. Therefore, star charts have to be plotted for a particular coordinate epoch or *equinox*, which is always that of a particular calendar year. The Tirion charts are plotted for equinox 2000, so the stars will be in exactly the plotted positions in relation to the grid system during that year, which is also when the cited position of Sirius in the previous paragraph applies. However, this only really matters to observers with precisely mounted telescopes equipped with setting circles; for most users of this work the very slight differences between the stars' current-year positions and that of 2000 is immaterial. It would also be instructive to compare the right ascensions and declinations of the stars on the Jamieson atlas with those on the Tirion; there is practically a two-century shift between the two.

We might also mention that in former times right ascension was also specified in degrees running eastward from the March equinox, with 1^h representing $15°$, 2^h equaling $30°$, and so on. This alternate system, which has somewhat fallen into disuse today, can be seen on the Jamieson charts along with the conventional hour-based scale. Yet in recent times there has been somewhat of a revival of the degree-based right ascension scale by computer users, who find its direct numbering system (albeit with decimal fractions of a degree) more convenient than the conventional time-based mixed-unit system. A computer can readily convert back and forth between the two.

The Ecliptic System

To show how ironically confusing things can sometimes get, there is another celestial coordinate scheme called *longitude*

and latitude which is *not* the equivalent of right ascension and declination (which is the heavenly equivalent of terrestrial longitude and latitude). It was the primary way of specifying celestial locations by Western societies during ancient and Medieval times, and uses the ecliptic as its "equator." On the Jamieson charts this older ecliptic-based coordinate grid is shown with dashed lines and runs at various angles against the right ascension and declination gridwork. Such dual-gridded charts were quite common during much of the 17th, 18th, and 19th centuries. The Tirion charts contain a vestige of the ecliptic system by calibrating that line for each 10° of celestial longitude. This earlier scheme has remained particularly useful for specifying the positions of the Sun, Moon, planets, and other solar system bodies such as comets, and—if truth be told—the casting of horoscopes for astrological purposes.

Other Coordinate Systems

Running approximately down the middle of the Milky Way band on the Tirion charts is another calibrated line of alternate dots and dashes. This is the *galactic equator*, and represents the approximate plane of our huge flattened Milky Way galaxy. It also has its own gridwork of galactic longitude and latitude (not shown) as well as poles; these poles are indicated on Tirion Charts 3 and 6 as crosses marked SGP and NGP, which mean respectively, South Galactic Pole and North Galactic Pole. The galactic coordinate system is a specialized scheme used by astronomers who study our Milky Way system and the distribution of certain objects in relation to it, both in space itself and against the celestial background.

Navigators make use of the altazimuth system, which stipulates the altitude and azimuth of a heavenly body in relation to the horizon. Azimuth is measured in degrees from north (0°), with east, south, and west being 90°, 180°. and 270°, respectively. Altitude is simply the elevation in degrees above the horizon, with the zenith being 90°. This scheme has a major defect for ordinary astronomical purposes in that the altazimuth coordinates of celestial objects change constantly as a result of the rotating Earth.

Also, navigators have modified the right ascension coordinates into their own Sidereal Hour Angle (SHA), which is numbered in degrees *westward* from the March equinox—the direct opposite of the already-discussed alternate astronomical degree system which increases eastward. With SHA, the 23^h circle becomes $15°$, 22^h is $30°$, and so on down the line.

Stellar Brightnesses

Even the casual skywatcher is aware of major differences in the brightnesses of the stars; the term used to express it is *magnitude*. The ancient Greek astronomer Hipparchus set up an arbitrary numerical scale for stellar magnitudes with six divisions, or steps. The brightest stars were designated as being first magnitude, the faintest as sixth. This was originally a relatively rough system based on eye estimates and survived for many centuries. After the appearance of the telescope in the early 17th century, astronomers were able to observe an enormous number of stars far beyond the naked-eye limit, and extended the magnitude scale further. Today's largest instruments can detect stars well beyond the 20th magnitude.

It wasn't until the 19th century that this magnitude scale was refined and placed on an exact mathematical basis. The distinguished British astronomer Sir John Herschel called attention to the fact that a typical first-magnitude star is just 100 times brighter than a sixth. In 1856 another British astronomer, Norman Pogson, first defined the magnitude system mathematically by stipulating that two stars that differ in brightness by a factor of exactly 100 shall differ in magnitude by exactly five (e.g. 1.0–5.0, 2.8–7.8, and so on). Pogson thus set up a logarithmic, or ratio, scale in which a difference of 1.0 magnitude represents a brightness difference of just over $2\frac{1}{2}$ (actually the fifth root of 100, or 2.512 . . .).

The accompanying table shows how the ratios of brightness and magnitudes compare. For example, how many times brighter is a magnitude 1.8 star than one of magnitude 4.4? Since their magnitudes differ by 2.6, we see in the table that this value corresponds to a brightness difference of 10.96— nearly 11 times.

For those with a mathematical bent, the formula expressing this relationship is

$$\frac{B}{b} = \left(100^{0.2}\right)^{m-M}$$

where B and M represent the brightness and magnitude, respectively, of the more luminous star, while b and m represent these values for the fainter star. This equation, incidentally, is easy to solve with one of those numerous inexpensive pocket scientific calculators.

This magnitude scale also extends into negative values; indeed, although Hipparchus and numerous others after him designated Sirius as a first-magnitude star, refined measurements in modern times places it in the –1 category; it's more precise value is –1.46 (with today's photoelectric photometers, astronomers can measure stellar magnitudes to hundredths and even thousandths; the best visual observers do well to detect a tenth-magnitude difference in stellar brightnesses). Extending the scale further into negative values, the brilliant planet Venus can gleam as bright as –4.6, the full Moon stands at –12.5, and the Sun at –26.5. Remember, each whole magnitude step represents a brightness difference of some $2\frac{1}{2}$ times, so, if it isn't already obvious, here is a mathematical warning that the Sun is one star we should never gaze at casually.

The Tirion charts show all stars down to about magnitude 6.5, which approximately represents the faintest normal eyes can detect under clear, moonless, pollution-free skies (an increasingly rare commodity these days). As is a common practice on present-day star charts, stars are shown as round dots

MAGNITUDE-BRIGHTNESS EQUIVALENTS			
Magn. Diff.	Light Ratio	Magn. Diff.	Light Ratio
0.1	1.10	3.4	22.91
0.2	1.20	3.5	25.12
0.3	1.32	3.6	27.54
0.4	1.45	3.7	30.20
0.5	1.58	3.8	33.11
0.6	1.74	3.9	36.31
0.7	1.91	4.0	39.81
0.8	2.09	4.1	43.65
0.9	2.29	4.2	47.86
1.0	2.51	4.3	52.48
1.1	2.75	4.4	57.54
1.2	3.02	4.5	63.10
1.3	3.31	4.6	69.18
1.4	3.63	4.7	75.86
1.5	3.98	4.8	83.18
1.6	4.37	4.9	91.20
1.7	4.79	5.0	100.00
1.8	5.25	5.5	158.49
1.9	5.75	6.0	251.19
2.0	6.31	6.5	398.11
2.1	6.92	7.0	630.96
2.2	7.59	7.5	1,000.00
2.3	8.32	8.0	1,584.96
2.4	9.12	8.5	2,584.9
2.5	10.00	9.0	3,981.1
2.6	10.96	9.5	6,309.6
2.7	12.02	10.0	10,000.0
2.8	13.18	11.0	25,119
2.9	14.45	12.0	63,095
3.0	15.85	13.0	158,489
3.1	17.38	14.0	398,107
3.2	19.05	15.0	1,000,000
3.3	20.89	20.0	100,000,000

whose sizes differ according to whole magnitude steps. Under this system, for example, any star from magnitude 1.50 to 2.49 is shown as second magnitude with the appropriate size dot; a third-magnitude symbol covers those stars between 2.50 and 3.49, and so on. Despite their being able to specify stellar magnitudes to hundredths or thousandths, today's astronomers will still often tend to refer to stars by rounded-off whole magnitudes in casual conversation (such-and-such is a "4th-magnitude star," etc.)

One of the attractions of old charts such as Jamieson's is their sometimes considerably more artistic method of portraying stars, with ornate multiple-point symbols, yet even these varied in size according to magnitude.

A
CELESTIAL ATLAS
by
Alexander Jamieson

STEREOGRAPHIC PROJECTION OF THE NORTHERN CELESTIAL HEMISPHERE ON THE PLANE OF THE EQUINOCTIAL.

PLATE I.

Published Feb.1.1822 by G.&W.B. Whitaker T.Tindell, & H.Butler London.

Drawn by A.Jamieson, A.M. 1822.

Plate I

We begin here our exploration of the starry heavenly vault with the first of Jamieson's picturesque atlas charts. As we go along, we will regularly refer to the Tirion chart that covers the same portion of the sky; his maps, however, mostly include larger segments of the celestial sphere than all but the very first and last Jamieson charts (Plates I and XXVIII).

The first of the Jamieson plates covers the entire northern hemisphere of the sky with the north celestial pole in the center and the celestial equator forming the outer rim. This is actually the way the sky appears at the Earth's north pole, with the celestial pole directly overhead (at the zenith) and the celestial equator coinciding with the horizon. Here every direction you face is south, no star rises and sets, each star moves parallel to the horizon at a constant altitude (which is the same numerically as its declination) as the Earth rotates. The only celestial objects that rise and set at the Earth's north pole are the Sun, Moon, planets, and other solar system bodies that move independently against the starry background; these motions are what causes them to rise and set at the pole, not the Earth's rotation. Yet the Sun remains above the horizon for six months at a time, the Moon for some two weeks each month, and the planets for months, years or decades at a stretch.

Notice the heavy ecliptic circle arching across the chart. It is calibrated with both celestial longitude as well as the Sun's approximate position along its length during the year. (This varies slightly from one year to the next, largely due to the difference in the number of days our years have: 365 in a common year, 366 during leap year.) Today we rarely find any kind of sky chart that has the ecliptic calibrated in calendar dates; however, this is virtually universal on planetarium projectors as well as on certain celestial globes. The range of dates along the ecliptic on Plate I runs from March 20th to September 23rd—the beginning of northern spring to the onset of fall. This is the six-month period during which the Sun is continuously above the horizon at the north pole.

Rather interesting is that on this Jamieson plate the ecliptic—rather than equatorial—system forms the primary coordinate grid, with a circle for each 10° of longitude and latitude indicated with lines of short dashes. However, a right ascension scale is included along the celestial equator around the periphery using both time and degree values. A declination "ruler" (called "Vernal Colure") can be seen extending upwards from the celestial pole. It touches the equator right at the vernal equinox point (March 20). The term "colure"— not often used today—refers to a right ascension circle that passes through one of the season points; there are three others on this chart without declination calibrations and they are 90° (or six hours) apart. With the aid of a strip of paper or dividers placed against the "Vernal Colure" calibrations and swung radially from the celestial pole, the declination of any star or object on this chart can be read off.

Notice the title Jamieson gave this chart, with the curved label along the upper rim: "Stereographic Projection of the North Celestial Hemisphere on the Plane of the Equinoctial." The first part of the title refers to the map projection used for this plate, which is a grid system that shows the constellation patterns with minimum distortion; the term "equinoctial" was formerly synonymous with the celestial equator and has also largely fallen into disuse, except at times by navigators.

Jamieson's Plate I, for some reason, is not plotted as accurately as his subsequent more detailed charts of individual sky areas. However, it nevertheless provides a useful overview of the sky north of the celestial equator. Compare it with Tirion's northern hemisphere of the sky on the stereographic projection, plus an extra 10° below the equator to provide an overlap with the southern index map (pages 102–3). However, Tirion's plotting precision is considerably superior!

PLATE II

Magnitude of the Stars

Booke 1 von 31 Strand

A. Jamieson 1820.

Plate II

Here is a more detailed look at the constellations in the more immediate vicinity of the north celestial pole, which is located at top center.

This chart, like the other detailed ones in the Jamieson set, has a complete dual grid system of both equatorial coordinates (solid) and ecliptic (dashed). Just below center, surrounded by Draco, the Dragon, is the north ecliptic pole, which is 90° from the ecliptic itself (which is considerably outside the boundaries of this map) or in a direction directly perpendicular to the plane of the Earth's orbit.

Just to the left of the north pole is Polaris, or the North Star, which is also at the end of the Little Bear's (Ursa Minor's) extended tail. Back in 1820, the coordinate epoch for which Jamieson constructed his work, Polaris was 1°39′ from the pole; for equinox 2000 (Tirion's), the precessional motion of the Earth's axis has crept the pole to within 0°44′ of the North Star. Refer to Tirion Chart 2, which incidentally, happens to cover a rather similar sky area—although slightly greater in extent—than this Jamieson plate. In the year 2102, the celestial pole will pass closest to Polaris, 0°28′ away.

The principal stars of Ursa Minor form the popular Little Dipper asterism, whereas towards the chart's right margin is the more prominent Big Dipper pattern, which forms the hindquarters and long tail of the Greater Bear, Ursa Major, which is featured on Plate VI. This famous Big Dipper asterism is called the Plough or Great Wain in England, and is regarded as some sort of wagon, carriage, or other vehicle in other countries and cultures. In our own country, the Big Dipper and North star are depicted on the flag of Alaska.

An odd astronomical anomaly of the two celestial bears is their long tails; one early Greek legend states that this occurred because when the king of the gods, Zeus, lifted these creatures into the sky, he grabbed them by their stubby tails (to avoid their teeth and claws) which stretched on the long pull up to heaven! However, as we shall see, these are hardly the only strange creatures that found their way into the sky.

One of these winds its way between the bears—the already-referred-to Draco. This is another ancient constellation, and although dragons were commonly pictured as hav-ing lizard-like bodies with limbs, the heavenly version has almost always been depicted as serpentlike. He also played a major role in early legends, including guarding the Garden of the Hesperides with its golden apples. In the sky he was given the crucial role of guarding the north ecliptic pole, a vital astronomical and astrological spot to earlier peoples because it represents the convergence of all the signs of the zodiac when extended northward; also, it should be remembered that to early Western cultures the ecliptic, not equatorial, coordinate system was the most important one.

At the upper left corner we see Cassiopeia, the mythological Queen of Ethiopia, while her husband, King Cepheus, lies between her and the Dragon. They figure in a prominent legend involving their daughter Andromeda and suitor Perseus, both of which are featured on the next plate (III).

This chart, like a number of other Jamieson plates, contains several obsolete constellations—ones no longer officially recognized and thereby excluded from modern sky maps. There is Custos Messium, the Guardian of the Harvests; and Tarandus, the Reindeer; both can be found immediately to the right of Cassiopeia. Another outmoded constellation on Plate II is Quadrans Muralis, the Mural Quadrant, located near the lower-right corner. This represents an astronomical instrument that was used to measure star positions from roughly the Renaissance period through the 19th century. We will encounter a number of other constellations based on instruments, gadgets, and other inanimate objects, of which some still exist, others do not.

On Plate II, as well as subsequent ones, it will be noticed that some constellation outline drawings are done more prominently than others. These are the "featured" groups on the particular chart, which on Plate II includes Ursa Minor, Cassiopeia, Tarandus, Cepheus, Draco, and Custos Messium. The other constellations on the plate, rendered in less conspicuous or more subdued style, are featured on other charts. In the original Jamieson work, each chart is accompanied by textual material not only discussing the "spotlighted" constellations on the plate, but there is also a listing of their member stars which includes their positions for 1820, along with other astronomical information.

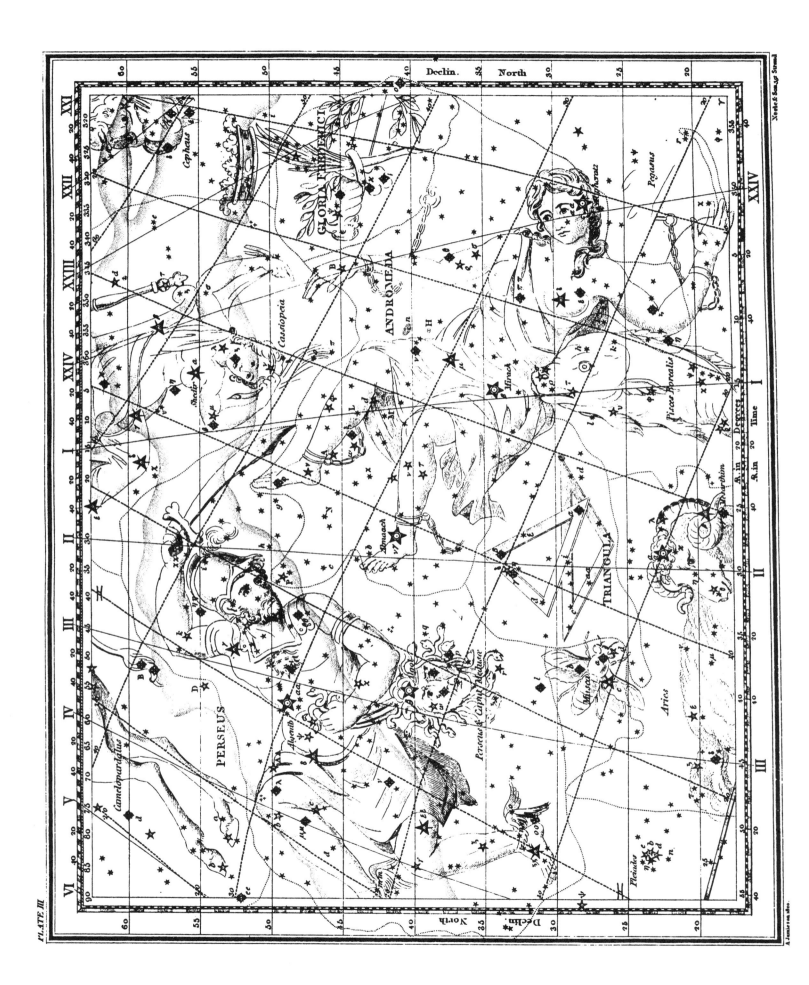

PLATE III

Plate III

Two important constellations hold "center stage" here: Perseus, the Champion; and Andromeda, the Princess. This part of the sky can be found around the uppermost third portion of Tirion Chart 3; yet the stars along the top of Jamieson Plate III are on Tirion Chart 1.

In the famous early Greek story, Andromeda's mother, Queen Cassiopeia (which can be found along the center of the top edge of this plate and whose main stars form a characteristic broad "W" pattern), boasted that her beauty exceeded that of the fabled Sea Nymphs. This enraged Sea God Neptune, who demanded that in retribution Cassiopeia sacrifice her daughter to Cetus, the Sea Monster (Plate XXIII), by chaining her to seacoast rocks in order for the beast to devour her. Otherwise, Cetus will ravage the coast. We see here the chains attached to Andromeda's outstretched arms, and for this reason she has sometimes been referred to as the Chained Lady.

As the story proceeds, just as Cetus approaches Andromeda and prepares to dispatch her, the Hero of the Story appears "in the nick of time"—Perseus. He was on a mission to find and behead the Gorgon Medusa, another type of mythological monster in the form of a lady with snakes for hair. Moreover, anyone who gazed at her face turned instantly to stone. (To avoid this, Perseus carried a shiny shield and took aim at the sleeping Gorgon's head by looking at its reflection in the shield.) While returning from this mission with his grisly trophy, Perseus was flying over the Ethiopian seacoast with the aid of winged sandals just as Cetus approached Andromeda. He swooped down, held the Gorgon's head in front of the Sea Monster, who upon gazing at it turned into an immobile rock sculpture of his former likeness. After thus rescuing Andromeda, Perseus married her and they "lived happily ever after." Cepheus, Cassiopeia, Andromeda, and Perseus have been long known as the Royal Family of the Sky because of this legend.

Astronomically, Andromeda is famous for a prominent galaxy that is situated among its stars. On the Jamieson plate it can be found as a hazy oval patch just under the letter "A" in the word "Andromeda." On Tirion Chart 3 it is labeled M31, its number in the famous Messier catalogue of deep-sky objects. For a number of centuries—actually until only after World War II—this object was usually called the "Andromeda Nebula." The term "nebula" was applied to any hazy non-stellar smudge-like object, whether an actual cloud of interstellar gas (a true nebula) or an enormous galactic system as is the one in Andromeda.

The Andromeda galaxy is the closest major galactic system to the one we live in, the Milky Way, and is a virtual next-door neighbor in terms of cosmic distances; it's just over two million light-years away. It's believed to have some 400 billion or more stars, which is quite a bit in excess of our home galaxy. On a clear, dark, moonless night far from light and other sky pollution, it can be glimpsed with the unaided eye as a fuzzy patch, which binoculars enhance. On long-exposure photographs made with sizable observatory telescopes, the Andromeda galaxy is a dramatic object indeed.

Plate II contains two obsolete constellations: Gloria Frederici, Frederick's Glory a decorative mace-like sword in honor of Prussia's Frederick, the Great, and Musca, the Fly; the first group—which is one of those featured on this plate—is near the right margin, while our fly is towards the lower left (it is not one of the "featured" constellations on this chart). Incidentally, there is still a fly in the sky, but in the southern heavens just beneath the Southern Cross (Plate XXVIII). Originally, when there were two of these creatures among the stars, the northern one (as shown here) was called Musca Borealis, the Northern Fly; the other was Musca Australis, the Southern Fly, which now is simply labeled Musca as there's no longer any ambiguity as to which is which.

Between Andromeda and Musca is a group called Triangula, the Triangles; today it is simply Triangulum, the (singular) Triangle. Here is an example, by no means the only one, of a constellation that changed its name over a period of time.

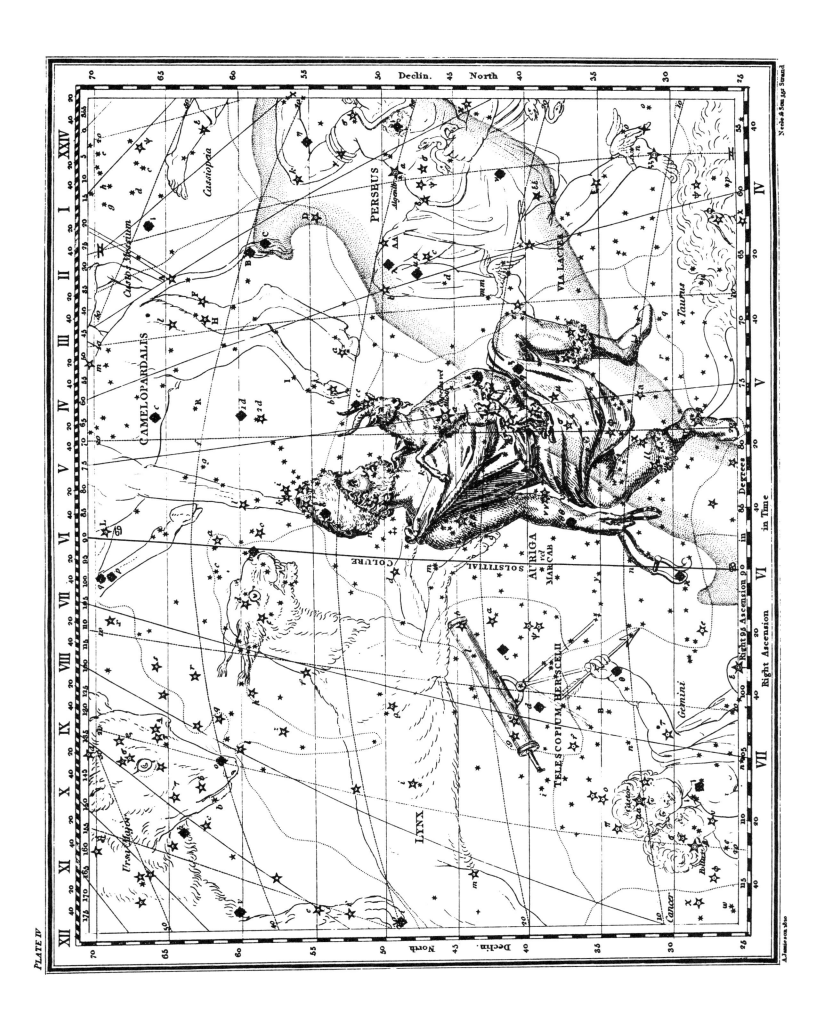

PLATE IV

Plate IV

Featured on this chart is the classic constellation Auriga, the charioteer, also called the Wagoner on some old maps. The area of sky covered by this Jamieson plate can be found at the very top of Tirion Chart 4, although the Jamieson version extends farther north.

Auriga is shown holding a goat and its kids, and these creatures are shown here, as well as on other old star maps, at a grossly disproportionate small size in relation to the human figure. The goat is no larger than a house cat and its kids fit neatly into Auriga's left palm! In certain types of early art, such creative exaggeration was not that rare, with gods and special heroes often rendered outsized.

The brightest star in this constellation is Capella, a prominent yellow luminary which dominates the overhead heavens on winter evenings as seen from mid-northern latitudes. Its name means "the Little She-Goat" in Latin since—as our chart suggests—it as been known as the "Goat Star" to a number of early peoples. Capella's Latin name is an exception in stellar nomenclature, since most of today's surviving appellations are of Arabic origin.

There are several early legends concerning our celestial charioteer, of which one of the better-known ones has him represent Erichthonius, a son of the mythological King Vulcan of Athens, who was credited with being one of the first to harness four horses to a chariot, that popular ancient vehicle. Incidentally, the transverse distance between this vehicle's wheels—or gauge—was often 4 feet, $8\frac{1}{2}$ inches (1,435 millimeters), a measurement that has survived to the present time as the most commonly adopted railroad gauge!

Another interesting sidelight is that during the 19th century some astronomers thought they detected a planet orbiting the Sun closer than the innermost known planet, Mercury, and even gave it the name Vulcan after the just-cited mythological ruler. We now know Vulcan does not exist; however, in the popular *Star Trek* stories it is the name of a fictitious planet somewhere in interstellar space which is the home of a highly logical pointy-eared race.

Jamieson omitted on Plate IV one of Auriga's principal naked-eye stars, Iota (ι), which is located in the Charioteer's left (to the right) boot. However; it can be seen at the top-center of Plate XIV; where Auriga's feet are visible below that chart's upper margin.

The prominent star in Auriga's other boot is Beta (β) Tauri, which has the name Elnath, and marks the tip of Taurus, the Bull's upper horn as seen on Plate XIV. However, in Jamieson's era and a number of previous centuries this star was regarded as "common" to both Taurus and Auriga; that is, belonging to both constellations. This is no longer the case, since today *no* star is shared by two constellations. This is a consequence of the creation of those official constellation boundaries by the International Astronomical Union, adopted in 1930, to which we earlier referred. Yet during the time of Jamieson, star charts—including his—often contained loose "unofficial" constellation boundaries which on his maps can be seen as curvy dotted lines wandering among the stars. These earlier boundaries were never exactly the same from one atlas to the next, and this sometimes caused confusion regarding to which constellation a certain star belongs.

In fact, in ancient and Medieval times something like 10 percent of the visible stars were not assigned to any constellation; they were labeled "unformed." After the Renaissance, astronomers such as Hevelius, Lacaille, and others created quite a collection of "gap filler" constellations out of a number of these unformed stars. We will encounter practically all on these Jamieson charts, a number of which are no longer officially recognized today.

One such group is just to the left of Auriga on Plate IV: Telescopium Herschelli (which is misspelled on this chart) and represents one of the smaller refractor-type telescopes of the illustrious German-English astronomer Sir William Herschel (1738–1822) who revolutionized observational astronomy, and, among numerous other things such as the discovery of legions of deep-sky objects, discovered the planet Uranus in 1781. He also made a number of telescopes both for himself and for others, with his largest one being a classic 48-inch aperture reflector at Slough, England. His son was Sir John Herschel, who we quoted earlier with regard to the type of constellation outline pictures contained on the Jamieson charts and who pretty much followed in his father's astronomical footsteps particularly in the Southern Hemisphere. The constellation Telescopium Herschelli was placed in the sky by the Austrian astronomer-priest Father Maximilian Hell, S.J. (1720–1792).

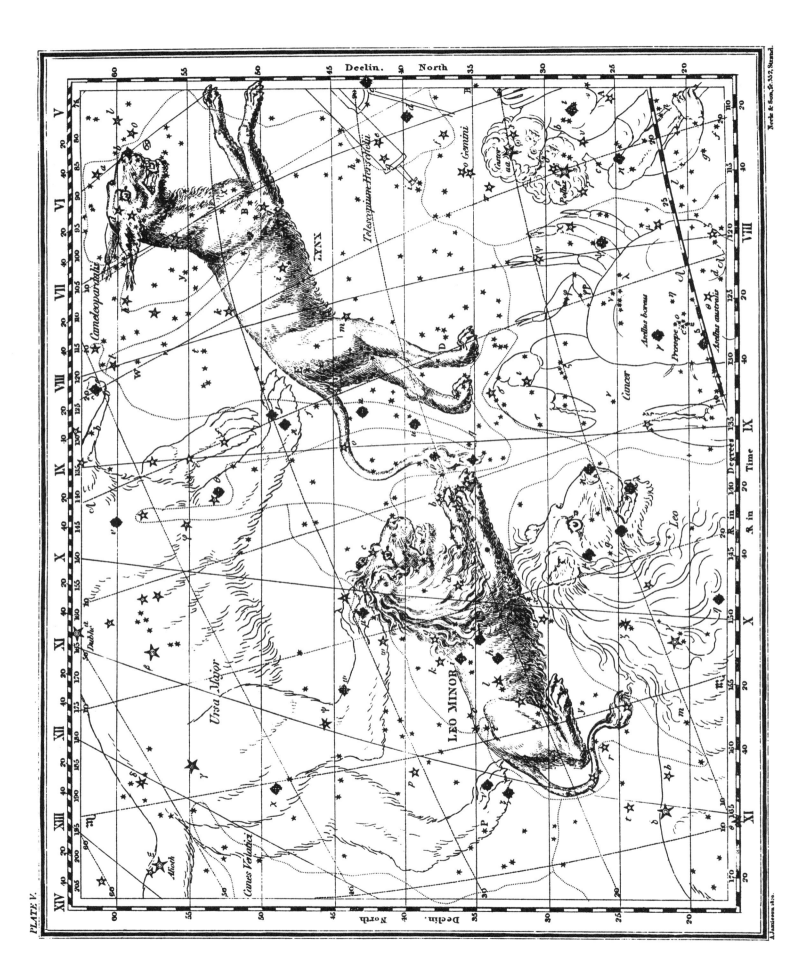

PLATE V.

Declin. ◯ North

Leo

LEO MINOR.

LYNX

Telescopium Herschelii

Ursa Major

Canes Venatici

Camelopardalis

o Gemini

Cancer

Arctus borealis

Arctus australis

Præsep.

Declin. ◯ North

Kœle & Son, Fc 352, Strand.

J. Aniscon 1822.

Plate V

Two celestial cats are the leading attractions on this chart: Leo Minor, the Small Lion; and Lynx, the Lynx or Bobcat. Both are relatively dim post-classical creations by the German-Polish astronomer Johannes Hevelius (1611–1687), who lived in the Baltic city of Danzig, now Gdansk in Poland, and produced one of the better-known old-time pictorial star atlases, his *Firmamentum Sobiescianum* of 1687. He was responsible for several other lesser constellations which we will encounter as we go along. However, Jamieson shows a rather strange type of lynx here with a head decidedly more canine than feline. Such misportrayals of living creatures in books wasn't that rare during previous centuries when knowledge of the natural world was quite a bit less complete than today.

The part of the sky shown here is overhead on April evenings for mid-northern latitudes and is also covered on the uppermost portion of Tirion Chart 5. There are relatively few bright stars here; nothing like those in the considerably more brilliant and star-spangled winter heavens, part of which is covered on the previous plate.

However, shown in the subdued style of non-featured constellations on a particular plate and found along the chart's margins are a few more prominent and better-known groups, at least in part, such as Gemini, the Twins (lower right); Leo, the Lion (lower left); and Ursa Major, the Great Bear (upper left). They are of great value in helping to locate Leo Minor and Lynx.

As we look at the two lesser constellations featured on this plate with their dearth of bright stars, we are actually gazing out into interstellar space at a steep angle to the plane of our home galaxy, the Milky Way system. The term Milky Way is most often applied to that hazy, somewhat smoky-textured cloud-like band that encircles the sky and which can usually only be seen at locations far from the atmospheric and light pollution found in populated areas. It passes through the center of the previous chart, Plate IV, and is portrayed on the Tirion maps as a green band. The reason this band exists in our sky is due to our location in that enormous flattened stellar "pancake" that represents the general shape of our galaxy. It is some 100,000 light-years in diameter and about 30,000 light-years thick at its central bulge and is believed to contain somewhere in the neighborhood of 200 to 300 billion stars (some astronomers place this figure even higher). When we look out along the plane of this pancake we see an enormous bunching together of billions of stars, individually too faint to be seen without a telescope, that combine to form that "milky" wreath encircling the sky.

However, the part of the sky on Plate V is in a direction away from the galactic plane, so we see considerably fewer stars here, bright or dim. As we go along, we will return to the topic of our galaxy and how it affects the appearance of the sky. The fact that the human race was able to acquire such a cosmic perspective represents one of the gigantic triumphs of civilization, and virtually all of it occurred within the past two centuries! The ancients who created our Celestial Picture Book couldn't in their wildest imaginings have begun to conceive the universe that we know today.

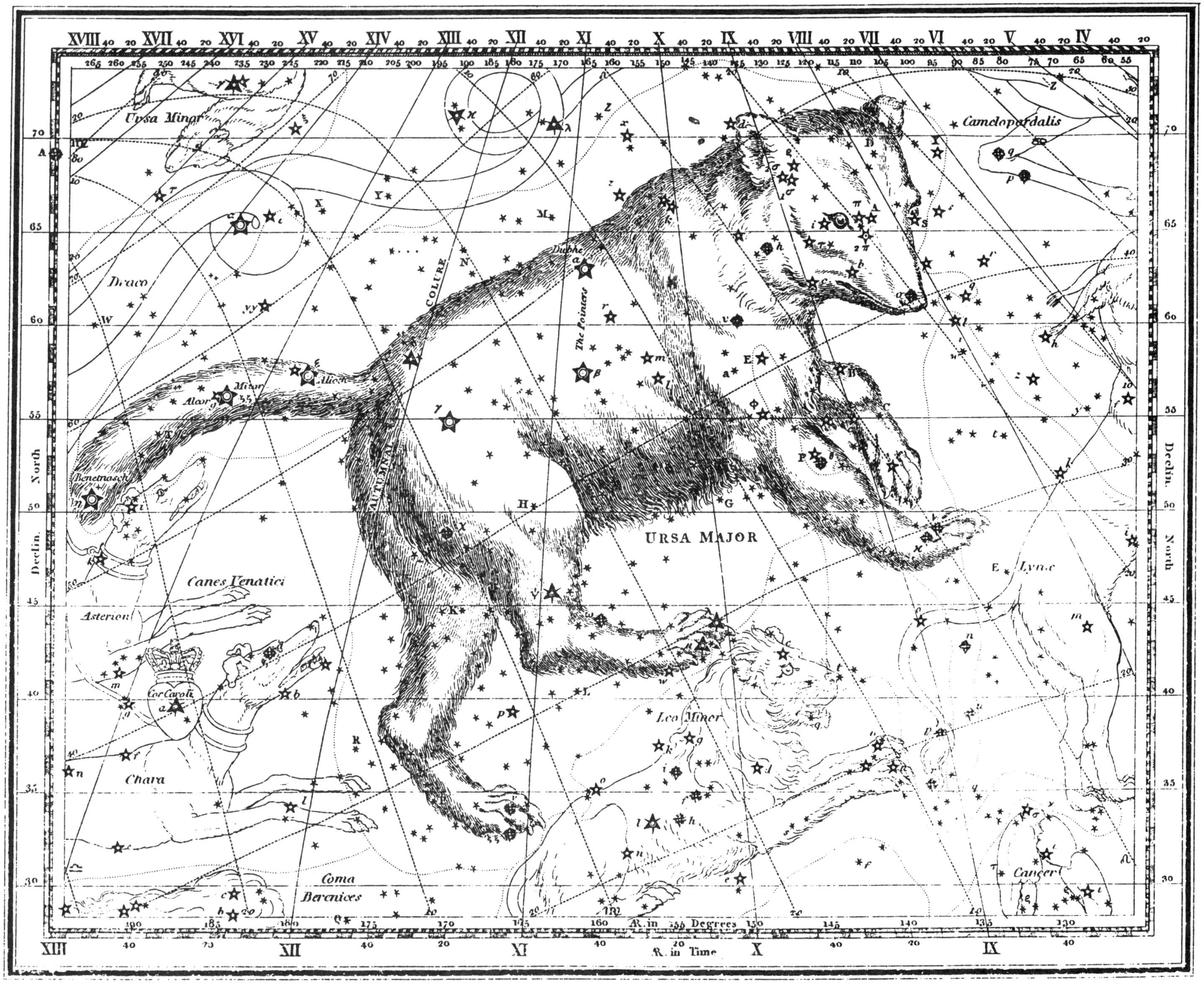

PLATE VI

Declin. North

URSA MAJOR

Camelopardalis

Lynx

E. Lyncis

Cancer

Leo Minor

Coma Berenices

Canes Venatici

Chara

Asterion

Cor Caroli

Ursa Minor

Draco

The Pointers

COLUER

Alioth

Mizar

Benetnasch

Alcor

A.R. in Degrees

R. in Time

Declin. North

Plate VI

One of the most famous of all constellations holds center stage on this map: Ursa Major, the Great Bear.

But the Bear's real claim to fame lies in its rear end! There we find that prominent Big Dipper asterism, which we already saw on Plate II; however, this chart shows the rest of the bear, unlike the other plate (which, nevertheless, better depicts the Dipper in relation to the other northern circumpolar stars, unlike here). We can find Ursa Major split up among three Tirion charts: the bottom of Chart 1; top of Chart 2, and the very top of Chart 5 (which shows the portion of Ursa Major below the Dipper).

The leading legend associated with Ursa Major has it originating in a love triangle involving Greek gods! (These deities had all the feelings and foibles of mortals.) The story has it that the King of the Gods, Zeus (Jupiter to the Romans), fell in love with a nymph called Callisto, for which, incidentally, one of the four major satellites of the planet Jupiter is named. Zeus' wife Hera (Juno to the Romans) hardly approved, of course, and using her godlike powers changed Callisto into a bear. In this form Callisto was vulnerable to being stalked and killed by hunters. Sure enough, a hunter named Arcas did show up, who happened to be Callisto's son. Overcome with emotion, Callisto ran over to embrace him, unmindful at the moment of her present form even as her son was raising and aiming a spear. At the last possible instant Zeus saw this, promptly changed Arcas into another bear, and raised the two of them into the heavens by their tails. It has sometimes been said that Zeus grabbed the creatures in this fashion to avoid their teeth and claws (why should it concern a god?) as we already indicated, and that this was responsible for their long tails. Callisto's son Arcas is commonly regarded to have become Ursa Minor, the Smaller Bear, which holds center stage on Plate II.

However, Juno managed to get a final revenge. She implored Oceanus, Ruler of the Sea, to forbid either bear to enter the water to bathe or refresh themselves; they were sentenced to circle in the sky endlessly. During the time of ancient Greece, even Ursa Major did this in its entirety as seen from that part of the world, but since then the precessional shift of the Earth's axis has carried the Great Bear farther from the northern pivot so that now it manages to immerse at least its lower body into the water during its circumpolar circuit as seen from the approximate latitude of Greece, 40°N, which is also about that of the most populous parts of the United States.

There is an interesting reference to this circling in Homer's *Iliad*, which goes back to the 9th century, B.C.:

Therein he wrought the Earth, and the Heavens,
*   and the Sea,*
The unwearied Sun and the full Moon,
And all the constellations with which the Heavens
*   are crowned,*
The Pleiades, the Hyades, the strength of Orion,
And the Bear, which they also call by the appel-
*   lation of the Wain,*
Which there revolves and watches Orion,
But is alone unwashed by Ocean's briny bath.

Also interesting is that Homer referred to the Great Bear as the Wain almost three millenia ago.

While the stars under discussion were a bear to virtually all our Middle East ancestors, it's rather remarkable that these same stars—at least those forming our Big Dipper—were *also* involved in a celestial bear to certain North American Indians. The creature itself was formed out of the four stars in the Dipper's bowl, with the three in the handle being hunters pursuing it in a never-ending chase around the sky.

Is it a coincidence that these Indians also saw a bear here? Possibly not. We know that the bear is one of the very oldest of the recognized constellations, and anthropologists now tend to believe that the New World Indian actually originated in the Old World, having migrated here over the land bridge that existed across the present Bering Strait thousands of years ago.

It seems that the prominent seven-star asterism in Ursa Major's haunches was viewed as a dipper or similar utensil largely by Americans. In fact, to runaway slaves in the period before the Civil War, it was the "Drinking Gourd," and members of that abolitionist movement called the Underground Railroad told escaping slaves who often preferred to travel at night that they should "follow the Drinking Gourd" in order to make sure that they keep heading north.

And this same pattern has long been used to tell or estimate time. In Shakespeare's *King Henry IV* (Part I, Act 2, Scene 1) a servant expresses concern about the group's tardiness by saying, "Heigh-ho! An't be not four by the day. I'll be hanged. Charles' Wain is over the new chimney; and yet our horse not packed." Charles' Wain is one of the names the British had for the Dipper stars.

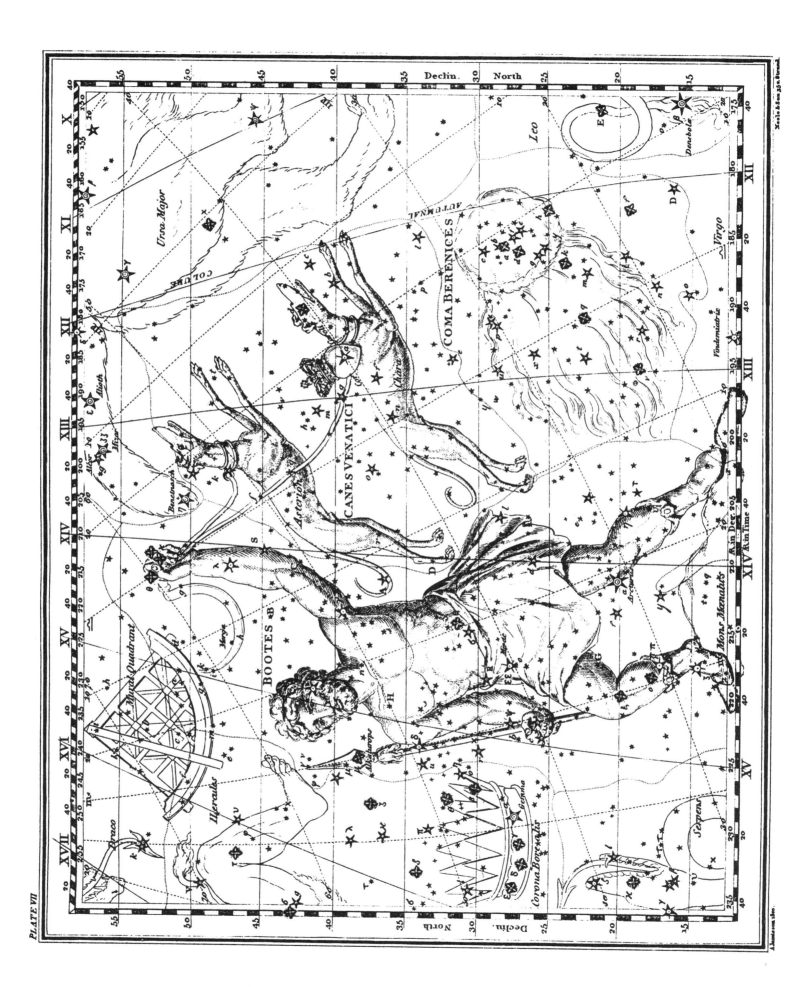

PLATE VII

Plate VII

Following the Great Bear—partially visible at upper right—around the sky is Bootes (pronounced Bo-OH-teez), the Bear Driver, also known as the Herdsman. In England, he has also been called the Ploughman, since they saw him following the Plough (Big Dipper). The sky area shown here corresponds approximately to the upper portion of Tirion Chart 6.

The origin of Bootes is shrouded in some uncertainty, since this individual has enjoyed several identities. Some authors, including Jamieson, have incorrectly identified him with Callisto's son Arcas, who we mentioned in connection with the previous plate. But Arcas, as we recall, became Ursa Minor, the Small Bear, according to most accounts. Bootes has even been confused with Orion, the Hunter, since some sky guides have called Bootes the Hunter. However, one way or another he has—at least in Western cultures—been regarded as the Bear Driver or Guardian, although some of the early Sumerians are said to have called him the Shepherd.

In fact, this constellation's brightest star, Arcturus, has a Greek name which plainly means "Bear Watcher," from the Greek word for bear, *arktos*. This, incidentally, is where we get our word "Arctic." Arcturus, shown here in Bootes' left knee, is a prominent yellow star that is a "landmark" in the spring evening sky and can be found by following the curve of the Big Dipper's handle (in the Bear's tail at the top center of the chart) southeastward about a Dipper's length.

During the 1933 Century of Progress exposition in Chicago, Arcturus played a major "high-tech" role (for the technology of the time) by turning on the lights of the fair. Its light was collected by the large 40-inch refracting telescope at Yerkes Observatory in Williams Bay, Wisconsin, and focused on a photocell which closed a circuit to trigger the main lighting control. What prompted them to do this was that at the time Arcturus was believed to be 40 light-years away (we now know it to be more like 36) and 40 years earlier Chicago had another big blowout, the huge Columbian Exposition. So, they thought, why not turn on the lights for the 1933 event with starlight that started its trip to Earth during the 1893 fair?

Plate VII features two other interesting constellations. We see Bootes holding the leashes of two hunting dogs, called Canes Venatici, that follow the Great Bear closely. They are another Hevelius creation, and have also been referred to as the Greyhounds by some, including Jamieson. Notice that these dogs have a name: Asterion and Chara, although they are seldom referred to by these appellations nowadays.

The brightest star in Canes Venatici is called Cor Caroli, Latin for "Heart of Charles." It refers to Charles I of England, who was "shortened by a head" during those stormy mid-17th-century political upheavals in that country. This resulted in a decade-long (1650's) interruption of the Monarchy by Lord "Protector" Oliver Cromwell. Upon the restoration of the Monarchy in 1660 with the accession of Charles II, his Physician, Sir Charles Scarborough, commemorated the first Charles by naming that star after him, or at least his heart, which Jamieson depicts as a crowned Valentine-type heart. (With apologies to our British friends, it might be mentioned that that heart was an awfully small one, for this ruler was among England's most narrow-minded and intolerant ones; and his demise—with all attending upheavals—is one of the events widely attributed to have started that country on the road to greater democracy.)

Another monarch is commemorated on this map, who, like Charles I, was a real—not mythological—ruler. It is Queen Berenice, wife of the Ptolemaic Egyptian King Euergetes, who ruled around 250 B.C. Egypt was then essentially a Greek province and enjoyed a true cultural "Golden Age," especially in its capital Alexandria. Directly under Canes Venatici we see Coma Berenices, the Hair of Berenice. This resulted from an incident where her husband went off to one of the battles against Babylon, and she vowed that if he returned safely, she would place her golden tresses in the Temple of Venus. He did, and she kept her promise. However, her hair soon disappeared from the temple and a very critical crisis was brewing. (Even in that "enlightened" culture, it was not unknown for rulers to vent their rage by arresting—and even executing—innocents). It was none other than Court Astronomer Conon who defused the situation by taking the Royal Couple outdoors one evening and showing them that striking star cluster near the Great Bear, shaped somewhat like an inverted letter "Y," and telling them that the gods were so taken by the beauty of her tresses that they placed it in the sky for eternity, and that cluster is it.

Nowadays, Coma Berenices enjoys some astronomical significance by being the constellation in which the north galactic pole is located. This point is marked NGP on Tirion Chart 6.

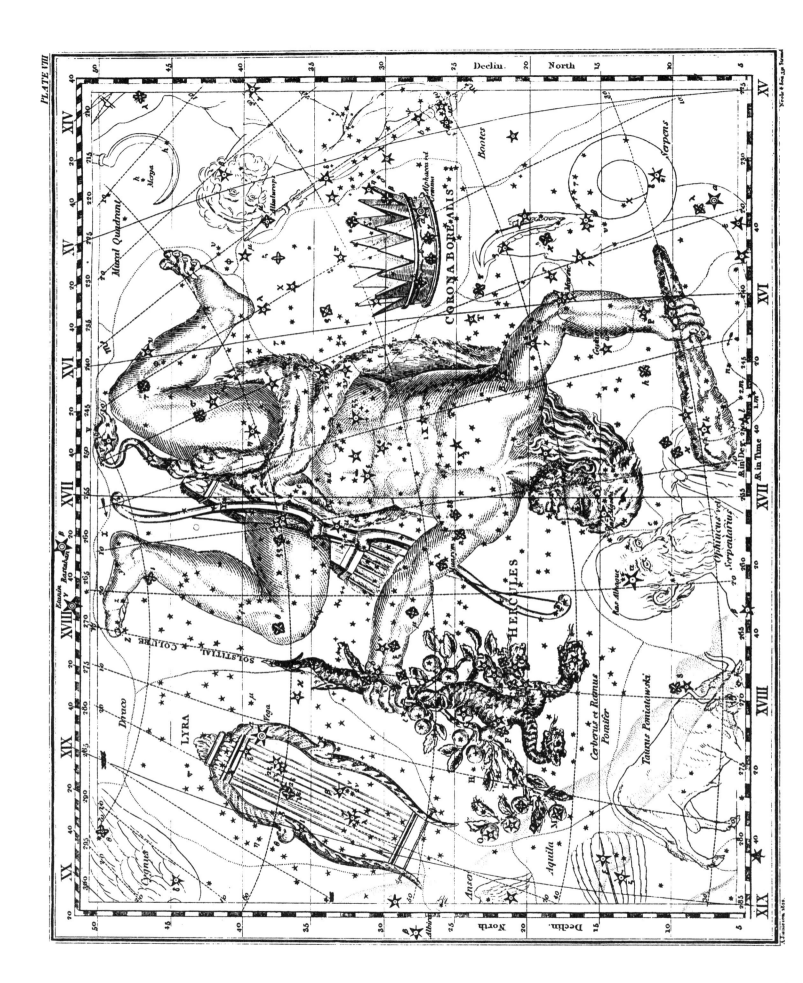

PLATE VIII

Plate VIII

Centered on this plate (which approximately corresponds with Tirion Chart 7) is one of the all-time legendary heroes and strong men, Hercules, also known to the Greeks as Herakles.

A Hercules-type "Superman" has been virtually universal in early Middle East cultures, as well as elsewhere, and this constellation is among the very oldest ones. Its earliest antecedent is believed to be the legendary Sumerian hero Gilgamesh who, among other things, slew a dragon called Tiamat as shown on one of their cylinder seals from before 3000 B.C. This dragon is the predecessor of today's Draco, which we saw on Plate II.

Although Jamieson doesn't obviously show it, Hercules has often been pictured as standing on Draco's head, since—as with Gilgamesh and Tiamat—he slew the Dragon as one of his exploits. And, as shown here, his heroic figure is portrayed in the traditional kneeling pose associated with him, indeed, to the ancient Greeks he was also known as Engonasin (the Kneeler).

But why is he upside-down? This mystery can be explained by the precessional shift of the sky in the five millenia since this constellation first existed in some incarnation. In the era of Gilgamesh, this figure appeared rightside up high in the northern heavens as seen from the Mesopotamian area. Today he is rightside up only from places south of about 15° north latitude. (The precession capabilities of a modern planetarium projector can readily reproduce these ancient skies.)

Hercules has customarily been portrayed—as here—with a lion's skin draped over him, a trophy from when he slew the ferocious Nemean Lion, often associated with the constellation Leo (see Plate XVII). Here, incidentally, we even have a Biblical tie-in with the Scriptural strong man Samson, who also slew a lion (with his bare hands) as described in the Book of Judges. In his left hand Hercules holds the three-headed serpent Cerberus as well as an apple branch.

But dispatching the vicious lion was but the first of twelve onerous labors he was "sentenced" to perform by King Eurystheus as punishment for having slain his wife Megara and their children in a fit of rage which was the result of a spell cast on him by the goddess Hera. Another was retrieving the Golden Apples from the Garden of the Hesperides which was guarded by Draco, whom he slew.

Hercules was a son of Zeus (Jupiter), which is one of the explanations of his powers, but not by Zeus' wife Juno; instead, his mother was Alcmene, one of Zeus' paramours. Ever-jealous Juno sent two serpents to kill the infant, but Hercules commenced his career early by strangling the snakes in his cradle. And, if that wasn't enough, Juno has been identified with the goddess Hera, who caused Hercules to kill his wife and children.

To the right, or west, of Hercules is a distinctive little constellation, Corona Borealis, the Northern Crown. It is most commonly associated with the jewel-studded crown of Ariadne, daughter of King Minos of Crete, who received it as a wedding gift from her suitor Bacchus. In fact, the brightest star in this constellation has often been called Gemma (the Gem), although today it is more commonly known as Alphecca.

On the other side of Hercules is Lyra, the ancient Lyre, one of the earliest type of stringed musical instruments. Lyra is associated with Orpheus, who played this instrument in such a way that he could charm any creature or human with it. One of the classic tales involving him and his lyre is his journeying with it to the underworld (abode of the dead) to try to charm its god, Pluto, to restore his wife Eurydice to life after she died of a snakebite. His musical skills succeeded in winning his wife's release; but on the condition that she follow directly behind him in the journey back to the upper world and that Orpheus not look back until they get there. Yet he couldn't resist, and so lost her forever.

Perhaps because of Orpheus' musical association, at least two major operas were based on his story: Monteverdi's *Orfeo*, and Gluck's *Orfeo ed Euridice*. Actually, Greek legends were a favorite subject for early operas and oratorios, including examples such as Handel's *Hercules*.

Lyra happens to have a brilliant beautiful star, Vega. It's pronounced *vee-ga*, not *vay-ga*, notwithstanding a certain auto manufacturer. It dominates the eastern evening heavens during summer, and forms a distinctive triangle with two other bright stars nearby, Deneb and Altair, which is popularly known as the Summer Triangle. Our solar system happens to be moving through interstellar space in the approximate direction of Vega; actually; the direction is closer to Hercules' hand where it grips Cerberus.

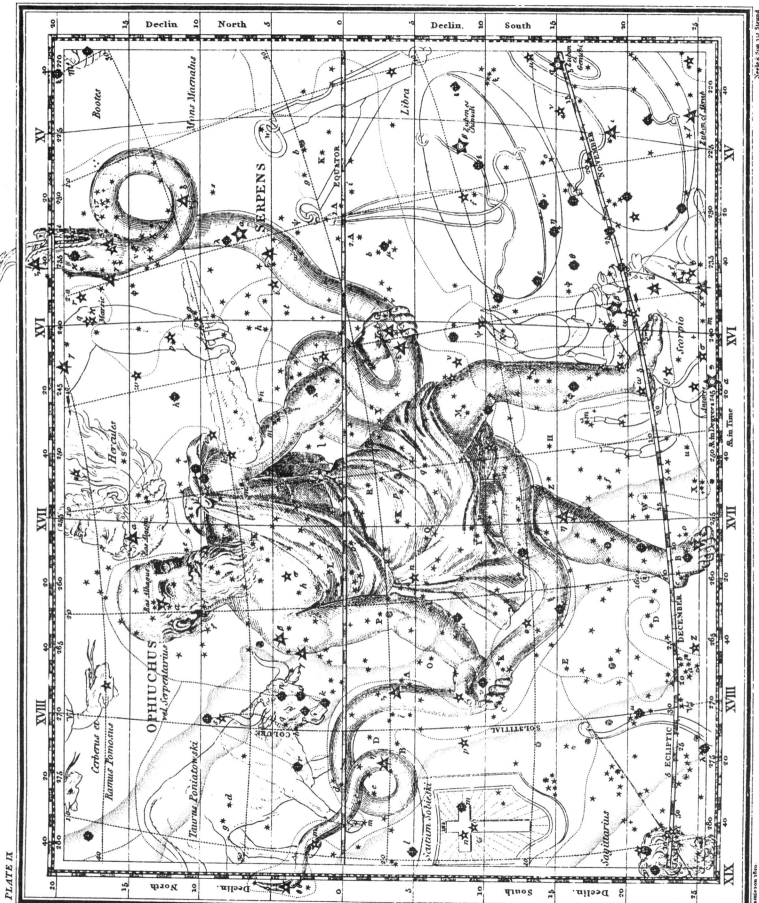

PLATE IX

Booles

Mons Maenalus

XV

XVI

SERPENS

Libra

EQUATOR

XVI

Hercules

XVII

Scorpio

XVII

OPHIUCHUS
vel Serpentarius

Cerberus &
Ramus Pomosus

XVIII

Taurus Poniatowski

SOLSTITIAL

DECEMBER

XVIII

Scutum Sobieski

Sagittarius

ECLIPTIC

XIX

Neele & Son 13.º Strand

A.Jamieson 1820.

Plate IX

Has the reader ever wondered how the serpent became a medical symbol? The plate presented here is one clue. It shows the ancient constellation Ophiuchus, the Serpent Bearer, which has in the past often been called Serpentarius as indicated on the chart's left under the "Ophiuchus" label.

The snake he is holding is a separate constellation called Serpens. Today this group has been officially split into two separate parts on either side of Ophiuchus: Serpens (Caput), its head; and Serpens (Cauda) the tail. This whole menage can be seen on Tirion Chart 7 just to the right of center. In fact, on the Tirion map we see how those official IAU constellation boundaries separate our snake.

Its holder, Ophiuchus, is most commonly regarded as representing the traditional Greek god of medicine, Aesculapius, and his serpent has become the classic symbol of the healing arts, having become the basis of the Caduceus symbol with a serpent (sometimes two) entwined around a winged rod. Aesculapius two daughters were Hygeia and Panacea, whose names have become familiar health-related words.

Our Greek god of medicine and his daughters are still invoked in the classic Hippocratic Oath physicians take upon graduating, whose opening sentence reads, "I swear by Apollo Physician and Aesculapius and Hygeia and Panacea and all the gods and goddesses, making them my witness, that I will fulfill according to my ability and judgment this oath and covenant:"

The early Mesopotamian Sun god Marduk has also been linked to Ophiuchus. Marduk was also credited with having slain the dragon Tiamat, as was the Mesopotamian strongman Gilgamesh, a predecessor of Hercules as described in connection with the previous plate.

Yet the leading legend pertaining to Aesculapius is that he became a super-skilled physician who, among his early feats, took the dismembered body of Hippolytus—which was torn apart by wild horses—and reassembled it back into a perfect, viable being. (Could it be that Aesculapius was also an original predecessor of Doctor Frankenstein?!) Finally, our physician was ready to try his capabilities on the ultimate medical skill: reviving the dead. This greatly alarmed Pluto, god of the Underworld, or Realm of the Departed, who felt that this upstart physician would dethrone him by depriving him of customers and reason for being. He appealed to the head god, Zeus, to do something about it, knowing that Zeus was concerned that his subordinate gods had no trouble in their respective realms.

So Zeus struck down Aesculapius with a thunderbolt, yet in recognition of this healer's otherwise unusually meritorious services gave him a permanent place in the sky along with his snake.

An interesting astronomical fact about this constellation is that although it is not—and never has been—a part of the zodiac, it most definitely is one from a de facto standpoint. Notice the way the heavy curved ecliptic line passes across both of his feet. Looking at Tirion Chart 7, we see that a considerably greater portion of the ecliptic is located in Ophiuchus than in neighboring Scorpius, an official zodiacal group. In fact, the Sun only spends about a week in Scorpius during late November, but takes some three weeks during the first part of December to cross non-zodiacal Ophiuchus.

We can also notice the precessional shift of the starry sky from 1820 to 2000, the equinoxes of Jamieson and Tirion, by noting the position of a starry triangle in the face of the small bull Taurus Poniatowski, marked o, k, and p by Jamieson and 67, 68, and 70 on Tirion Chart 7. On the Jamieson map this grouping is to the right of the 18–hour circle (marked XVIII), while on the Tirion chart it is to the immediate left, or east, of that line. This represents the 180–year precessional shift of the starry sky between the epochs of these two sets of sky maps.

Incidentally, Jamieson labels those stars by the lower-case Roman letters originally assigned by Johann Bayer in 1603; Tirion uses their Flamsteed numbers—the preferred system today for fainter naked-eye stars. Still fainter stars are usually referred to by their number in some catalogue or listing.

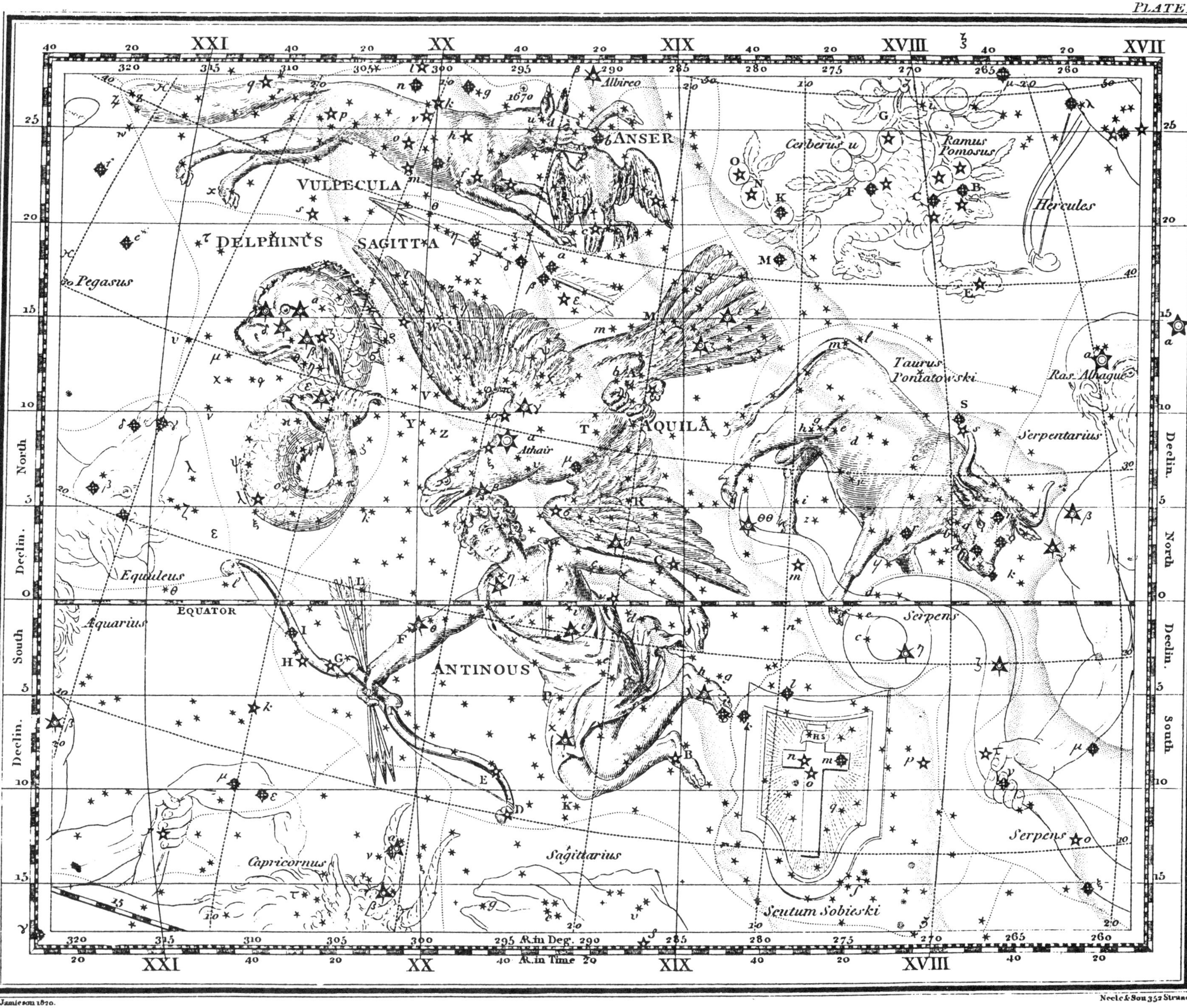

PLATE X

Declin. North   Declin. South

Hercules
Ramus Pomarius
Cerberus
Taurus Poniatowski
Serpentarius
Serpens
Serpens
Scutum Sobieski
Sagittarius
Antinous
Capricornus
Aquila
Atthair
CANSER
VULPECULA
SAGITTA
DELPHINUS
Pegasus
Equuleus
Aquarius
EQUATOR

Neele & Son 352 Strand
A Jamieson 1820.

Plate X

Going directly eastward from Ophiuchus along the celestial equator we come upon Aquila, the Eagle, which happens to lie squarely in the middle of one of the Milky Way's richest summer stretches. Its brightest star, Altair, is virtually a next-door neighbor as stars go, being a mere 16-or-so light-years away. Here is an example of a star that appears bright mainly because of its proximity.

The portion of the sky on Plate X is basically left of center on Tirion Chart 7 as well as along the central portion of the right margin on his Chart 8. (Here is a good indication of the generous overlaps Tirion allowed among his charts, which greatly simplifies finding one's way around the heavens and which other star atlases have sometimes been very skimpy about, largely to save work and paper. On the other hand, Jamieson also has significant overlaps on his maps.)

Our Eagle was a special bird to the ancient Greek gods, and was a special favorite of Zeus himself, who kept this creature at his side and used it to carry his thunderbolts. Other early peoples regarded this constellation as a falcon, or vulture, which, like Aquila, belong to the raptor (birds of prey) family.

Jamieson shows Aquila carrying the young boy Antinous, which is how this bird has traditionally been shown on old star maps. Antinous is a now-defunct group which represents another actual, instead of mythological, individual. Astronomical writers have long described him as a special favorite of the Roman Emperor Hadrian.

Immediately to the east (left) of our Eagle is Delphinus, the Dolphin, whose four main stars—in the creature's head—form an attractive compact stellar quadrilateral. On the Jamieson map, as well as other oldtime pictorial renditions, Delphinus hardly resembles the small member of the whale family we know dolphins to be.

But there is little doubt that the ancients were aware of the intelligence and affinity for humans displayed by this creature. A prominent legend concerning Delphinus involves his rescuing the renowned musician Arion (not to be confused with Orion, the Hunter).

The story goes that Arion was aboard a ship returning from a recital in Sicily and carrying treasures his appreciative audience there gave him in reward. The roughneck crewmen wanted to get their hands on it all, and decided to throw Arion overboard. The latter pleaded to be allowed to play a final melody on his harp first, which he was permitted to do. The music attracted a school of playful dolphins, so Arion jumped overboard and was carried to shore by one of these creatures. From there he went to Corinth (the vessel's destination) and awaited the surprised crewmen, accompanied by authorities who helped him recover his possessions.

Directly above Aquila is Sagitta, the Arrow, another ancient, if compact, group. It has various stories associated with it, of which one describes it as the missile Apollo used in killing the one-eye Cyclops human monster; another legend associates Sagitta with the arrow Cupid aims when he wants to make someone love-struck.

Plate X contains two constellations created by that famous 17th-century Danzig astronomer Johannes Hevelius: Vulpecula et Anser, the Fox and Goose; and Scutum Sobieski, King Sobieski's Shield (another actual person, a Polish ruler). Today these groups are known simply as Vulpecula and Scutum, as indicated on modern maps such as Tirion's, as well as listings such as that on page 71.

While the Fox and Shield have gained official astronomical status and thus remain among the roster of recognized constellations, another post-Renaissance group on Plate X was eliminated: Taurus Poniatowski, The Bull of Poniatowski, which we mentioned in connection with the previous plate and which is also named after a Polish king. This little bull is attributed to the Polish priest Father Poczobut, who is said to have been influenced by the fact that those stars in the beast's face form a V-shaped asterism not unlike the Hyades cluster in the face of the "real" heavenly bull—Taurus.

PLATE XI.

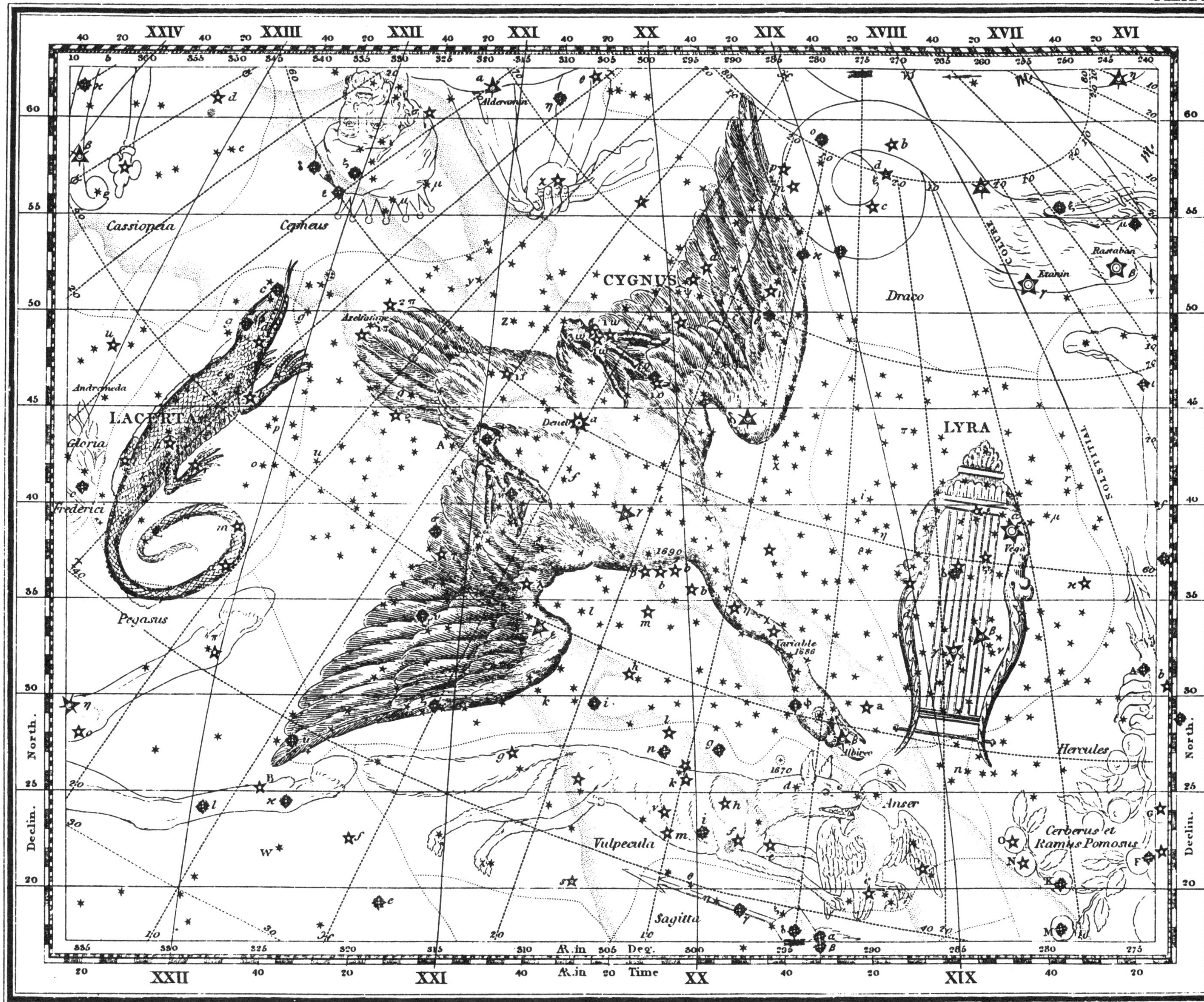

A Jamieson 1820

Neele & Son fc. 352 Strand.

Plate XI

The sky area on this chart includes the greater portion of the well-known "Summer Triangle" asterism, which consists of the bright stars Vega, Deneb, and Altair. The first two, situated in Lyra and Cygnus respectively, are shown here, while Altair is on the previous plate in Aquila. The entire Summer Triangle is visible in the upper-left corner of Tirion Chart 7, while the sky area on Plate XI is included in both the aforementioned corner of Chart 7 and the upper-right corner of Chart 8. The Summer Triangle is prominent in the eastern sky as it gets dark on summer evenings.

Cygnus, the Swan, is the main feature on this plate, its principal stars forming a cross-shaped asterism whose upright runs the length of the bird's body, while the crossarm extends across from wing to wing. This pattern is known as the Northern Cross, an alternate unofficial name for Cygnus, which is easy to see at the upper-right corner of Chart 8. (The Southern Cross, on the other hand, is an official constellation in itself which has the name Crux.)

The brightest star in Cygnus is Deneb, whose name derives from the Arabic word for tail. Although Deneb is usually described as being in the Swan's tail, on the Jamieson chart and a number of other oldtime pictorial renditions the star is clearly in the bird's body *near* but not *in* the tail.

We mentioned in connection with the previous plate that Altair (the southernmost member of the Summer Triangle) is a "next-door neighbor" just $16\frac{1}{2}$ light-years away. Vega is somewhat further at 26 light-years, but Deneb is anything but a next-door neighbor; it's something like 1,600 light-year into the interstellar void. This means that the light by which we see it at present started its journey to us during the last days of the Roman Empire! Deneb is among the remotest of the naked-eye stars, and the fact that it appears as bright as it does (first magnitude) despite its distance makes it among the most luminous stars in our galaxy. It's over 50,000 times brighter than our Sun, being one of those rather rare (percentage-wise) hot giant blue-white luminaries which are sprinkled around the arms of spiral galaxies—including our home system, the Milky Way—and which contribute to making these arms appear as prominent as they do. Such stars are more common in the winter sky, particularly in constellations such as Orion.

Along the neck of the Swan we find one of the Milky Way band's richest portions which in binoculars forms a glorious sight—a dusting of seemingly countless stars with brighter stellar jewels liberally interspersed. Here we are looking along the length of our home galaxy's local spiral arm—the one the solar system is located in—which astronomers, not surprisingly, call the Cygnus arm. Additionally, the Cygnus area is one of the places where the Milky Way band appears to be split into two parts, as shown on Tirion Charts 7 and 8. This "split" is due to the vast amounts of interstellar dust and debris in the plane of our galaxy's disk which blocks the light of more distant stars behind it.

Incidentally, the star in the Swan's beak—Albireo—is a well-known gorgeous orange-and-blue double star that can be detected as such with low telescopic, as well as binocular, magnification. It is one of the best illustrations of how stars can differ in color.

How did the Swan get into the sky? The leading legend associated with it has to do with Phaeton, the son of the Sun god Helios. While yet a young lad, Phaeton was chided by his friends and associates to prove that he really is the son of Helios, so he asked his father to—as teenagers have done to this day—"lend him the keys"; in other words, to be permitted to drive his father's vehicle (the Sun chariot). Phaeton was unable to handle its frisky horses, who drew the chariot virtually out of control on a wild ride here and there, including close enough to Earth to parch large areas of its surface, leaving barren deserts. Finally, Zeus was outraged at this escapade, and hurled one of his thunderbolts at the lad, who fell into the river Eridanus (now a constellation of its own) where he was changed into a swan so he wouldn't drown.

Near the left margin of Plate XI is Lacerta, the Lizard, another post-classical constellation attributed to Hevelius, whose stars form a zigzag pattern.

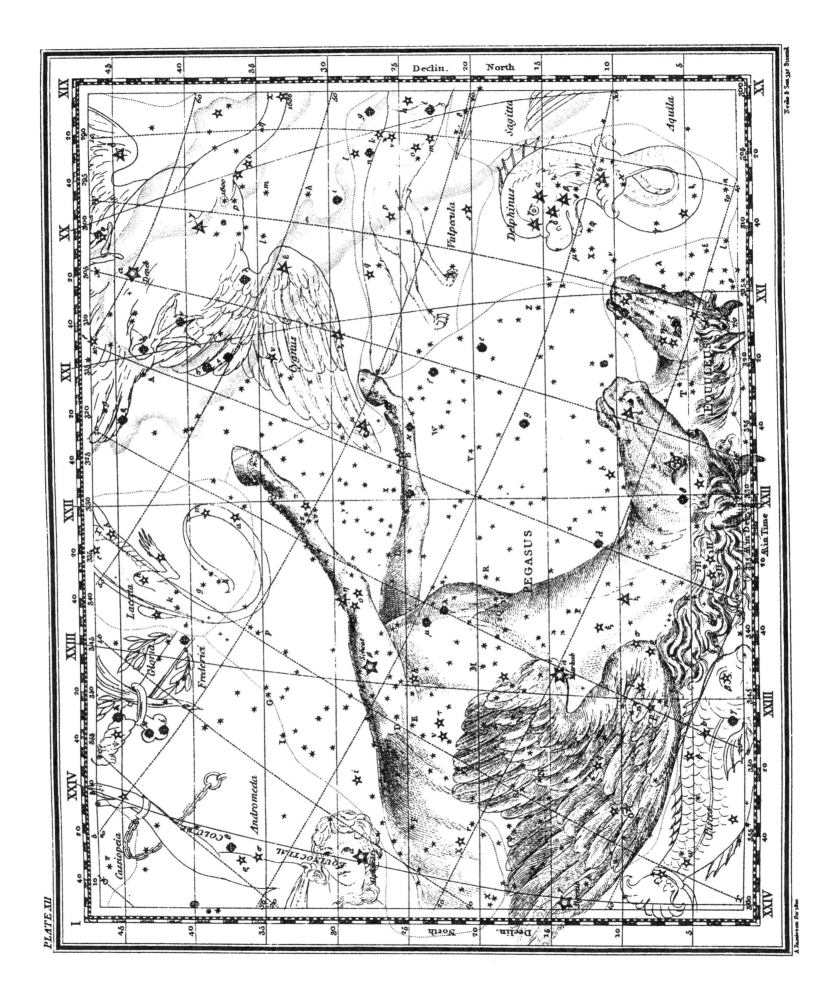

PLATE XII

Plate XII

The ancients, particularly the Greeks, had quite a mythological menagerie of strange "half-and-half" or composite animals, including flying non-flying creatures. Several of these found their way into the sky as constellations, such as the specimen presented here: Pegasus, the Flying Horse, which can also be found on Tirion Chart 8. In fact, the sky area covered by Jamieson's Plate XII closely matches the entire upper half of Tirion's Chart 8.

The best-known celestial "landmark" associated with this constellation is a prominent square of second and third magnitude stars in the beast's body which on popular star maps is often labeled "Great Square of Pegasus." The shape of this asterism is better shown on the Tirion chart because of the superior map projection employed. However, only three of those four "Great Square" stars belong to Pegasus at present. The one at upper left, Alpheratz, belongs strictly to Andromeda (whose head is visible near the left margin) and is borrowed simply to complete the square. Yet in former times Alpheratz was indeed shared by the two constellations; there were also a number of other "shared" stars in the sky, as well as "unformed" stars that do not belong to any constellation. Today, every star belongs to *one* constellation; none are shared and none are "unformed." This is the result of those official IAU constellation boundaries which are delineated on the Tirion maps.

Pegasus is associated with several ancient legends, including the one told in connection with Plate III where the hero Perseus rescues the chained princess Andromeda after flying over the seacoast where she is confined. Although Perseus is often described as being able to fly because of his winged sandals, other versions of the story places him on the back of Pegasus.

Another legend associated with our flying steed has to do with his living on Mount Olympus among the gods and that he seldom came down to Earth. And here he again became involved in a slay-the-monster adventure, this time involving another reckless youth like Phaeton, but named Bellerophon.

He decided to kill another "composite" creature called the Chimera, which had a lion's head, goat's body, and dragon's tail. (Here we have the origin of our word "chimera" or "chimerical," referring to something really wild, fantastic, or "far out.") Bellerophon spent an entire night in the Temple of Minerva, imploring the goddess to lend him divine assistance for this task. He succeeded, because in the morning Bellerophon found Pegasus nearby, as well as a golden bridle in his hand which he would need to harness and mount the horse.

On the back of Pegasus Bellerophon was able to slay the Chimera, and then, intoxicated by his sudden success, decided he was given broad godlike powers. So he rode the horse to its home atop Mount Olympus. Zeus, the ruler of it all up there, was astounded at the youth's audacity, so he sent a gadfly to sting Pegasus, who then bolted and caused Bellerophon to fall to Earth, thereby suffering injuries that made him lame and blind for the rest of his days.

Among other things, Pegasus has formerly enjoyed the status of serving as the symbol or "logo"of the Mobil Corporation for a number of years. And, believe it or not, this creature was even more "chimerical" to certain ancients who added a fish's tail to its rear end! (Talk about the ultimate aerial-amphibious animal.) In fact, the large sky area below Pegasus and extending some distance left and right is the ancient Celestial Sea, which we will come to further on.

Notice the head of another horse near that of Pegasus: Equuleus, the Little Horse, or Colt, often—as here—shown only by its head. Incidentally, on old maps only the front portion of Pegasus itself was usually portrayed. Equuleus was the horse that Mercury (the Messenger of the gods) gave to the youth Castor, who then gave it the name Celeris, from which we get our word "celerity," meaning speed.

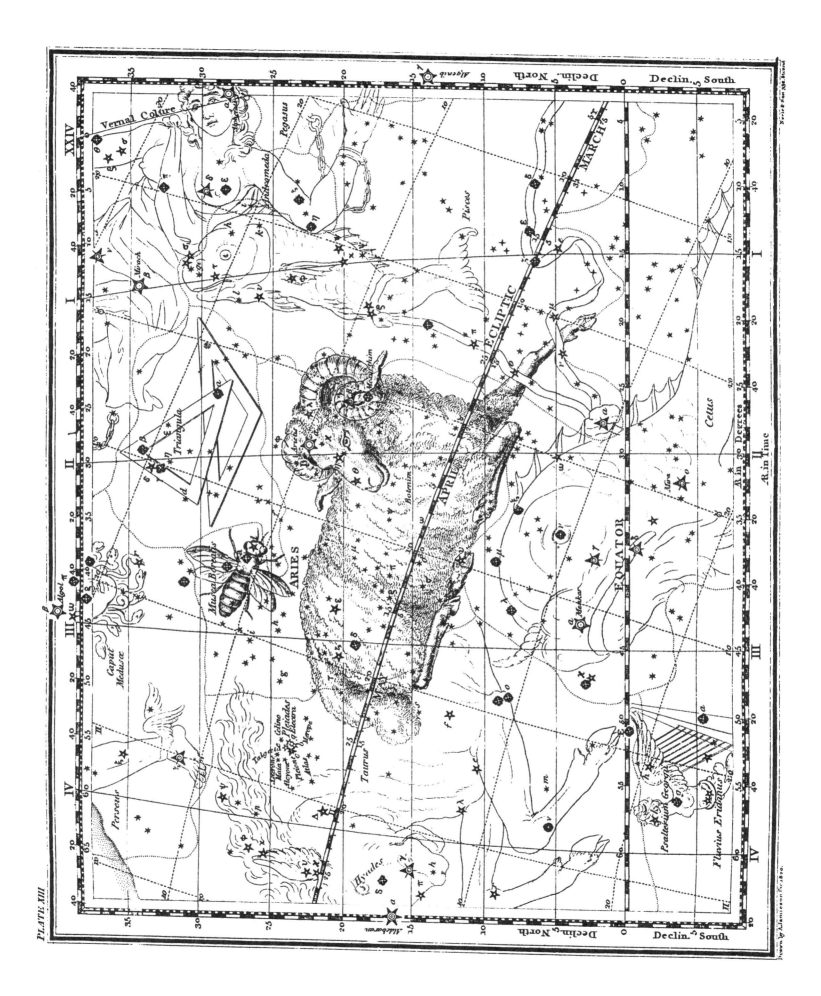

PLATE XIII

Plate XIII

A very important zodiacal constellation holds "center stage" on this plate: Aries, the Ram, which has traditionally been associated with the coming of spring. Even Chaucer, in his *Canterbury Tales*, refers to "the yonge Sonne, Hath in the Ram his halfe cours y-ronne." It simply means that the Sun passes through this part of the sky at this time of year, whose inception is the vernal equinox.

This is also the point where the ecliptic crosses the equator as the former ascends northward; on our chart here this intersection is just beyond the right-hand margin, but is centrally located on Plate XXII. Also, the part of the sky shown here can be found in the upper portion of Tirion's Chart 3.

The equinox point now lies among the stars of the next zodiacal constellation to the west of Aries, or Pisces, the Fishes. However, the *sign* of Aries—which represents the first 30° of longitude along the ecliptic eastward from the equinox—also lies almost completely within the stars of Pisces. This is the result of the precessional shift of the sky over more than two millenia, which has similarly caused all the other zodiacal signs to shift westward from the constellation of the same name. Here we see that the sign of Aries only reaches as far as the Ram's chest, where the sign of Taurus begins (indicated on the ecliptic by the symbol ♉). However, in this instance the sign of Taurus manages to extend well into the constellation of Taurus, the Bull, all the way to a point just above the beast's mouth, where the sign of Gemini (indicated by the symbol ♊) begins. It should be noted that the signs and corresponding constellations of the zodiac never exactly coincided, because the star pictures varied in extent along the ecliptic, while the signs have always been of exactly the same width—30° each.

Astrologers still use these signs, and our Jamieson chart (as well as the others that include the ecliptic) make it clear what it means to "be born under a particular sign," or what it means "to be an Aries," etc. We see that the first 30° of longitude—which covers the sign of Aries—corresponds to the month-long period from about March 20 to April 20; the dates are marked underneath the ecliptic line, and they indicate the Sun's approximate location on those dates.

It is rather interesting that present-day navigators still recognize the sign of Aries, after a fashion, by referring to the vernal equinox point as simply "Aries," which is how it is listed in their nautical and air almanacs. However, it should be pointed out that calling this point the "vernal" equinox reveals a bit of many-centuries-long Northern Hemisphere chauvinism, because in the Southern Hemisphere it becomes the autumnal equinox. It is precisely for this reason that astronomers and navigators now prefer to refer to this equinox by the month it occurs in—March equinox—and the other season points are similarly labeled by their months, not seasons.

The Ram itself has a rich lore behind it, being traditionally associated with the legendary Ram of the Golden Fleece who, among other things, carried the children of King Athamas, Helle and Phrixus, on its back to escape their jealous father. However, while crossing that strait separating Greece from Asia Minor (now Turkey), Helle fell off the Ram's back and landed in the water, which has been named the Hellespont after her. Her brother arrived at the intended destination Colchis safely. Aries was later sacrificed to Zeus (Jupiter) and its unique golden fleece was preserved. It became the object of the legendary expedition by Jason and the Argonauts using that amazing ship, the Argo, which is described in connection with Plate XXV.

Aries has also been linked to the two major spring religious festivals—Easter for Christians and Passover for the Jews—since the Sun is in this part of the sky at that time and the Paschal Lamb holds a central role for both holidays. However, both are movable festivals; that is, their date of occurrence on the civil calendar varies by about a month.

Plate XIV

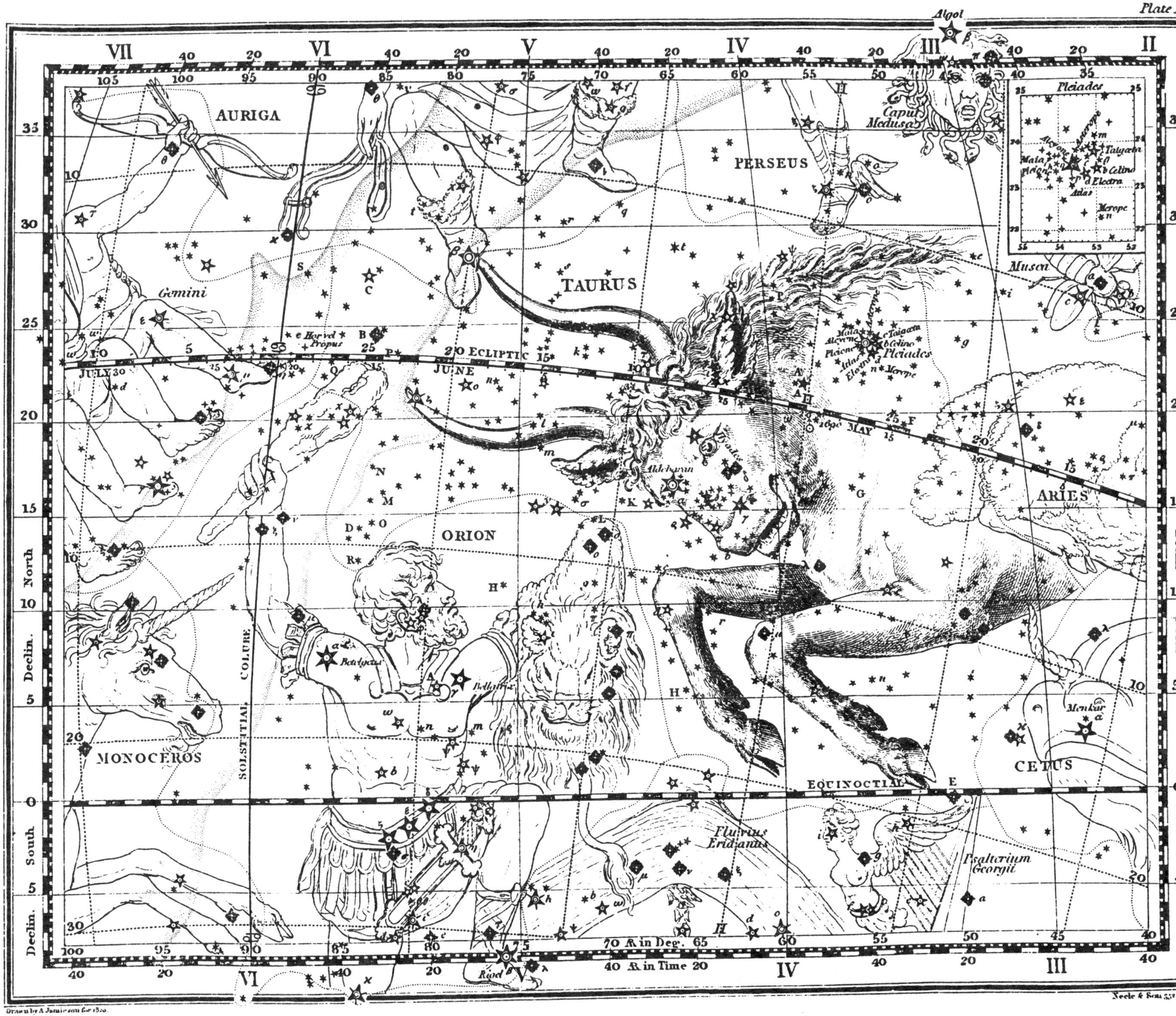

Drawn by A. Jamieson for 1820.

Neele & Son 352 Strand

Plate XIV

Here we have one of the best-known parts of the sky, with Orion, the classic celestial Hunter-Warrior confronting Taurus, the Bull, traditionally the second zodiacal constellation. However, Plate XIV actually only features our bovine creature; Orion "officially" belongs to Plate XXIV, along with several other groups. The upper portion of Tirion's Chart 4, except along its top and left areas, approximately covers the same sky area as Plate XIV.

Taurus is perhaps best known for its two prominent naked-eye open clusters: the Hyades and Pleiades. They can be found, respectively, in the Bull's face and shoulder area. The Hyades, along with the orange-hued first-magnitude star Aldebaran, forms a neat V-shaped asterism, while the Pleiades looks like a tiny dipper (and is sometimes mistaken for the Little Dipper by laypeople).

Aldebaran, located in the Bull's right eye, is not physically part of the Hyades cluster, but by a remarkable coincidence lies in precisely the right direction in space to complete that V pattern. The Hyades stars (some 130 light-years away) are almost twice as far as Aldebaran (70 light-years). Both the Hyades and Pleiades are, as we said, open clusters; the term "open" refers to such a cluster's open or loose appearance, and such objects populate the spiral arm portion of our galactic plane, which is why they are found mainly along the Milky Way band in the sky.

The main stars of Taurus, including the Hyades cluster, form an even longer and narrower V-pattern that extends to the tip of the Bull's horns. The star in the upper horn, Beta Tauri or Elnath, was already encountered back on Plate IV in connection with Auriga, the Charioteer, in whose right leg this star is situated as well as in Taurus' upper horn. As we said, for a long time Elnath was common to both constellations, but such a situation cannot exist today, and the star now belongs strictly to Taurus.

The star in Taurus' lower horn, Zeta (ζ), is just over a degree southeast of the well-known Crab Nebula, which is the first object in the Messier Catalogue and thus has the designation M1 and can be found and is therefore labeled on Tirion's Chart 4. This is a special type of gaseous nebula known as a supernova remnant; it is the remains of a star we on Earth saw appear as a brilliant "new" star in the year 1054 where the Crab Nebula is now situated. The star itself exploded some 6,000 years earlier (it being about 6,000 light-

years away), the result of which appeared to eyes on Earth as that brilliant supernova. These are actually massive stars that literally blow themselves to bits as the result of a heavy collapsing iron core, and the cataclysmic ensuing explosion creates all chemical elements heavier than iron which are then "re-seeded" into space to perhaps eventually become parts of new stars and planets. An object like the Crab Nebula is the beginning of this re-seeding process; in terms of cosmic time the explosion—occurring some seven thousand years ago—took place only "yesterday." Any reader wearing gold jewelry might be interested in knowing that since this heavy metal was formed during a supernova explosion, they are actually wearing a cosmic souvenir or a piece of a supernova.

Look closely along the curved ecliptic line on the Jamieson Plate at the May 20 position where the symbol X can be found with the date 1690 next to it. This is a symbol for the planet Uranus, which was sighted and recorded at this location as but a star on December 23, 1690 by John Flamsteed, England's first Astronomer Royal. He never suspected it to be anything else. It was almost a century later, in March 1781, that the celebrated English astronomer William Herschel recognized this object in his telescope as being non-stellar by its tiny disk. Yet he thought he found a new comet, and it was some time before the motion of this object revealed it to be a new planet beyond Saturn.

Our celestial Bull is another very ancient constellation with an extensive body of lore behind it. One of its earliest antecedents was the bull-god Apis of the ancient Egyptians, and various images—bas relief and other—of this bovine deity with a human body and bull's head has regularly appeared in Egyptian art. To the Greeks Taurus was the bull that Zeus transformed himself into to swim from Phoenicia to Crete with Princess Europa on his back. Upon arriving on the island he changed back into his regular self, and this impressive display of his ability to change form so readily helped him win Europa as his bride. (Yet she was far from being Zeus' only bride, whether simultaneous or successive, not to mention his vast assortment of paramours.)

Incidentally, recall that Zeus was Jupiter to the Romans, whose name has been appropriately applied to what we now know to be the largest planet, which the ancients had no way of knowing. One of its four largest satellites is called Europa; the others are Io, Ganymede, and Callisto.

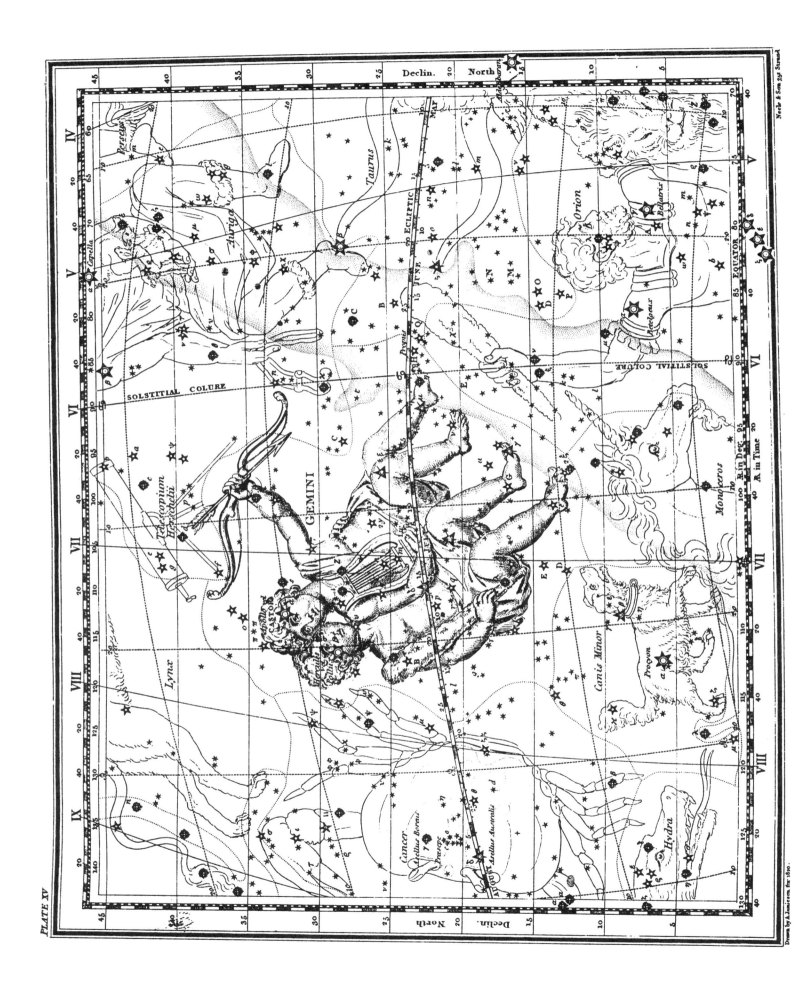

PLATE XV

Plate XV

Moving eastward along the zodiac we next come across Gemini, the Twins. Their names, top to bottom, are Castor and Pollux, which are also the names of the two brightest stars in this constellation which are located in the Twins' heads. The sky area on this Plate can be found in the upper-left portion of Tirion's Chart 4.

The constellation of Gemini is presently virtually entirely within the sign of Cancer, with the constellation of that name being the next zodiacal group as we continue eastward; it is featured on the next Plate (XVI). Here is but a further example of that zodiacal sign-constellation displacement, the result of the precessional movement of the heavens, which was discussed in connection with Aries (Plate XIII).

Above the twin Castor's left toe is the point on the ecliptic where the Sun is located at the beginning of Northern Hemisphere summer. This point has traditionally been known as the summer solstice, which the Sun reaches at the present time on June 21st or 22nd. (Actually, the date on which this occurs is also called the summer solstice.) However, in view of the simple fact that this is the winter solstice for folks "down under" (in the Southern Hemisphere), here again it might be better to call this point—or date—the June solstice. Notice also that here is where the ecliptic reaches its greatest distance north in the sky and that after the June solstice it—and the Sun that follows it—begins dropping southward again. This is why Northerners see the Sun's daily altitude decrease day by day after the summer solstice. Here is a fundamental astronomical phenomenon anyone can notice.

The summer—or June—solstice point is also the beginning of the sign of Cancer, indicated by the symbol ♋. When the Sun is at this point it is also $23\frac{1}{2}°$ north of the equator, or directly over that latitude circle called the Tropic of Cancer, which indeed is named after that zodiacal sign. If we go $23\frac{1}{2}°$ south of the equator we encounter the Tropic of Capricorn, named after the sign of Capricorn, which is presently among the stars of Sagittarius and shown on Plate XX. The Sun appears over this latitude circle on December 21st or 22nd, the date of the December solstice or the beginning of northern winter and southern summer. In fact, the Sun can appear at the zenith (directly overhead) only at places on Earth between the tropics of Cancer and Capricorn—nowhere else.

The constellation of Gemini, regardless of what it was called, was regarded as the Twins by just about all early Middle East peoples. However, the foremost legend associated with this pair is the Greek one in which they are twin sons of Zeus with one of his many paramours, this one being Ledo, the wife of King Tyndarus of Sparta. To woo her, Zeus this time changed himself into the form of a swan.

Our heavenly Twins were special heroes to sailors, and one of their mythological adventures was serving as crew members on Jason's voyage with the Argonauts seeking the Golden Fleece. Since ancient times sailors have often sworn by the Gemini twins, which gave rise to the familiar oath we often hear, "By Jiminy!"

The main stars of this constellation form sort of a tall gatelike pattern with the stars Castor and Pollux at the top. Indeed, one way the Japanese have viewed this star grouping is as a celestial version of their torii type gates. They also called Castor Gin Boshi (Silver Star) and Pollux was Kin Boshi (Golden Star), descriptions based on these stars' colors. This stellar pair was also known to them as Neko-no-Me (Cat's Eyes) because of how this bright side-by-side stellar pair appears when descending the western heavens, as during spring evenings.

During such spring evenings, when all those brilliant winter stars are leaving us one by one, Castor and Pollux sort of "bring up the rear" of the parade and are the last of that group to set. They even suggest the two marker lights on the back of a railroad train that bring up its rear as it disappears down the track.

PLATE XVI.

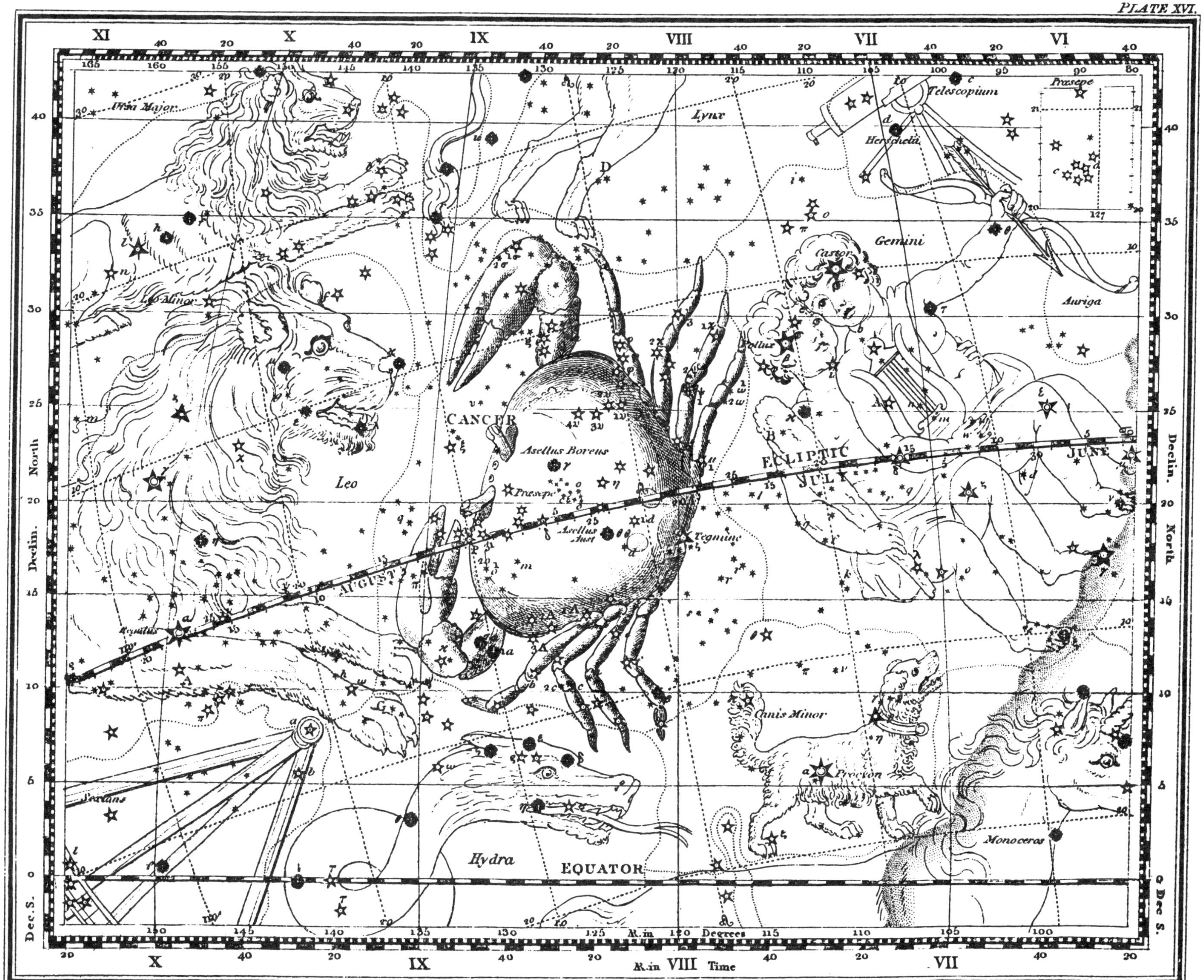

Declin. North

Dec S.

Dec.S. Declin. North

Plate XVI

Here we have one of the two faintest of the zodiacal constellations: Cancer, the Crab. The other faint one is Pisces, the Fishes, which appears on Plate XXII. Neither contains any star brighter than fourth magnitude. Cancer can be found in the upper-right portion of Tirion's Chart 5.

As we said in connection with the previous Gemini plate, in classical times Cancer was situated at the sky location the Sun reaches at the beginning of summer, which is where the sign of Cancer still begins. The former location of this constellation, at the summer solstice point, has been offered as one explanation as to why it was placed there. When the Sun reaches that location in the sky, it has ended its half-year-long northward journey in the heavens (although its motion is more eastward than northward) and will now reverse its direction and head southward for the next half year, just as a crab can reverse itself and readily walk in both directions.

Interesting also is the fact that Cancer is one of two arthropods in the zodiac; the other is Scorpius, the Scorpion (Plate XIX). These are insectlike animals with a hard exterior "skeleton" and jointed multi-legs. Insects, which must have six legs to fall into that category, are by far the largest division of the arthropod phylum. Some early star charts and atlases even show Cancer as a crayfish or lobsterlike creature, which is incorrect. There is even a further arthropod association with this constellation. Certain early peoples such as the ancient Egyptians and some on the Indian subcontinent pictured this grouping as a beetle—a definite insect.

However, as we indicated, the ancient constellations still recognized today are portrayed pretty much as the Greeks saw them. Their mythological background for Cancer was that it was the crab that ever-jealous Hera once sent to bite to death Hercules, the son of her wayward husband Zeus. When Cancer bit Hercules, the Strong Man was engaged in one of his classic twelve labors: battling the Hydra serpent-monster (whose head is visible immediately below Cancer and is featured on Plates XXVI and XXVII). Cancer's bite was no more than a mere annoyance to Hercules, who forth-with crushed the creature with his foot. Legend has it that because the Crab suffered this less-than-heroic fate in carrying out its assigned task, Hera placed it in the sky as one of the less-prominent constellations.

Just because a constellation is faint, it doesn't follow that it's necessarily uninteresting. Cancer contains another well-known open star cluster of the same type as the Hyades and Pleiades in Taurus, but less prominent. Located right in the middle of the constellation, it has the name Praesepe as well as the designation M44, as it is labeled on the Tirion chart. M44 means that it's the 44th object listed in the famous Messier catalogue of deep-sky objects. The Praesepe cluster is often popularly known as the Beehive, or sometimes the Manger. Under ideal sky conditions, it is visible to the unaided eye as a hazy patch, while in a binocular it appears as an attractive swarm of stars, which no doubt is how it became known as the Beehive. However, the Manger is actually the more nearly correct name; in fact, the two stars above and below the cluster to its left are known as the "Two Asses," which are feeding from the Manger. The name of the upper star is Asellus Borealis (The Northern Ass) and the lower one is Asellus Australis (The Southern Ass). However, Jamieson labels the first star "Asellus Borus," and applies the label "Asellus Aust." to the wrong star; he has it next to Theta (θ), whereas it should apply to Delta (δ), immediately to the left and sitting right on the ecliptic. Yet on the previous and following plates—XV and XVII—where Cancer appears near the margins, this star is correctly labeled.

Some of the ancients even used the Praesepe cluster as a sort of weather indicator. Pliny, among others, mentioned that if it is invisible in a clear sky, rainy weather would follow. This was no doubt the result of the fact that haze or moisture in the air, which often precedes precipitation, can prevent Praesepe from being seen. However, nowadays one would have to be in a location that enjoys unusually fine skies—far from light and other pollution—to be able to use this cluster as a weather predictor.

PLATE XVII

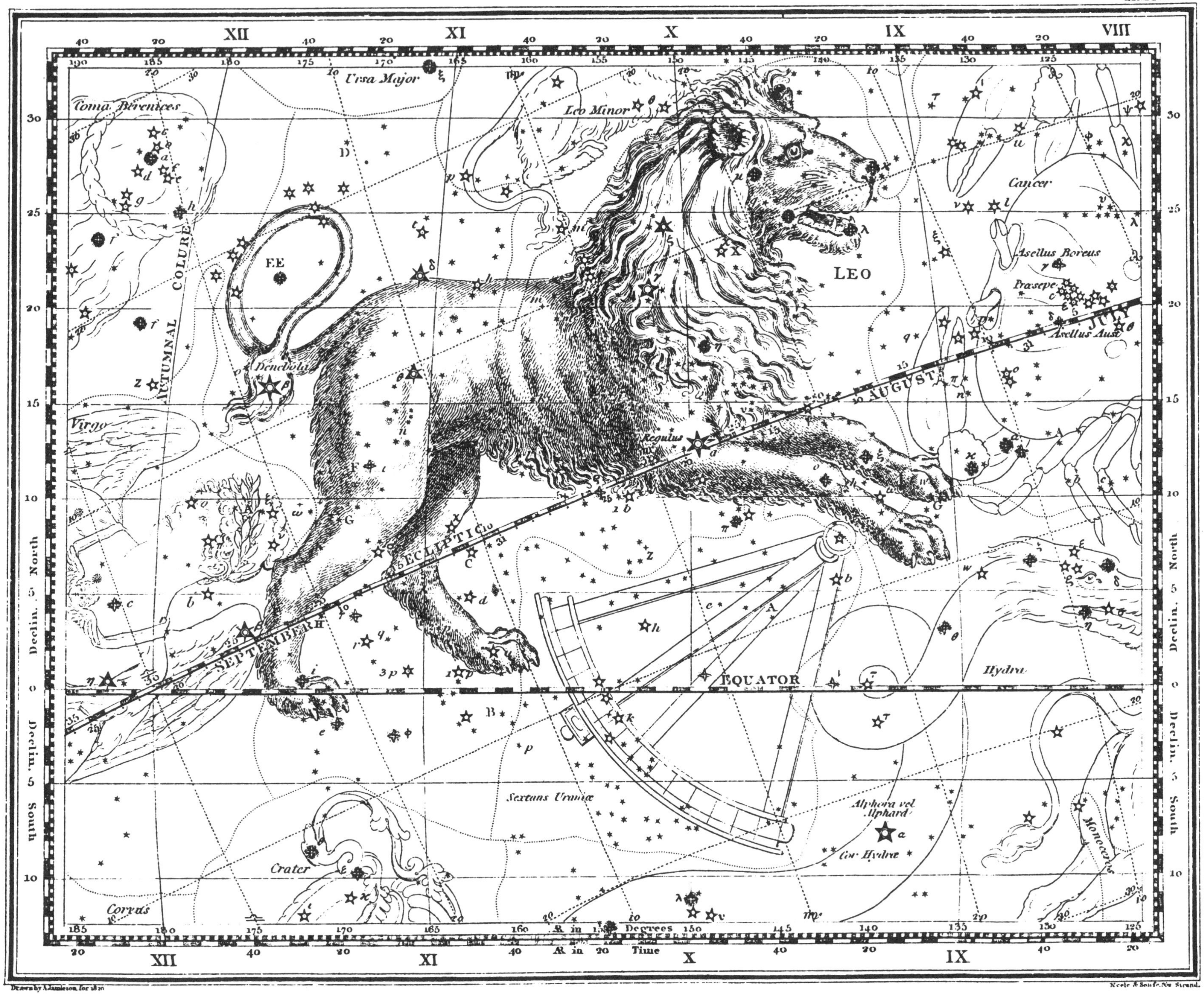

Drawn by A. Jamieson for 1820

Neele & Son sc. 352 Strand.

Plate XVII

Here is another truly ancient constellation: Leo, the Lion, another group whose origins trace way back to early Mesopotamia over five millenia ago. It can be found towards the upper-left of Tirion's Chart 5 not far from the center.

Back in that remote era the stars of the Lion were situated at the summer solstice point. Recall that, as described in connection with the previous plate, the Crab was at this solstice during the time ancient Greece flourished. Being the so-called "King of the Beasts," the Lion was originally placed in this exalted position at the zodiac's highest location. Yet even more significant was the fact that this fierce creature was associated with the fierce heat of summer—which is indeed just that in the Middle East—and the Sun was regarded as acquiring added strength when among the Lion's stars.

The early Egyptians adopted the Lion as a symbol for the Sun when its heat is most oppressive, and further associated these creatures with summer because they then wandered into the cooler Nile valley to escape the heat. Since this was also during the time of the year the Nile overflowed its banks and made the land on either side suitable for agriculture, the highly superstitious Egyptians associated the Lion with the precious annual irrigation that made their land fertile. As a result, their water sluices often had the head of a lion on them, from whose open mouths the water flowed. This no doubt was the origin for all those lion-head water spouts and fountains down through the centuries.

Yet to the Greeks the celestial Lion was that highly vicious Nemean beast which caused great destruction and havoc among the people of the Valley of Nemea. It had an impenetrable hide which no arrow, spear, or other weapon could penetrate. It remained for our heroic Strong Man Hercules to kill this beast, which was the first of his twelve famous labors. Not having any luck with whatever weapon he tried to use, Hercules strangled the animal with his bare hands and then wore its skin as a trophy. This tale is similar to the Old Testament account, in the Book of Judges, in which Samson also strangles a lion with his bare hands.

The brightest star in Leo is Regulus, which in Latin means "Little King," a diminutive form of the word *rex* (king). Here is one of the relatively few instances of a Latin star name; most of them are Arabic. Regulus is often described as being in the Lion's heart, but Jamieson has it in its upper right front leg. Regulus is at the bottom of a pattern of stars, in Leo's front portion, popularly known as the Sickle because of its shape; it is also sometimes likened to a backwards question mark.

Regulus was known to the ancient Persians as one of the four Royal Stars of the Heavens; the other three are Aldebaran in Taurus (Plate XIV), Antares in Scorpius (Plate XIX), and Fomalhaut in Piscis Austrinus (Plate XXI). Some 4-5 millenia ago, each of these stars was more or less in the vicinity of one of the equinoxes or solstices, so they were regarded as the "Guardians of the Heavens." Since that time the precessional shift of the heavens carried these stars some distance from those season points.

Here again, by comparing the Jamieson and Tirion renditions of Leo, we can see the extent of the precessional shift from the years 1820 to 2000. Notice that on the opposite chart Regulus is just to the right (west) of the 10-hour right ascension circle (labeled X along the top and bottom margins); on Tirion Chart 5 it is to the left (east) of that line.

The third-brightest star in Leo is Denebola, at the tip of its tail. We first encountered the name "Deneb," deriving from the Arabic word for tail, as the name of the star in the tail of Cygnus, the Swan, on Plate XI.

Directly below Leo is one of the so-called "modern" constellations: Sextans, the Sextant. Jamieson labels it with its original longer name, Sextans Urania, the Celestial Sextant. This constellation is another Hevelius creation of the late 17th century, and he here commemorates one of those huge six-foot-radius instruments he used to observe star positions with surprising accuracy for a device with only naked-eye sights. This instrument was not the same as the much smaller hand-held navigator's sextant of today.

PLATE XVIII

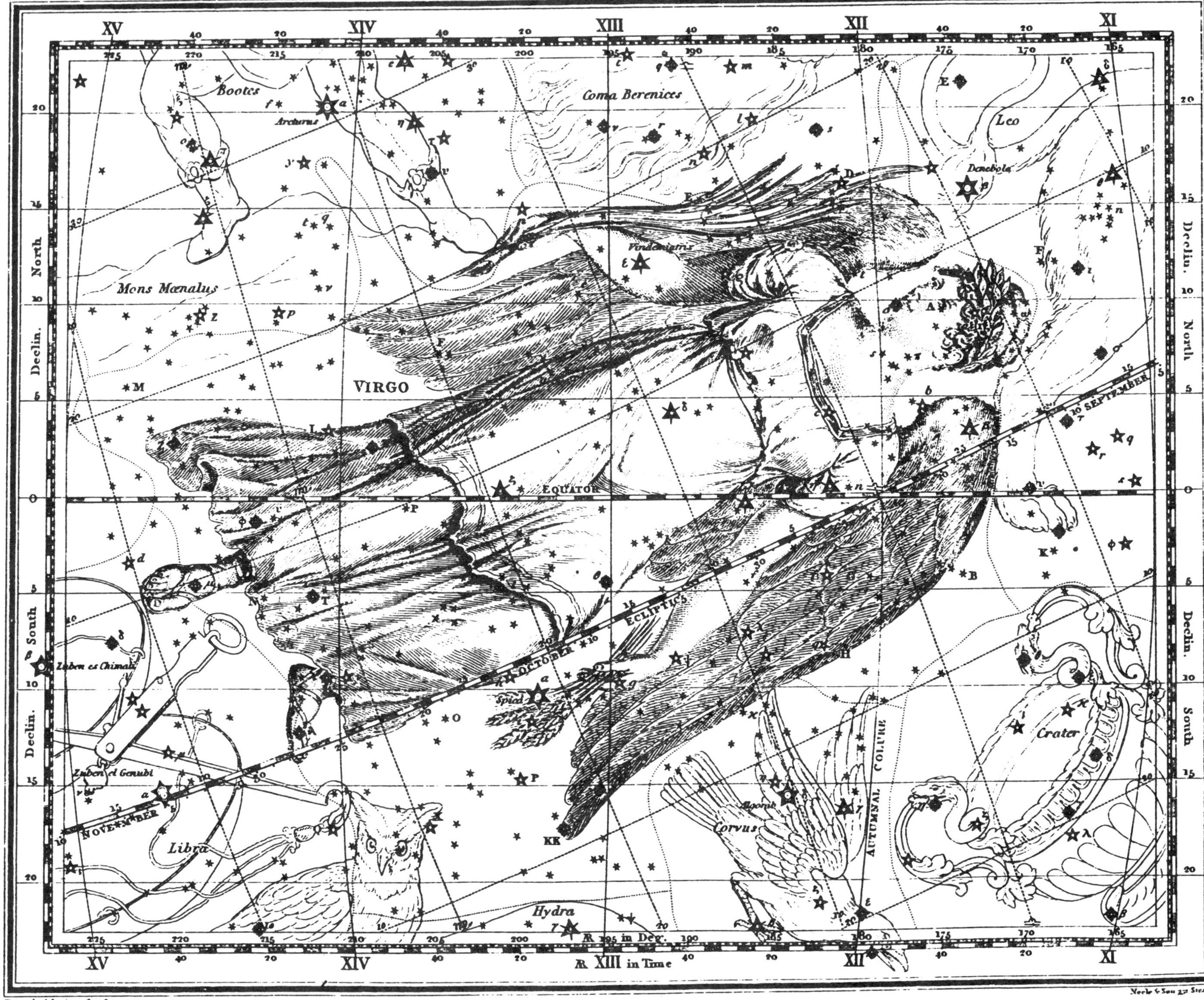

VIRGO

Plate XVIII

Next along the zodiac is the last of the three women in the sky: Virgo, the Virgin or Young Maiden. (The other two are Cassiopeia and her daughter Andromeda, which we encountered on Plates II and III, respectively.)

Virgo can be found in the middle of Tirion's Chart 6, and, although it isn't apparent at first glance, it is the second-largest constellation in the entire sky, based on those official constellation boundaries shown on the Tirion maps with short dashes. The largest star group is Hydra, the Water Serpent, whose tail is directly beneath Virgo (a small portion is just visible at this plate's lower edge) and which is featured on Plates XXVI and XXVII.

Our young lady of the sky is located right by the autumnal or September equinox, where the ecliptic again crosses the celestial equator. The Sun reaches this point on September 22–23, at which time day and nights are again of equal length everywhere in the world (excepting the poles) just as they were during the vernal equinox six months earlier. And, again because of that precessional shift of the sky since ancient times, although the September equinox is among the stars of Virgo it marks the beginning of the sign of Libra, whose symbol (♎) appears at the equinox point, but whose constellation is the next one along the zodiac and partly visible at this chart's lower left edge.

Virgo has been associated with more than one ancient theme, of which the two main ones are as the Goddess of Agriculture, Fertility, and the Harvest—Ceres to the Greeks (the origin of the word cereal)—as well as Astraea, the Goddess of Justice. On this plate we see the accoutrements of both roles: she is holding a sheaf of wheat in one hand and a palm branch in the other. And near her feet are the Scales (Libra), the traditional symbol of justice; a Virgo-like woman, complete with flowing robes and holding a set of scales, is a familiar constituent of several state seals. The leading legend concerning Astraea is that originally she mingled with ordinary mortals on Earth during a long-ago "golden age" when humankind did not know corruption, violence, or war. As these traits started entering the picture, she decided she wanted nothing further to do with the human race, and so left the Earth for the heavens. As the Goddess of Agricul-

ture, this constellation traces back to the ancient Egyptian agricultural goddess Isis. One of the legends involving her was that she was once pursued by a monster called Typhon, and while fleeing him caused the grain in her hand to be scattered across the heavens to become the Milky Way band. Finally, Virgo is generally visible in the evening sky during those months when the Earth produces its bounty. The location and visibility of a particular constellation has—as is the case here—been a not infrequent factor to those who originated it.

The brightest star in Virgo is first-magnitude Spica, whose name in Latin means "Ear of Grain," as our plate clearly reveals. And in her right forearm, near the palm branch, is another harvest-related star with the pretty name Vindemiatrix, another Latin appellation which means "Female Grape Gatherer"; compare it to our word "vintage." Here is an interesting example of how more comprehensible Latin—and Greek—star names are than Arabic, since English, along with a number of other Western tongues, has roots in both those classical languages. Both Latin and Greek, along with the major Western linguistic families such as Teutonic, Romance, and Slavic, are part of that large group called Indo-European. Arabic, on the other hand, is to us a considerably more exotic language (from the Semitic family) and star names that derive from that tongue are often condensed corrupted versions of an original Arabic phrase. One reason Arabic star names have become so dominant is because these people played a major role in keeping astronomical knowledge alive during the Dark Ages.

Right by Virgo's right shoulder, between the stars Vindemiatrix and Denebola in Leo, is that amazing gathering of galaxies often referred to as the "Virgo Cloud," of which only a few of its brightest members are included on Tirion's Chart 6. It's a cluster of thousands of galaxies some 50 million light years away. Galaxies, like stars, tend to be sociable, and are often found in such gatherings. Our home galaxy, the Milky Way system, is part of a small conglomeration called the Local Group; it includes among its about two dozen members such well-known neighbors as the Magellanic Clouds and the Andromeda galaxy.

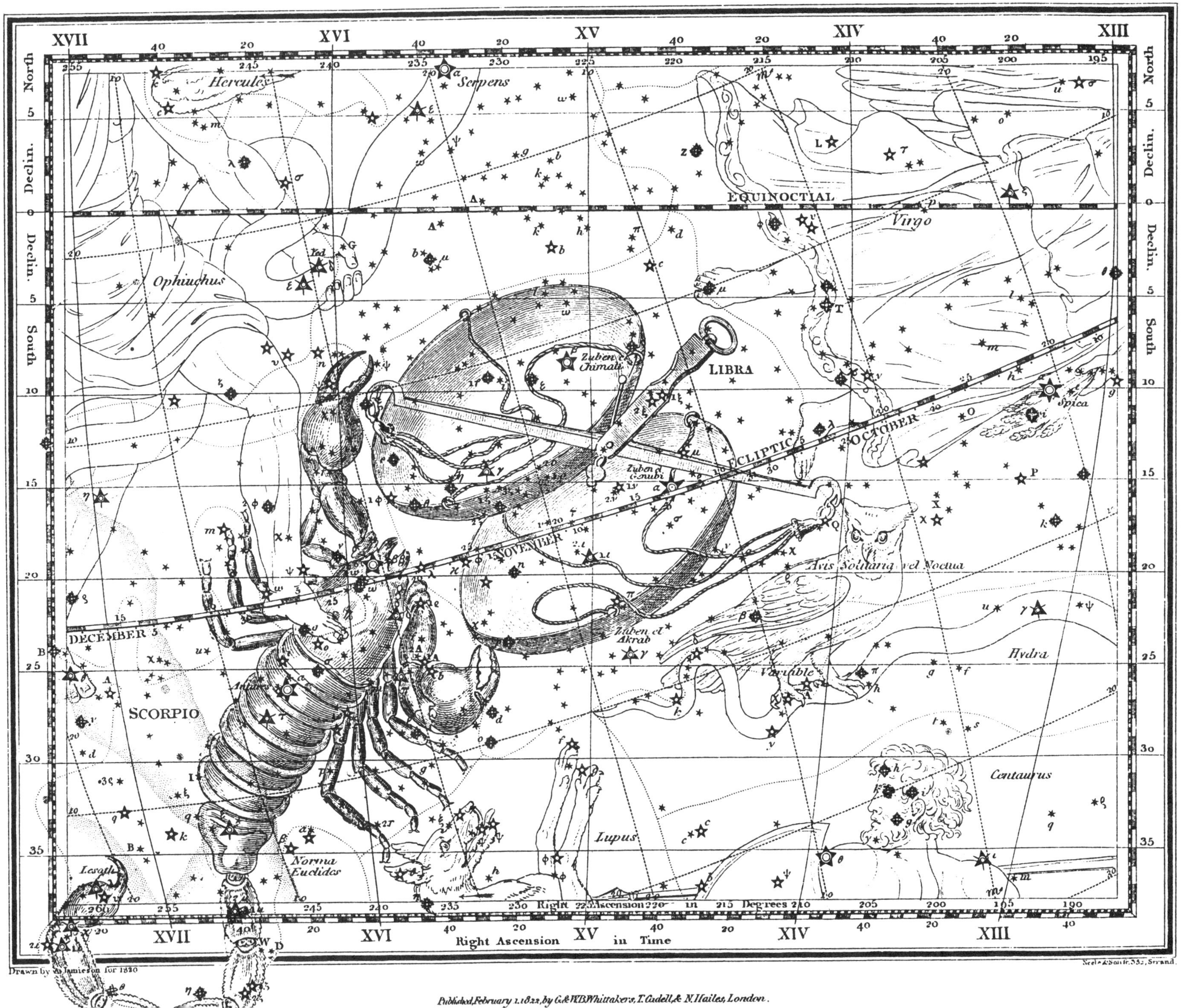

PLATE XIX

Published February 1.1822, by G.&W.B.Whittaker, T.Cadell & N.Hailes,London.

Plate XIX

Here is a two-for-the-price-of-one plate featuring two zodiacal constellations: Libra, the Scales; and Scorpius, the Scorpion. Jamieson labels the latter group by a now-obsolete name, Scorpio, which is still how that sign is called by astrologers. Yet the correct current name of the constellation is Scorpius, which is how it appears on modern maps, including Tirion's. The Scorpion can be found near the bottom-right corner of Tirion's Chart 7, whereas neighboring Libra is located in the bottom-left section of Chart 6; the head of Scorpius is at that chart's lower-left margin.

Libra has the distinction of being the only inanimate member of the zodiac, despite the term "zodiac" deriving from the Greek for "circle of animals." (Yet, for that matter, there are humans in this group as well.) However, the stars of the Scales were originally part of neighboring Scorpius, with the present Scales' stars being in that creature's originally longer claws. Indeed, the names of Libra's two brightest stars are carryovers from their original role: Zubenelgenubi and Zubeneschamali, which in Arabic respectively mean Southern Claw and Northern Claw. Jamieson has these names slightly different—Zuben el Genubi and Zuben es Chimali. These stars also have a set of alternate names that have appeared on some charts: Kiffa Australis and Kiffa Borealis. These are Arabic-Latin hybrids that actually refer to Libra as such; they mean, respectively, Southern Pan and Northern Pan [of the scales]. The Latin words Australis and Borealis, for south and north, are familiar to many; they appear in constellation names and the name of the large southern continent Australia.

Scorpius is perhaps the most magnificent of all the zodiacal constellations, but it's rather unfortunate that for many Northern Hemisphere residents it appears too low in the southern part of the sky, if it isn't actually obscured by the southern horizon itself. Notice the subdued style with which Jamieson portrays the creature's lowermost portion—the curve of its tail which extends below the map's bottom margin. That is the part of the Scorpion that never rises at all from the latitude of London ($51\frac{1}{2}°$N.).

To see this constellation well, one must go south of about 35° north latitude—and the farther south, the better. Scorpius is a splendid pattern of stars whose hook-like shape does somewhat suggest that creepy little arthropod. One of the main legends associated with this animal is that it was the creature that stung the mighty hunter Orion to death. This mythological enmity is associated with the mutual placement of these two constellations. As seen from most locations in the Northern Hemisphere, they never appear in the sky together; when Orion is above the horizon, Scorpius isn't—and vice versa. This little poisonous creature was sent by the goddess Juno, one of whose strongest traits was jealousy which was not just limited to affairs of the heart. She couldn't stand the adulation Orion was receiving, and so sent the creepy creature—which our hunter could have crushed under his heel—to sting him to death in such a humiliating manner. It's rather remarkable that such a splendid group of stars—none of the main ones in the pattern are fainter than third magnitude, which makes the group easy to see even from built-up areas—was made into a constellation representing such a small, somewhat loathsome animal.

Because of its distinctive hook-like shape, certain South Sea islanders, such as the Maori's of New Zealand, regarded these stars as being the Great Fishhook that was used by their god Maui to rescue their island home from the bottom of the Pacific Ocean. Of course, in that part of the world—indeed, anywhere in the Southern Hemisphere—this constellation rises quite high in the sky and even appears overhead for places such as New Zealand. From such areas this constellation is indeed a splendid sight!

Scorpius' brightest star is first-magnitude Antares, a well-known red supergiant right in the heart of the creature. Its name is a Greek one meaning "Rival of Mars." Ares was what the Greeks called the God of War, which was Mars to the Romans. (Here is the origin of the term "martial," which refers to war or combat: martial arts, martial law, and so on.) The name Mars was given in ancient times to that famous planet due to its ruddy or bloody color, and the similarity of their hues is why Antares acquired its name. In fact, even the Mayas, in the tropical Americas, associated the stars of this constellation, and particularly its bright red star, with its God of Death, and the planet we call Mars with death and violence. Indeed, they regarded this red wanderer as having originated here, and whenever any other planet passed through this constellation, it was regarded as an ominous omen.

Antares is a star in the latter stages of its life, when an increase in its core energy has caused it to expand enormously into a huge bloated globe of gas so immense that if we were to replace the Sun in our solar system with this star, its outer portions would reach well beyond the Earth's orbit to that of its namesake planet—Mars.

PLATE XI

Declin N. 0 Declin 0 South

XVII

SCORPIO

Norma Euclidis

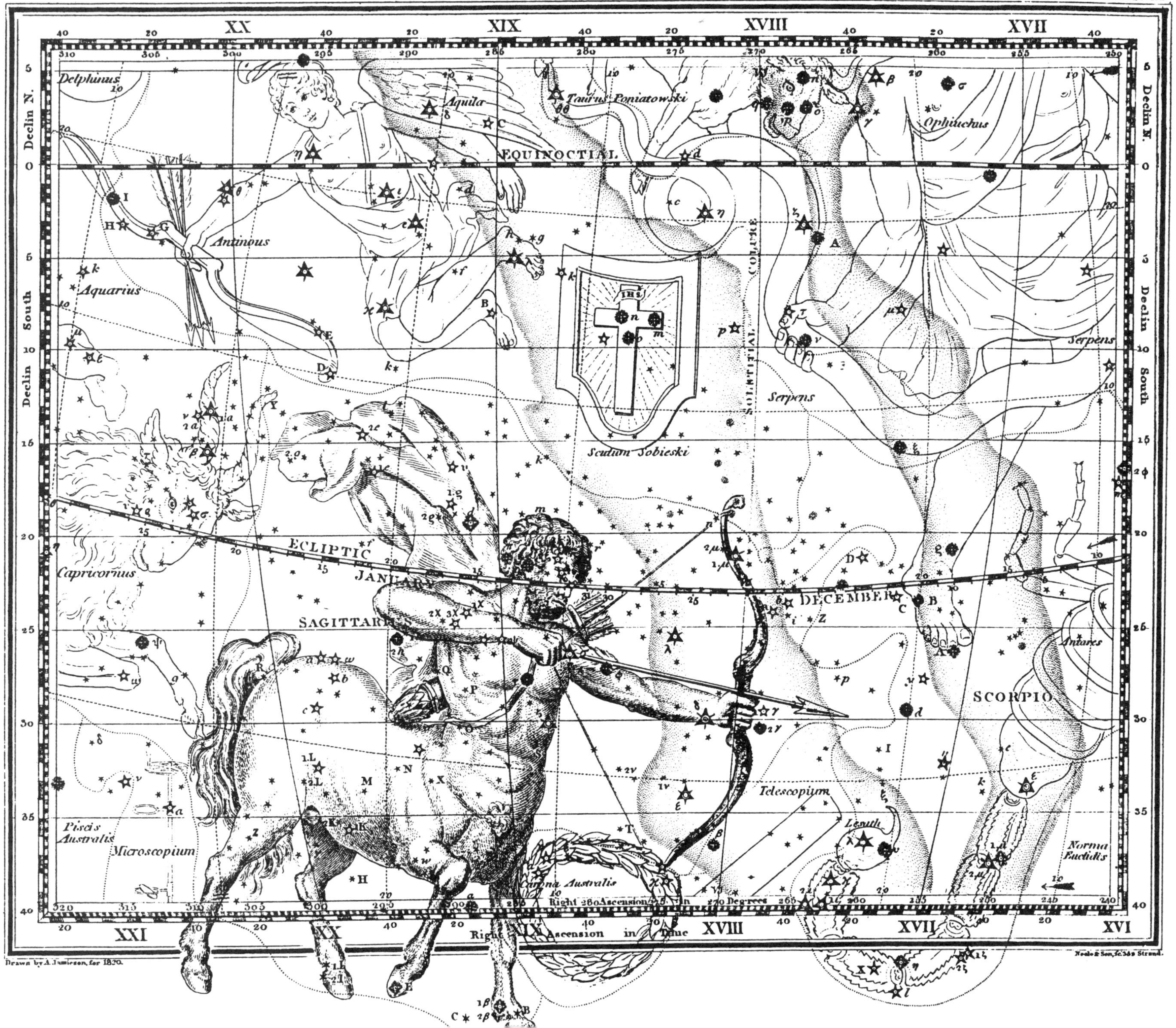

Ophiuchus

Serpens

DECEMBER

Telescopium

SOLSTITIAL COLURE

Scutum Jobieski

Corona Australis

Right Ascension in Time

SAGITTARIUS

ECLIPTIC JANI

EQUINOCTIAL

Aquila

Antinous

Microscopium

Piscis Australis

Delphinus

Aquarius

Capricornus

Declin 0 South Declin 0 South Declin N.

Drawn by J. Emslie for 1830.

Plate XX

We have arrived at the lowermost reaches of the zodiac, where the ecliptic dips down to its winter or December solstice position. Here we find Sagittarius, the Archer, which can also be found at the bottom-center portion of Tirion's Chart 7.

On the date of the winter solstice, December 21–22, Northern Hemisphere observers see the Sun crossing the sky at its lowest altitude during the year, after which its elevation will gradually increase day by day until it reaches its maximum six months later at the summer or June solstice. Although the December solstice is presently occupied by the stars of Sagittarius, this point in the sky continues to mark, as it did for the ancients, the beginning of the sign of Capricorn. That is the name by which this zodiacal sign is still called, although the corresponding constellation (on the next plate and partly visible on this plate's left edge) is now officially called Capricornus, which represents the Sea Goat. Since the Sun enters the sign of Capricorn when it reaches the December solstice point, the latitude circle on Earth over which it is then directly overhead, $23\frac{1}{2}°$ south, is called the Tropic of Capricorn, as we earlier indicated.

The archer represented by Sagittarius is another one of those fanciful half-and-half creatures the ancients, particularly the Greeks, were quite adept at creating. He is one of two centaurs in the sky, those horse-man hybrids. The other is represented by the constellation Centaurus, whose head is visible at the lower-right corner of the previous plate (XIX), and in its entirety on the final Jamieson star map, Plate XXVIII.

In the Greek legends, the centaurs were mostly creatures of great wisdom and knowledge, who, among other things, were teachers of the gods. They were even quasi-deities themselves who enjoyed certain divine traits such as immortality. Some centaurs became the ultimate in hunters and warriors, such as the one represented by Sagittarius, being far more efficient than a mere man on horseback. Sagittarius is commonly pictured—as here—aiming an arrow at the heart of the neighboring Scorpion; indeed, one legend has him avenging the death of fellow hunter Orion, whom, as we recall, the Scorpion stung to death.

Sagittarius has also been linked to the most famous of the legendary centaurs, Chiron, who included among his numerous skills and talents that of the healing arts. However, he managed to die as the result of being accidentally struck by a highly toxic arrow shot by Hercules. Despite his medical skill, Chiron was unable to remove the poison from his body, which caused him intense, unbearable pain even though it could not kill him. He therefore pleaded with Zeus that he be released from his suffering by being allowed to die, and his wish was granted.

Some classical authorities associated Chiron not with Sagittarius, but with the other celestial centaur represented by the constellation Centaurus, maintaining that our Archer was a more ordinary and more roughneck centaur.

While it would take an unusually creative imagination to see a centaur formed by the stars of Sagittarius, it so happens that the main stars of this constellation—the ones in and around the bow and arrow—form a remarkably convincing picture of a teapot, which has become a widely-recognized asterism in this constellation.

When we look at the direction of the stars of Sagittarius, we are gazing towards the center of our home galaxy, the Milky Way system. As a result, that smoky-looking band of billions of distant stars appears brightest in this constellation, particularly just above the position of the center of the Archer's bow in the Jamieson plate. This brightest portion of the Milky Way is also located directly over the "spout" of the Teapot asterism in Sagittarius, and even suggests a puff of steam from that utensil. To the Greeks, the prominent Milky Way in this part of the sky was pictured as billowing smoke rising from Ara, the Altar, a constellation directly beneath Scorpius and found on Jamieson Plate XXVIII. Directly beneath Sagittarius is the ancient constellation Corona Australis, the Southern Crown, which on the Jamieson plate opposite partially protrudes below its bottom edge. While some have linked it to the Northern Crown (Plate VIII), Corona Australis has most often been regarded as one of the leafy wreaths worn by ancient gods and special individuals—in this case Sagittarius.

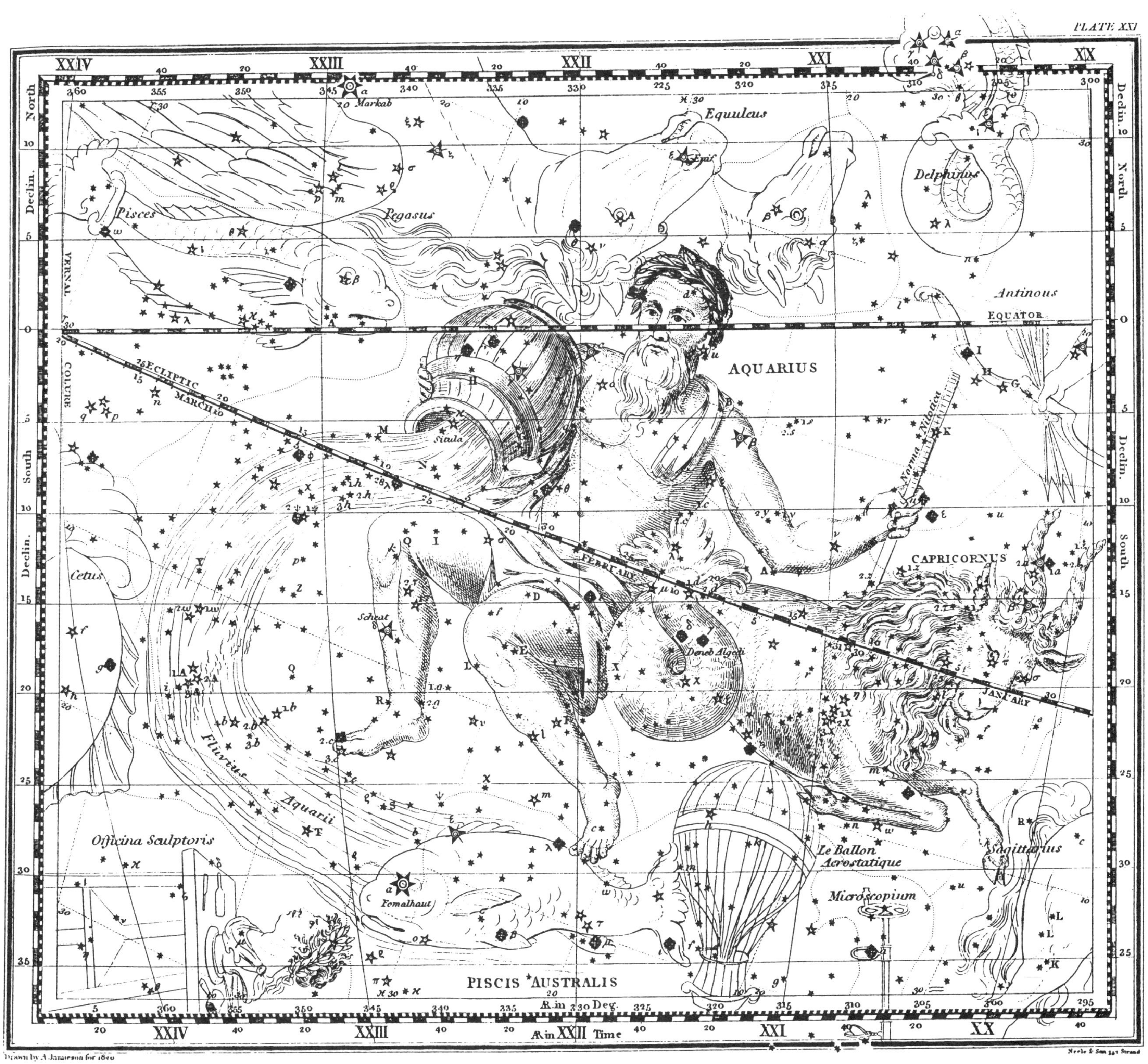

PLATE XV

Declin. North   Declin.   South

Delphinus

Antinous

EQUATOR

AQUARIUS

CAPRICORNUS

Equuleus

Sagittarius

Le Ballon Aerostatique

Microscopium

Norma Nilotica

Dor. Algedi

Jani Ani

Pegasus

Markab

FEBRUARY

ECLIPTIC

MARCH

Fomalhaut

PISCIS *AUSTRALIS

R. in 330 Deg.

R. in XXII Time

Fluvius   Aquarii

Officina Sculptoris

Cetus

Pisces

VERNAL   COLURE

North   Declin.   South   Declin.

Morie & Son 19% Strand

Drawn by A. Jamieson for this

Plate XXI

On this plate, and the next three, we have arrived at a part of the sky that since the earliest Western eras—meaning all the way back to the Mesopotamians—was known as the Celestial Sea. This is because the constellations located here, including those featured on this chart, are of a watery nature or are associated with the sea. On this plate Capricornus, the Sea Goat (already referred to in discussing the previous plate); and Aquarius, The Water Carrier, hold center stage. They can be found just below the center of Tirion's Chart 8. This Celestial Sea occupies a major portion of the southern part of the sky on fall evenings.

During that remote five-millenia-ago era to which the Celestial Sea traces back, Aquarius was situated at the winter solstice point which, as we saw in connection with the preceding plate, is now in Sagittarius. That was the time of year of wet rainy weather, which was also a contributing factor in placing a constellation in this location representing a man pouring water out of a jug; the stream of water is traditionally pictured as cascading into the mouth of Piscis Austrinus, the Southern Fish, another member of the Celestial Sea. Visible at bottom-center, this creature should really be shown with an open mouth. Still another member of this watery group is Delphinus, the Dolphin, at this plate's upper-right corner, and which was officially featured back on Plate X.

Aquarius is a prime example of a group of stars that by no stretch of the imagination even begins to suggest the "star picture" these stars are supposed to represent. Indeed, most constellations are like that, and those who doubt this statement need only look at the various Jamieson plates. The Mesopotamians also pictured the Man With a Jug as being the source of their life-giving waterways, the Tigris and Euphrates rivers. Somewhat around the same time the ancient Egyptians regarded their annual Nile flooding as being caused by the Water Carrier dipping his jug into the river to refill it. Incidentally, the Nile and Tigris-Euphrates river systems were crucial in making those parched lands habitable and suitable for agriculture. Indeed, high school and college world history students are all too familiar with the term "Fertile Crescent," which refers to a roughly arch-shaped stretch of territory extending from the Nile region at its western extremity to the Tigris-Euphrates area at its eastern end. This region has long been regarded as the cradle of Western civ-

ilization (and Biblical events), as well as the place where the earliest still-recognized constellations originated, including the zodiac.

The early Arabs had an interesting variation on Aquarius in which the Water Carrier was a mule instead of a man. This was largely due to their prohibition against pictorial renditions of the human form, not unlike the Old Testament prohibition against "graven images."

Below and to the right of our Water Carrier we come to yet another of those half-and-half creatures of the ancients: Capricornus, the Sea Goat. As we already indicated, around the time ancient Greece flourished, this constellation marked the winter solstice location, just as Cancer at the time stood at the summer solstice. Around the same time period, some 2–3 millenia ago, certain Oriental peoples regarded this constellation (our Capricornus) as being the Southern Gate of the Sun, with its opposite number, Cancer, being the Sun's Northern Gate.

Like Aquarius, Capricornus traces back to that early Fertile Crescent period, yet the most commonly related legend pertaining to it comes—as is so often the case with our constellations—from the Greeks who associated it with their god Pan, also known as Bacchus. The story goes that Pan and some fellow gods were having a festive feast—or bacchanalia (that word even derives from this deity)—when that famous monstrous giant Typhon appears, who shows up at crucial junctures in other legends. To escape him, everyone there changed themselves into some animal, yet Pan panicked (and "panic" also comes from his name) and leaped into the adjoining river feet-first before he finished changing himself into a goat. The portion of his body already immersed thus became fish-like! This sight so amused Zeus that he forthwith placed this odd hybrid in the heavens for eternity.

Directly beneath Capricornus is one of those "modern" (post-classical) constellations attributed to the 18th century French astronomer Joseph Jerome de Lalande: the no-longer-recognized Hot Air Balloon, created to commemorate that famous Montgolfier ascent. (Like steam locomotives, this device has reappeared, albeit as a passtime.) Rather atypically, Jamieson labels this constellation in French, whereas constellation names have traditionally been in Latin, by which this constellation has been called Globus Aerostaticus.

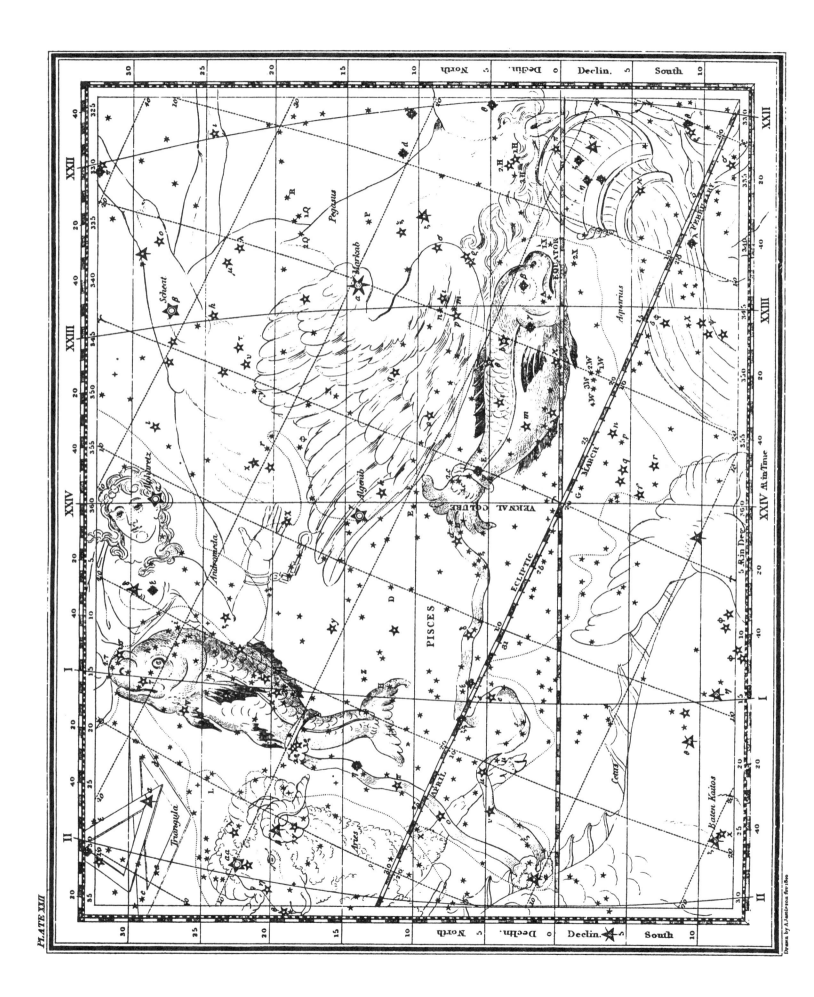

PLATE XXII

Drawn by A.Jamieson for 1820

Plate XXII

We have now reached the last of the zodiacal constellations—Pisces, the Fishes—and have returned to the vernal equinox point, which marks the beginning of the sign of Aries, as we earlier mentioned; the head of that constellation (the Ram) is noticeable at this plate's left edge. Pisces, very much a member of the Celestial Sea, has traditionally been depicted as two fish whose tails are tied together by a cord—a rather odd image! Pisces is one of the zodiac's two faintest constellations; the other is Cancer. Neither contains any star brighter than fourth magnitude. Our Fishes can be found to the above-right of center on Tirion's Chart 3, as well as at the middle of the left edge of Chart 8.

Were we here to again address that perennial question as to whether the stars of Pisces suggest the star picture they are supposed to form, one could offer a somewhat qualified yes. The lower portion of the constellation contains a stringlike row of stars which does represent the cord that extends to the lower creature, commonly called the Western Fish. A second starry string extends upward to the Northern Fish. This constellation somewhat resembles a huge tilted letter "V" at whose bottom is the star called Alrescha or Al Rischa, Arabic for "The Knot." It refers to the knot tying together the two cords; however, this star name is not on the Jamieson chart.

If Pisces is a faint star group that hardly hits one in the eye, its location is relatively easy to pinpoint because of its proximity to the prominent Square of Pegasus, which is directly above the Western Fish while the Northern Fish is to the left of the Square. In fact, the shape of the Pisces pattern even suggests the shape of a giant tweezer about to grab the Great Square—like a tong about to pick up a huge sugar cube! Such do-it-yourself imagery can at times be quite helpful in locating or learning constellations.

Speaking of Pegasus, it is rather interesting—and ironic—that this Pisces plate shows the Great Square of Pegasus more correct, or less distorted, than Plate XII on which Pegasus is featured. This is because on the Pisces chart the Great Square is near the center where the curved coordinate grid distorts it less. Finally, since we're referring to Pegasus here, it is worth mentioning again that to some early people it was a member of the Celestial Sea by having the tail of a fish—a la Capricornus.

And speaking of Capricornus, the leading legend concerning Pisces is not unlike that pertaining to the Sea Goat. The two fishes were originally the Goddess of Love, Venus, and her son Cupid. They were strolling along a river one day when our Typhon monster again chose to show up, as he was wont to do in these legends. So, as the Capricornus party did, they changed themselves into fishes—completely, not partially—and swam away. (We presume without being tied together by that cord.)

Pisces is also the location of one of the leading theories as to what the Star of Bethlehem might have been—assuming it was a real astronomical event. In 6 B.C. the planets Mars, Jupiter, and Saturn formed a compact group within this constellation and this would have been considered significant, even by the Magi who, among other things, were practicing astrologers. One reason such an occurrence would have been significant was that Pisces was a sacred part of the sky to the Hebrews of the time.

The Pisces plate also shows quite graphically how the Sun's daily altitude in the sky greatly increases from late February to late April—about a month before and after the vernal equinox. Similarly, on Plates XVII and XVIII (Leo and Virgo) we see the corresponding solar altitude decrease during the months before and after the autumnal equinox.

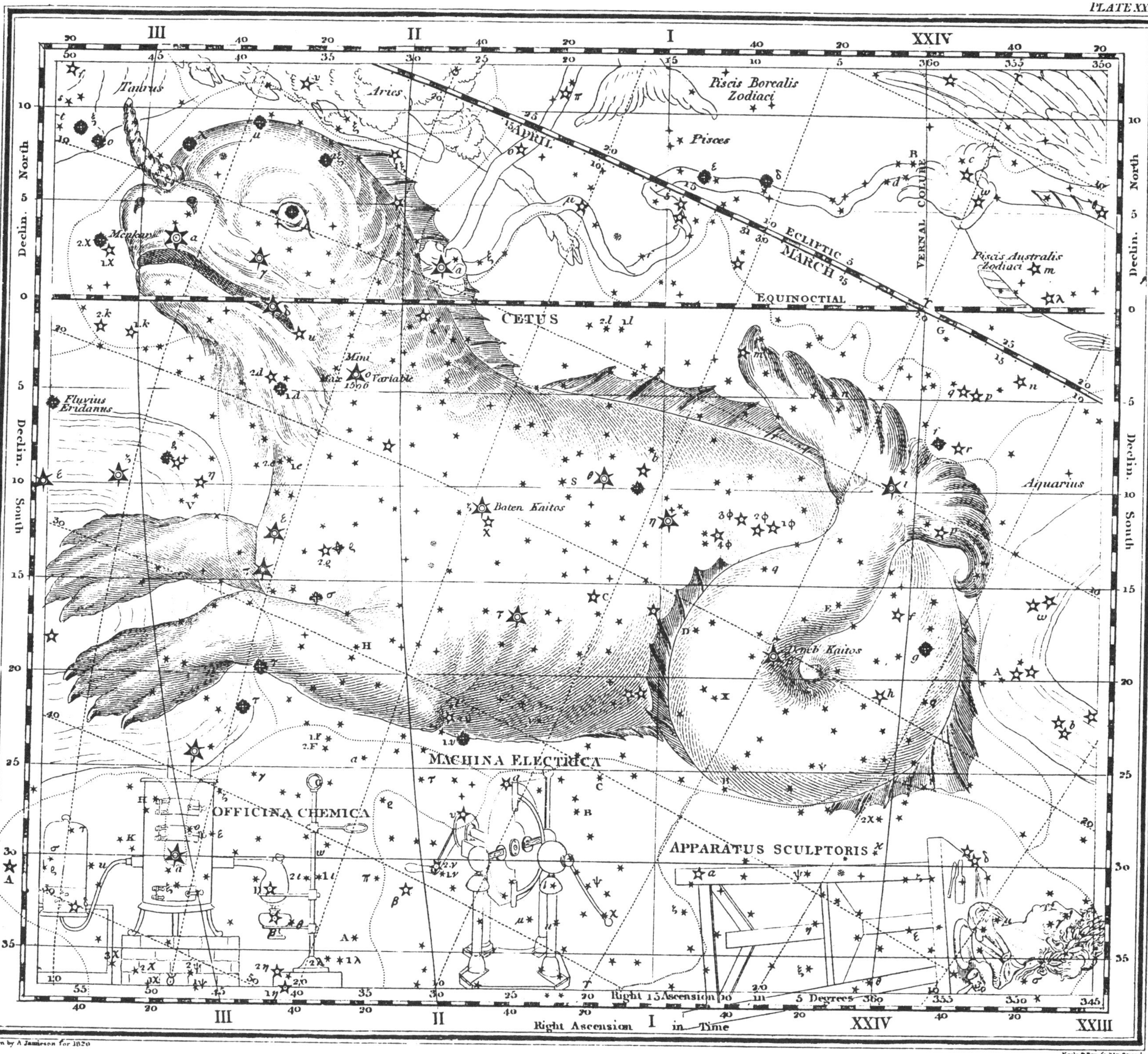

Drawn by A. Jamieson for 1820

Neele & Son sc. 352 Strand.

Plate XXIII

The interesting beast that all but fills up Plate XXIII is Cetus, the Sea Monster. This constellation is most often referred to as the Whale, yet what kind of whale looks like what is pictured here? The sky area covered by this chart is but a short hop downward and to the left from the previous Pisces plate, with considerable overlap between the two. Notice, for example, the vernal equinox intersection involving the equator and ecliptic on both maps. Notice also that here Jamieson labels the two members of the adjoining Pisces pair "Piscis Borealis Zodiaci," and "Piscis Australis Zodiaci." These mean, respectively, "Northern Zodiacal Fish" and "Southern Zodiacal Fish." However, the latter is not what it's called today, it being the Western Fish. As is his practice, Jamieson shows Pisces in the subdued style of an adjoining (non-featured) constellation on this Cetus chart. The huge denizen of the deep featured here can be found a bit below center on Tirion's Chart 3.

Throughout history—and even today—the sea has been regarded as the abode of the strangest forms of life, much of it imaginary and whimsical, among which have been sea monsters of every size, shape, and description. Yet it's not all imaginary. Certain forms of pelagic (oceanic) life—particularly those which live at great depths—are very strange, and some of them look absolutely weird. And who has not heard of the famous Loch Ness Monster, a controversy that refuses to die. When the early Middle East civilizations created the Celestial Sea, they placed some strange creatures within it; did we not already encounter a strange submersible goat?

We even have the Old Testament account of Jonah being swallowed by a whale, except that the Bible refers to it simply as a "great fish," which some have linked to Cetus. We know today, of course, that whales are not fish, but mammals—the largest there are. What is interesting, however, is that the scientific name of the whale family is *Cetacea*, deriving from the Latin word for whale, Cetus, which is also the name of the constellation. However, the important point is that what has usually been pictured as the constellation Cetus is not what we today know whales to be.

We have already encountered Cetus in discussing Plate III in which it is the Sea Monster sent by Neptune to devour Princess Andromeda. We recall that the hero of the story, Perseus, flew overhead just in time to turn Cetus into stone by holding up the head of Medusa for him to gaze at.

In the neck of the Monster is one of the truly remarkable stars in the heavens—Mira, another Latin star name which means "Wonderful" (and from which words such as "miracle" derive). However, on the Jamieson chart it is incorrectly labeled "Mini." Such errors were not uncommon back in those days when such artwork had to be hand engraved from materials supplied by its creator; indeed, errors of this type, as well as inconsistencies from one plate to another, are not uncommon in such old star maps. The reason this star was called "Wonderful" is that it is visible for several months, then disappears for a few months more, then reappears again in a brightening-dimming cycle ranging from about 3rd to 9th magnitude that takes an average of 334 days to go through. The discovery of this star's variability is attributed to the Englishman David Fabricius in 1596 (the date is even marked by Jamieson). Yet the writer seriously wonders if it is possible that this now-you-see-it, now-you-don't star went unnoticed by the innumerable sky watchers during the numerous centuries prior to Fabricius.

Today, of course, we know that Mira is far from unique. It is one of thousands of known long-period variable stars which are basically red giants undergoing internal instabilities towards the end of their life cycles. But at the time Mira's peculiar nature was discovered, it did seem like a miraculous star. Indeed, the noted 17th-century Danzig astronomer and celestial cartographer Johannes Hevelius even wrote, in 1662, a book about this star: *Historiola Mirae Stellae*, "A Short History of the Wonderful Star."

Beneath Cetus are some interesting modern constellations. Left to right, they are: Officina Chemica, the Chemical Equipment (now known as Fornax, the Furnace); Machina Electrica, the Electrical Machine; and Apparatus Sculptoris, the Sculptor's Apparatus (as if the last two names really need to be translated). Of the three, the middle one is no longer recognized as a constellation. It was created by the noted German astronomer Johann Elert Bode at the beginning of the 19th century when electricity became one of the truly high-tech wonders of the time.

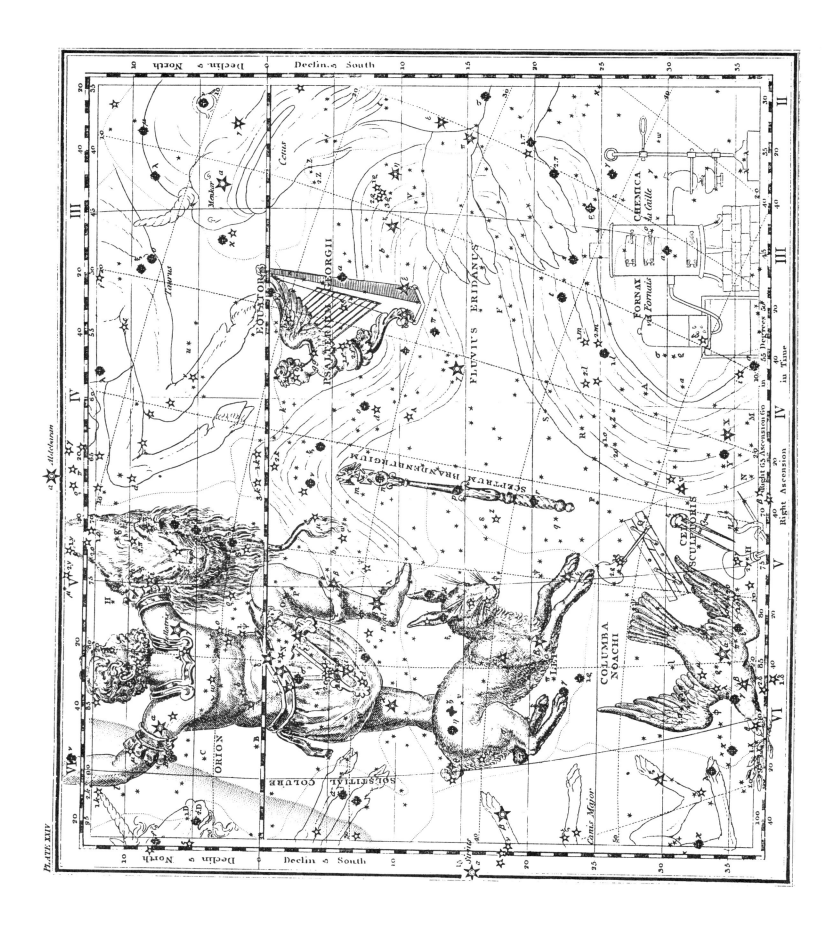

PLATE XXIV

Plate XXIV

We have finally arrived "officially" at what is almost universally regarded as the sky's most magnificent constellation: Orion the Mighty Hunter. Although this is the plate on which Jamieson features this star group, we already encountered it back at the bottom portion of the Taurus chart (Plate XIV). Indeed, that Taurus map must be consulted in order to see the uppermost portion of our Hunter, particularly his upraised club, which is beyond this plate's upper margin. And Orion manages to occupy a commanding position right in the center of Tirion's Chart 4, surrounded by his constellation entourage, such as the two dogs Canis Major and Canis Minor (which are on the next plate—XXV), and Taurus, the Bull.

What really makes Orion unique—and is indeed its trademark—is that almost perfect row of three almost equally bright and separated stars marking the Hunter's belt. This stellar trio even has a catchy set of names (not indicated by Jamieson); they are, left to right, Alnitak, Alnilam, and Mintaka. Back in the Introduction, we cited that Biblical quotation from the Book of Job that refers to Orion's belt. But that's hardly the only place in literature this splendid star group gets mentioned. We quoted an excerpt from Homer's *Iliad* in connection with Ursa Major on Plate VI. And then there are these well-known lines from Tennyson's poem *Locksley Hall*.

> Many a night from yonder ivied casement ere I
> went to rest,
> Did I look on great Orion sloping slowly to the
> west.
> Many a night I saw the Pleiads rising thro' the
> mellow shade,
> Glitter like a swarm of fireflies tangled in a silver
> braid.

It should be noted that his "many a night" couldn't have occurred any time during the year. If Tennyson saw Orion sloping towards the west around his bedtime, it most likely took place around February or March. Similarly, his seeing the Pleiads (Pleiades) rising is something that occurs in the evening during the latter part of the year.

Orion's mythological exploits were legendary. He was a truly heroic figure in ancient lore who has often been labeled the Giant Hunter, implying that he was of considerably greater size than ordinary men, even a sort of demi-god. It is therefore hardly surprising that such a magnificent group of stars—which even suggests a majestic standing human figure—became the constellation representing this special individual. A number of early accounts, even of pre-Greek ancients, associates the Hunter one way or another with the Sun or Sun God.

In one of these stories Orion falls in love with Merope, daughter of King Oenopion, who strongly opposed their marriage. He tried all sorts of delaying tactics, including sending Orion on various missions to separate him from Merope. When this didn't work, he assigned Orion the task to rid his land of all its most dangerous wild beasts, no doubt hoping it would be the end of that unwanted suitor. This Orion successfully accomplished, it being virtually a sport for him. After the King continued to stall, Orion ran off with Merope, but was captured and brought before the King, who had him blinded. The sightless hunter wandered around aimlessly for a while, until he fortuitously encountered the forge of Vulcan, who had sympathy for the Mighty Hunter, and helped guide him to the Land of the Sun—the place where it rose each day. By facing its intense rays, Orion's sight was restored.

Scorpius and Orion, despite being mythological adversaries as discussed in connection with Plate XIX, are similar star groups astronomically. Both are composed largely of hot blue giant stars—among the very brightest in our galaxy—and both contain a first-magnitude red giant star (Antares and Betelgeuse, respectively) that contrast strongly with the bulk of the group's other stars. When we look towards Orion, we're looking towards the brightest stars in our part of our galaxy.

Directly under the Hunter is Lepus, the Hare, an ancient pattern which, representing a commonly-hunted creature, has thus been linked to Orion. One of the interesting ways in which this constellation was regarded is its being linked to the Moon, perhaps in disguised form.

Beneath Lepus is Columba, the Dove, here labeled by its old name Columba Noachi, or Noah's Dove. This post-classical constellation was created in the 17th century by Jacob Bartsch. Immediately to its right is what Jamieson labels Cela Sculptoris, the Engraver's Tools; today it is simply Caelum, the Engraver's Tool. Additionally, two obsolete constellations honoring royalty are centrally placed on this plate: Psalterium Georgii, the Harp of George III of England, and Sceptrum Brandenburgium, the Scepter of [the house of] Brandenburg. The Harp is attributed to the Austrian astronomer Father Maximilian Hell to honor England's third German (Hanoverian) monarch, while the Scepter was created by the 17th-century Prussian astronomer Gottfried Kirch.

Finally, taking up a large part of Plate XXIV is the large non-featured constellation Eridanus, the River, which officially belongs to Plate XXVIII, the final Jamieson star chart on which he gathers a large number of Southern Hemisphere constellations. Eridanus is the easternmost member of our Celestial Sea (even if rivers are supposed to flow into seas).

PLATE XIV

Declin ♋ North   Declin ♋ South

ORION

EQUATOR

MONOCEROS

CANIS MINOR

Procyon

CANIS MAJOR

SOLSTITIAL COLURE

Sirius

LEPUS

COLUMBA NOACHI

ARGO NAVIS

PIXIS NAUTICA

Hydra

Declin ♋ North   Declin ♋ South

Right Ascension 100 in 9.4 Degrees 120

Right Ascension VII in Time   VIII

Drawn by A. Jamieson for 1820.

Neele & Son Gr 352, Strand.

Plate XXV

Moving eastward from Orion—here visible at upper-right—we come across his two dogs, Canis Major at the bottom and Canis Minor near the top. Yet this plate, ironically enough, appears to be dominated by Monoceros, the Unicorn, a rather faint constellation (no star brighter than fourth magnitude) which, like Columba (lower right), is attributed to Jacob Bartsch. The sky area covered by this plate approximately coincides with the left-central portion of Tirion's Chart 4.

Back on Plate XI we pointed out the so-called Summer Triangle made up of the bright stars Vega, Deneb, and Altair. On this plate there is another prominent stellar triangle composed of the stars Sirius, Procyon, and Betelgeuse which, respectively, are in Canis Major, Canis Minor, and Orion. This is a nearly equilateral triangle called the Winter Triangle; it stands out better on Tirion's Chart 4.

Sirius in the Large Dog's nose, enjoys the distinction of being the brightest star in the entire night sky, yet one would never guess it from the Jamieson chart; instead notice how it appears on the Tirion map. One should really say that Sirius is the brightest *appearing* star in the sky because, for example, the main stars in Orion—including his belt—are actually far brighter than Sirius, yet much more distant. They range from over 500 to more than 2000 light-years away; Sirius is only 8.7 light years—virtually a next-door neighbor as stars go—thereby owing its brightest-star distinction primarily to its proximity.

Because of its location in the Greater Dog, Sirius has long been known as the Dog Star. In fact, a number of centuries ago it rose just before the Sun around the beginning of August, which coincided with the summer's hottest period. This is one reason these became known as the Dog Days, which was also attributed to the way dogs are sometimes driven mad by the heat. It was also believed in ancient times that Sirius' rays added to the Sun's helped bring about the Dog Days. The name of this star, incidentally, comes from the Greek "seirios," meaning searing or scorching, no doubt inspired by this star's brilliance.

The rising of a star just before dawn is known as its heliacal rising, from the Greek word for the Sun, "helios," and to the ancient Egyptians the heliacal rising of Sirius—which they called Sothis—was of special significance. In that era this took place around the beginning of summer, and Sothis'

initial appearance in the dawn heralded the annual flooding of the Nile, which provided crucial irrigation and renewal of topsoil for agriculture in what would otherwise be dried-up desert land.

If we move up the eastern edge of our Winter Triangle we arrive at Canis Minor, the Small Dog with its bright star Procyon. This name is also of Greek origin and means "Before the Dog." This refers to the way Procyon rises before Sirius and the rest of Canis Major (which is what is meant by "the" dog) as seen from most Northern Hemisphere locations. Procyon is sometimes called the Little Dog Star, and, like Sirius, it can also legitimately be called a cosmic next-door neighbor, being only 11.3 light-years from us.

To the left of the Large Dog is one of those quaint no-longer-recognized constellations representing a mechanical device, the creation of which became a temporary late-18th-century craze. It is the Printing Press, which Jamieson labels by its French name, although it was better known as Officina Typographica in Latin—which actually more nearly means Printing Apparatus or Office. This rather faint constellation was created by the German astronomer Johann Elert Bode at the end of the 18th century to commemorate that great Gutenberg invention $3\frac{1}{2}$ centuries earlier. Shown are both the old-fashioned hand press at right and the type storage case at left; this latter item has become a popular "Yuppie" artifact as spice storage cabinets and such.

A major ancient constellation is partially visible in the lower-left corner: Argo Navis, the Ship. This was the famous mythological vessel that was involved in numerous exploits, including carrying the Argonauts in quest of the Golden Fleece, as related in connection with Plate XIII. Although this constellation officially belongs to Plate XXVIII, its upper portions can be better seen here and on the next plate. At present Argo Navis no longer exists as an intact ship. Largely because of its huge size and complexity, it has been officially split up into four component parts: Puppis, the Stern (the part next of Canis Major); Vela, the Sails; Carina, the Keel; and Pyxis, the Mariner's or Nautical Compass. The last constellation is shown by Jamieson as such and labeled by its former longer name Pyxis Nautica. This same group has also been called Malus, the Mast; the reason for it is obvious on the plate.

PLATE XXVI.

Declin. 5 North   Declin. 0 South

VIII

Monoceros

Machina Typographica

ARGO NAVIS

PYXIS NAUTICA

Cor Hydræ al Alphard

SEXTANS

HYDRA

FELIS

ANTLIA PNEUMATICA

SEPTEMBER

Leo

Virgo

CRATER

Corvus

Centaurus

Declin. 5 North   Declin. 0 South

Right Ascension in Time

Right Ascen 8,150 in 245 Degrees

Drawn by A. Jamieson for 1820.

Neele & Son 352 Strand

Plate XXVI

Ever since Plate XXIII, we have been sliding almost exactly eastward as if these charts were on a huge filmstrip moving to the right. Additionally, the bottoms of these "filmstrip"-like maps approximate the southern horizon of London. Here we come to the sky's largest constellation, Hydra, the Water Serpent, one so lengthy that it has to be spread across two Jamieson plates—both this and the next one. Its head is directly under Cancer (see Plate XVI) and the tail falls right beneath Libra (Plate XIX), so it spans four zodiacal constellations! The part of the sky on this map approximately corresponds to the portion of Tirion's Chart 5 just a little below its center.

Because of its length, our Water Serpent practically spans the southern part of the sky on spring evenings. However, despite what some writers say, the stars comprising this constellation do not form a natural or obvious serpentlike pattern, unlike the western portion of Eridanus, the River, which is noticeable at the right on Plate XXIV and lower-left portion of Tirion's Chart 3. Here is another illustration of the not-often-appreciated fact we've been stressing that the stars of the great majority of constellations do not form a pattern that suggests what the star picture is supposed to represent.

In fact, Hydra is in one of those relatively star-poor parts of the sky, and its brightest star is second-magnitude Alphard. In Arabic it means "The Solitary One," an apt name for this star which stands so apart from other bright stars.

There are actually two water serpents in the sky. The other one is a considerably smaller one near the south pole called Hydrus and not visible from most Northern Hemisphere locations. Hydra is actually female, while Hydrus is male. Also, our large female creature featured here is of ancient origin, while the smaller male one is a Johnny-come-lately pattern created by Keyser and introduced in 1603 by the famous stellar cartographer Johann Bayer in his epochal *Uranometria* star atlas.

Some have linked Hydra to the ancient Mesopotamian monster Tiamat, the same one Draco, the Dragon, is supposed to trace back to. Yet the most common legend associated with this creature identifies it with the multi-headed Lernean serpent-monster that normally concealed itself in swampy areas and periodically emerged to cause death and destruction among the populace. Disposing of this creature was the second of Hercules' celebrated labors. However, every time he knocked off one of the creature's heads, several others grew in its place. (Here is the origin of that familiar expression "Hydra-Headed Monster" in referring to something unmanageable, such as the tax system!) Finally, Hercules was able to destroy all the heads but one with fire; this last one he buried under a huge rock from which the creature could not extricate itself and so starved to death. The father of the Hydra was supposed to be another celebrated monster which we already encountered—Typhon. One legend states that the gods, acting together, were able to eventually subdue, if not kill, the creature who, among other things, breathed fire and smoke as part of its arsenal of destruction. So when the gods decided to bury it under Mount Etna in Sicily, Typhon could still make its presence felt through periodic volcanic eruptions.

On the back of Hydra is another ancient constellation: Crater, the Cup, which is described in association with the next plate. And directly beneath the Serpent is the obsolete constellation Felis, the Cat, placed there by the 18th-century French astronomer Joseph Jerome de Lalande, who even said, "I am very fond of cats. I will let this figure scratch on the chart. The starry sky has worried me quite enough in my life, so that now I can have my joke with it." He might also have mentioned that he formed this constellation out of stars so faint that one really needs feline eyesight to see it.

At the bottom is a "modern" inanimate constellation attributed to another 18th-century French astronomer, Nicolas Louis de Lacaille, one of a group of constellations representing mechanical devices he placed in the southern heavens as a result of a stay at the Cape of Good Hope between 1750 and 1754. It is Antlia, the Air Pump, here labeled by its originally longer name Antlia Pneumatica.

Notice that on this plate Jamieson labels the Printing Press—at right—by his own Latin name, Machina Typographica. Recall that on the previous plate he labeled it in French. Here is another example that such inconsistencies were far from unusual on star maps of the period.

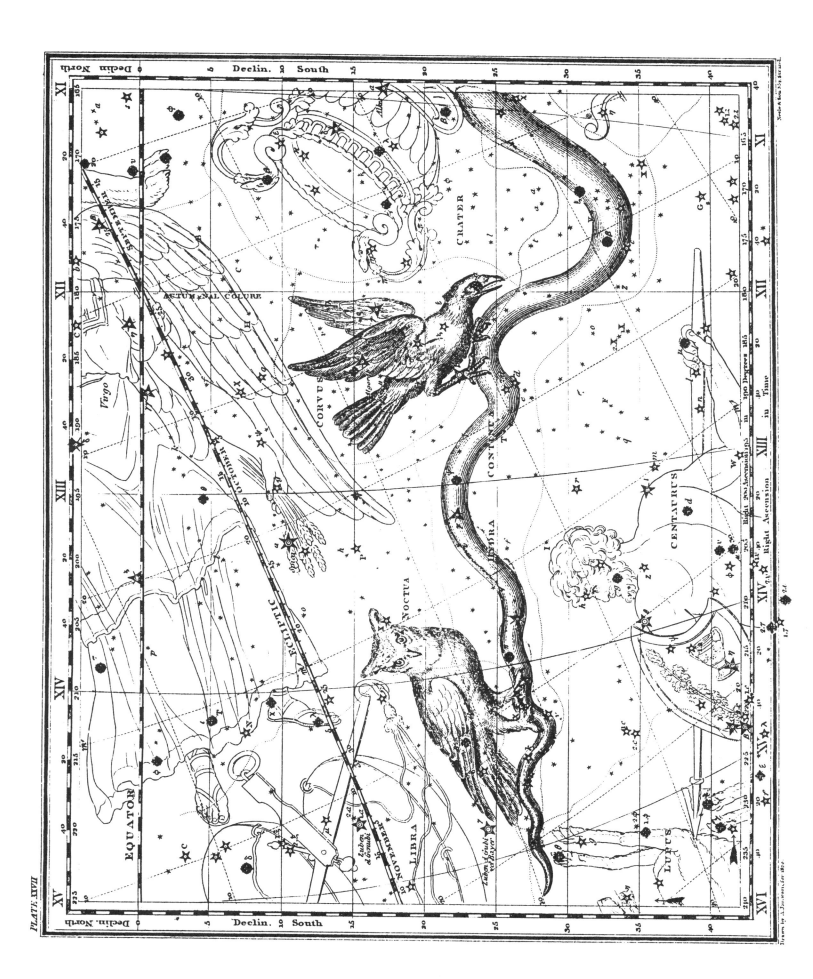

PLATE XXVII

CRATER

Declin. 9 South

Declin. North

CORVUS

HYDRA CONTINVED

NOCTVA

LIBRA

CENTAVRVS

LVPVS

EQVATOR

Virgo

ASTVMNAL COLVRE

ECLIPTIC

Right Ascension in Time

Right Ascension in Degrees

Drawn by A.Jamieson, for 1820.

Plate XXVII

As we said, Hydra is so long that Jamieson had to spread it across two charts, and here we see its tail, which he labels Hydra Continua. This part of the sky can be found at the bottom center of Tirion's Chart 6.

Two birds are perched on Hydra's tail. Corvus, the Crow, remains a recognized constellation, while Noctua, the Owl, does not. (Compare its name to the word "nocturnal," referring to night.) The Crow is an ancient group which has also been called the Raven. Both it and the adjoining constellation Crater, the Cup, which is better seen on the previous plate but still visible here at the right, are associated with the famous Greek god Apollo. One of Corvus' tasks was to serve this god as a scout, servant, and messenger—and also as a spy on certain occasions. These included instances when Apollo was interested in a member of the opposite sex and wanted to be sure of her fidelity, even if to the gods themselves fidelity was a silly idea. We recall that these gods frequently had liaisons with ordinary people.

On one occasion it happened that the object of Apollo's interest was not faithful to him, as reported by the Raven. As a result he grew so enraged that he changed the bird from white to black, and this was an explanation for the present color of this species.

In another story, Apollo asks Corvus to fetch him some water in the cup which became the constellation Crater. While away on this errand, the bird spots a highly appealing fig tree with ripening fruit. He decides to wait until the fruit is ready to eat, and indulges himself. Finally, he remembers the errand he is supposed to be performing, and gets the water and brings it to Apollo with the alibi that a water serpent prevented him from getting at the water. Apollo immediately sees this for the bold-faced lie it is, and in his anger places bird, cup, and serpent in the sky together. Here is but another illustration of how the ancients often placed constellations in the sky not because the stars suggest an obvious likeness, but according to a systems approach dictated by some story or legend.

The main stars of Corvus form a distinctive quadrilateral of nearly-equally-bright third-magnitude stars. This pattern, which to some suggests the mainsail of a small sailboat, really stands out in this star-poor part of the sky, and its two upper stars point almost directly to the first-magnitude star Spica in neighboring Virgo.

Although we have been saying that, by and large, constellations do not look like what they are supposed to represent, Crater, the Cup is somewhat of an exception. Its faint stars do form a sort of goblet-shaped pattern which suggests a wine glass. Yet the constellation itself—as here—has most often been shown as a two-handled chalice-like vessel. Crater is an exception to another common conception; namely, that constellations representing inanimate objects must be of modern origin. Crater clearly is not. Incidentally, its Latin name, meaning "cup," has also been applied to those countless cup-shaped holes on the surface of the Moon and other solar system bodies.

The origin of our other bird on this chart—Noctua, the Owl—is shrouded in a bit of mystery. Several authors attribute it to Elijah H. Burritt and his famous *Geography of the Heavens* atlas and guidebook, which first appeared in 1835. What is especially interesting is that the constellation figures in Burritt's atlas strongly resemble those of Jamieson, although Burritt's star-plotting accuracy is decidedly inferior. Yet our Owl clearly exists in the Jamieson work, suggesting that this is where it first appeared. Also, Jamieson does not mention Noctua at all in his text. Also, in the late 18th century another bird was formed at the location of our Owl: Turdus Solitarius, the Solitary Thrush. On certain old maps it appears instead of Noctua; among these its Bode's major *Uranographia* of 1801.

All this points out that tracing down information about star and constellation lore is sometimes not that simple. And this Jamieson work itself provides a number of examples of internal inconsistencies, not to mention variations between what it contains and other atlases and sources.

STEREOGRAPHIC PROJECTION OF THE SOUTHERN CELESTIAL HEMISPHERE ON THE PLANE OF THE EQUINOCTIAL.

PLATE XVIII.

Magnitudes of the Stars.

Drawn by A. Jamieson A.M. 1822.

Plate XXVIII

We have arrived at Jamieson's final star chart showing the mythological constellation figures, this plate being an overall general one of the entire southern hemisphere of the sky from the celestial equator to the south pole. The approximately central portions of this plate correspond with Tirion's Charts 9 and 10.

Jamieson decided not to continue his series of rectangular detailed sectional maps below the approximate declination of the horizon of London. Another reason may have been that the star groups in the far-southern heavens around the south celestial pole have very little early lore associated with them, since this part of the sky was not visible to the early Middle East civilizations from whence the classical constellations derive. Note the circle on this chart labeled "Horizon of London." The sky area inside of it cannot be seen from the latitude of that city.

The present Plate XXVIII, like Plate I (which is the same type of general map of the northern celestial hemisphere), is not as complete, nor is it plotted with the same degree of accuracy, as the individual sectional plates in between. However, we must again emphasize that none of these Jamieson charts are as accurate as those of Tirion, which should always be consulted in order to get an accurate rendition of the starry scene. It wasn't really until the 15th century that Europeans began sailing down below the equator into the Southern Hemisphere and got to see those "new" stars around the south celestial pole they couldn't see back home. There was, therefore, a substantial constellation gap in those far-southerly skies which only began to be filled by the early 17th century. However, various Southern Hemisphere natives formed their own patterns and constellations, quite different from our own.

The first group of south-polar constellations were Keyser creations and introduced by Johann Bayer in his classic *Uranometria* atlas of 1603. They include: Apus, the Bird of Paradise; Chamaeleon, the Chameleon; Dorado, the Swordfish; Grus, the Crane; Hydrus, the [female] Water Serpent; Indus, the [New World] Indian; Musca, the [Southern] Fly (originally, Apis, the Bee); Pavo, the Peacock; Phoenix, the mythical Phoenix Bird; Triangulum Australe, the Southern Triangle; Tucana, the Toucan; and Volans, the Flying Fish. Keyser largely followed the ancient tradition of creating constellations that represent animals or humans (there is one inanimate object—the Southern Triangle).

Thus the southern constellation roster remained for another century-and-a-half until Lacaille, during his Cape of Good Hope sojourn, introduced the following 14 new constellations, all representing inanimate objects: Antlia, the Air Pump; Caelum, the Sculptor's Chisel; Circinus, the Drawing Compasses; Fornax, the Chemist's Furnace; Horologium, the Clock; Mensa, the Table Mountain (named after a formation at the Cape of Good Hope); Microscopium, the Microscope; Norma, the Carpenter's Square; Octans, the Octant; Pictor, the Artist's Easel; Pyxis, the Mariner's Compass; Reticulum, the Reticle; Sculptor, the Sculptor's Apparatus; and Telescopium, the Telescope. As we already saw, some of these constellations originally had longer names.

The groups introduced by both Bayer and Lacaille managed to survive to the present time, yet some of the later creations, such as the Printing Press and others, mercifully fell by the wayside.

Although the southern heavens largely lack the lore and traditions of the northern, by a twist of fate it so happens that some of the most splendid starry sights are situated down there. Even though we described Orion as the most magnificent constellation, it so happens that—at least in the author's opinion—the most splendid part of the sky is situated at the Southern Cross and its immediate vicinity. Within a sky area smaller than that occupied by the main stars of Orion, there exists here four brilliant first-magnitude stars, two in the Southern Cross (Crux) and two in neighboring Centaurus. One of the latter two is Alpha Centauri (also called Rigil Kentaurus) the nearest star to us after the Sun—at 4.3 light-years—and the third brightest appearing star in the sky. Extending westward from the Crux-Centaurus area is a band of brilliant stars along the southern Milky Way that extends all the way to Orion. Here we also find the sky's second-brightest star, Canopus, which is invisible to a large portion of Northern Hemisphere residents.

We don't have enough space here to describe all those southern splendors, yet a good sampling of them appears on the appropriate Tirion charts and accompanying listings. Anyone interested in celestial observing should not pass up an opportunity to travel to the Southern Hemisphere. The celestial sights observable from there will well repay the trip.

Finally, as if to prove the maxim that you cannot have everything, despite the splendors that exist in the southern skies, one thing it lacks is a prominent "South Star" like Polaris. The area around the south celestial pole is barren of bright stars; the closest naked-eye star to that pole is fifth-magnitude Sigma (σ) Octantis, which can be found on Tirion's Charts 9 and 10.

About the Modern Universe

Although this volume is not intended to be a formal introduction to the science of astronomy, we still wish to offer a basic description of the true nature of what the star charts in this book actually portray. Tirion's *Bright Star Atlas* which follows is based upon the Yale *Bright Star Catalog, 4th Edition*. This atlas plots the positions of all the stars in that catalog and represents virtually all the stars with a visual magnitude 6.5 or brighter, which is what the average dark-adapted human eye can see under ideal conditions. If you are middle aged or older you will be able to see fewer of the fainter stars because your iris has lost some of it's ability to "open up" to admit more light.

Opposite each of the ten *Bright Star Atlas* charts you will find tabular data. These lists were compiled by Brian Skiff with the aim of providing a reasonably consistent selection of the brightest examples of each class of deep-sky objects, double and variable stars visible in common hand-held binoculars and the smallest telescopes. In addition, all Messier objects are included, even though many do not meet the selection criteria outlined below. Many of the best examples of types of variable stars fall below the limit for this atlas and would not normally have been plotted. A selection of these variables that are brighter than 10.0p (photographic) at maxima are included to make the list more comprehensive.

The Stars

Despite the fact that the human race gazed up at the starry firmament for millenia, it wasn't until only a century-and-a-half ago—in the 1830's—that mankind was first able to penetrate the "third dimension" of the vast stellar universe. At that time the distance to a nearby star was first measured by means of a very delicate triangulation technique called parallax measurement; the star's tiny apparent shift against the more remote stellar background, which results from the Earth's orbital motion, was detected. This enables the star's distance to be calculated.

These distances are incredible. The star that's truly closest to us—our Sun—is only about 93 million miles away, or some 150 million kilometers. The next nearest star, Alpha Centauri, is about 25 trillion miles from us. With millions, billions, and trillions being tossed around with such abandon these days (especially with matters such as government expenditures, to which the term "astronomical" is aptly applied), one tends to lose touch with what such numbers represent. So here's a better way of picturing how far the nearest nighttime star is. Light from the Sun takes only about $8\frac{1}{2}$ minutes to reach our eyes; from Alpha Centauri it requires some $4\frac{1}{3}$ years!

Most of the stars we see when we look up at night without a telescope—those making up the constellations that form the main theme of this book—are but tens, hundreds, and but a few thousand light-years into the inky interstellar void. Yet our Sun, with its family of planets, one of which we live on, is one of perhaps 300 billion or so other suns that make up the galaxy we live in, the Milky Way system. This enormous cosmic pancake is some 100,000 light-years across and about 30,000 light-years thick at its center. Like a great number of the larger galaxies, its outer portions have a spiral shape, and we are situated along the inner edge of one of the Milky Way's spiral arms. Those fortunate enough to reside in or have access to locations far from the ubiquitous light pollution of populated areas can see that ghostly, smoky, "Milky Way" band arching across the heavens. This band, shown in green on the Tirion charts, represents the combined light of billions of remote stars in our galaxy that individually are too faint to be seen without a telescope. Although the term Milky Way (or Via Lactea in Latin on some old charts) has traditionally been applied to this band in our heavens, today it also refers to our home galaxy.

Our Sun is a rather average star in certain respects. Although it's considerably larger and brighter than the great majority of stars populating our galaxy, of which most are red dwarfs, it's also smaller and fainter than practically all the stars we see with the unaided eye at night, or those forming the constellations. These latter types of stars, numerically but a small percentage of the stellar population, are the "celebrities" of our galaxy. Like human celebrities (also small in number, percentagewise) they are known—or visible—over considerably greater distances than the "average citizens" such as the red dwarfs.

Stars also come in a variety of colors—all the way from red for the coolest ones to blue-white for the hottest. Their surface temperatures range from roughly $3,000°C.$ ($5,000°F.$) for the "cool" red stars to about $35,000°C.$ ($60,000°F.$) for the hottest. But these values are only for their surfaces. In their cores, where stars are fiery nuclear furnaces that convert light elements into heavier ones while releasing enormous quantities of energy, temperatures range in the tens to hundreds of millions of degrees!

Double Stars

Like the human population, most stars are "married"; that is, they have a companion—even in certain cases two, three, or more. Single stars like the Sun are in the minority. (However, a few astronomers believe that there's a possibility the Sun might have a remote, hard-to-detect faint red-dwarf companion. Also, the giant planet Jupiter is sometimes called a "stillborn star"—a body with the makings but not the mass to become a genuine self-luminous star.)

Some of these double stars are splendid sights in a telescope, and a good selection of them are listed in the accompanying tables. A few of these pairs show beautifully contrasting colors, such as Albireo in the constellation Cygnus, which has an orange and blue component. True double stars—those gravitationally tied together—are called binaries. These stars actually orbit one another, or around a common center of gravity between them called the barycenter. Because of this orbital motion, the relative separations and orientations of binaries change over periods of time, and depending on circumstances, noticeable changes can be detected over intervals of years, decades, centuries, or millenia. This is why double star listings often have a year or "epoch" included that indicates exactly when the listed values apply.

The doubles were selected by Brian Skiff using the following criteria: the brighter star's visual (V) magnitude is brighter than or equal to 6.50 so all the pairs will have their primaries listed in the Yale *Bright Star Catalog*; the fainter star visual magnitude is brighter than or equal to 8.00; separation between 2.0 and about 30 arcseconds. A special effort was made to include what Skiff calls "61 Cygni-type pairs," which are relatively bright, nearly equal pairs with separations around 20 to 40 arcseconds (61 Cygni's specifications are V=5.2 and 6.0, 30 arcseconds separation). Although not of interest at high power, they are often resolvable in sharp binoculars, and in very low power telescopes are frequently beautifully set in their star fields. Pairs with large magnitude differences (difficult to view with low-power instruments) were excluded, particularly those of smaller separations. Up-to-date separations were found in the 1984 edition of the *The Washington Double Star Catalog* by Worley and Douglass. Nearly all the pairs have been measured within the last two or three decades, quite recent enough since their motions are generally very slow at these wide separations. Position angles have been omitted because they are of minimal interest in visual observation. If the year 2000 is given for the date of the measure, this indicates a pair with a published orbit. A few very wide pairs (having arcminute separations) also have 2000 in the date column: for these (mostly optical pairs), proper-motions were accounted for up to that date. Magnitudes are from the Yale *Bright Star Catalog* (YBS), with amendments from Wallenquist's *Catalogue of Photoelectric Magnitudes and Colors of Double and Multiple Systems,* and (south of −25° Dec) from the photoelectric-scanner photometry of Hurly and Warner. Many pairs were eliminated as a result of the accurate data in these sources, their historical (WDS) magnitudes being too bright compared to their photoelectric magnitudes. Magnitudes for even very bright stars were often shifted by several tenths of a magnitude. Star names are from the YBS.

Variable Stars

Another special type of star is the variable star, one whose light changes periodically—and sometimes drastically—on a more-or-less regular cycle. There are two broad classes of variables: extrinsic and intrinsic.

The extrinsic variables comprise the eclipsing binary stars: a close pair of stars whose orbital plane is nearly in our line of sight, such that they block each others light wholly or partially on a regular cycle. The best known eclipsing system is Algol in Perseus (β Persei, Chart3). Its brightness drops by 1.3 magnitudes and brightens again over the course of a few hours about every three days.

Nearly all the intrinsic variables are stars that pulsate different amounts at varying rates. The changing sizes of these stars accounts for the change in brightness and (to a lesser extent) temperature. Three groups are common on our lists: Miras, semiregulars, and Cepheids. The Mira stars are cool red giants showing very large magnitude changes over the course of a year or so. Mira itself (o Ceti, Chart 3) has an extreme range of eight magnitudes with an average cycle length of about eleven months. Amateurs continue to make a valuable contribution to astronomy by following the changes in these stars, which are not strictly predictable or periodic.

The semiregulars comprise a variety of cool, luminous stars (giants and supergiants) that pulsate like Miras, but usually have a smaller range. As their name suggests, their variations are often cyclic, but not so strongly periodic as in the Miras. The Cepheids are hotter supergiant stars that pulsate predictably with periods from days to weeks.

The variable stars were selected from a list prepared by Janet Mattei of the American Association of Variable Star Observers (AAVSO) and published in the 1989 *Astronomical Almanac*. They include the brightest variables of all types with ranges exceeding 0.5 magnitude. A few of the stars have a maximum brightness below the Atlas limit, but are included because they represent important classes of variables. The tables include the magnitude ranges (extremes for the Miras), the Julian Date of maximum, and the period. The periods of most of the eclipsing variables and Cepheids are known to high precision (often to within a few seconds of time), whereas those given for the long-period Miras and semiregulars are merely typical for the star and can vary considerably from the value listed—one reason they are important to observe!

Denizens of the Deep Sky

Much more than mere stars fill our firmament. There are innumerable nebulae, clusters, and galaxies, of which some of the most prominent and easy-to-observe examples are shown on the Tirion charts and listed in the tables. The five major categories of these non-stellar or "deep-sky" objects are open clusters, globular clusters, diffuse nebulae, planetary nebulae, and galaxies. For those who are interested, we have here included certain technical details pertaining to the compilation of the tables.

Open Clusters

The open clusters populate the plane of our galaxy, particularly the spiral arm areas. The Pleiades and Hyades clusters in Taurus (Tirion Charts 3 and 4) and Praesepe cluster in Cancer (Chart 5) belong to this category. These are usually loose aggregations of young, often hot blue, stars. Open clusters typically have only hundreds of members, so their individual stars are observable. We might regard the youngest of them as stellar "nurseries" of newly-born stars. Since they are located mainly in the plane of our Milky Way galaxy, it is not surprising that in the sky they are found largely along the Milky Way band.

The open clusters brighter than integrated V magnitude 7.0 are included in the tables, with a few exceptions. Some open clusters with a single dominant star were omitted. Diameters and magnitudes are from *Sky Catalogue 2000.0, Volume 2* or Lynga's *Catalogue of Open Cluster Data.*

Globular Clusters

Stars in globular clusters are much more numerous than in open clusters; they can have up to hundreds of thousands or even over a million members, and are found outside the galactic disk in a roughly spherical halo suggesting moths around a bright light. In a sense, globular clusters are miniature galaxies of their own which are similar in structure and composition to true spherical galaxies. These objects could be regarded as stellar senior citizen communities which, unlike open clusters, have older stars. Photographs of globular clusters suggest that they are packed solidly with stars, which is only an illusion arising solely from the limited angular resolution of the photos. In a telescope most globulars look like out-of-focus fuzzy disks, but the larger and brighter ones show sprinklings of individual stars.

Globular clusters brighter than integrated V magnitude 7.0 are included, with a few exceptions. Messier globulars below the magnitude cutoff were preserved. Magnitudes are from a 1984 compilation by Webbink, which he believes are good to a few percent; they often differ considerably (almost always brighter) from those given in older catalogs but probably better represent the state of the art in this matter. Diameters are from a list by Alcaino.

Diffuse Nebulae

Diffuse nebulae, such as M42 in Orion (Tirion Chart 4) contain the raw material, gas and dust, from which stars are born; indeed, in M42—which is popularly known as the "Orion Nebula"—stars are being born at present, so these objects could be regarded as stellar maternity wards. In fact, certain open clusters such as the Pleiades still have dust material among their stars. Like open clusters, diffuse nebulae are found in the spiral-arm portions of galaxies, and, consequently, largely along the Milky Way band in the sky. Many of these objects—like M42 in Orion—glow by both fluorescence (energy from stars within causes their gases to glow) as well as reflected starlight.

The tables include a selection by Brian Skiff of bright diffuse nebulae. He also provides rough integrated magnitude estimates, but no claim is made as to accuracy; no actual measures exist in the literature. Most of these are naked-eye or binocular objects, at least from a truly dark site, i.e. they are objects that do not require a sky-suppressing "nebula" filter to see them, although they may be enhanced by such filters.

Planetary Nebulae

Planetary nebulae are so called because the first objects so termed were disk-like (N3242, N6210) and not because early telescopes had inferior optics as speculated by some writers. This is an unfortunate misnomer, because these objects have *nothing* to do with planets. What they really represent are the roughly spherical cast-off outer portions of certain stars late in their lifetimes. The Ring Nebula in Lyra (M57) and the Dumbbell Nebula in Vulpecula (M27)—both on Tirion Chart 7—are leading examples of this type of object.

With but a few exceptions planetaries brighter than visual magnitude 10.0 are included in the tables. The magnitudes were provided by Jack Marling, who summed published fluxes for the emission lines intermixed with the dark-adapted visual response function; the magnitude zero-point was determined by a similar computation using an absolute flux calibration of Vega (which comes out on this system at magnitude –0.13). A judicious selection was made of the dimensions given for each object in the catalog of Perek and Kohoutek, attempting to provide the most modern measure of the brighter portion of the object, excluding extremely faint outer haloes many objects possess.

Galaxies

Galaxies are huge star systems like our own Milky Way numbering up to over 100 billion. They stretch to the limits of the visible universe, and perhaps beyond. Yet the "sociability of the stellar universe," or the tendencies of stars to gather together, also applies to galaxies because there are innumerable clusters of galaxies. The most prominent example is the well-known "Virgo Cloud." It's situated between the main stars of Leo and Virgo and contains thousands of member galaxies. Tirion's Chart 6 shows but a handful of Virgo Cloud members. The two closest galactic systems to us are the Large and Small Magellanic Clouds. They are "satellite" galaxies of our Milky Way and both can be found on Tirion's Chart 9 labeled LMC and SMC, respectively.

Galaxies are classified among three basic types depending on their appearance: elliptical, lenticular, or spiral. The ellipticals are characterized by a smooth appearance lacking bright star clouds or nebulous star-forming regions. The degree of their apparent elongation is expressed by a number ranging from zero for circular objects to 6 for the most elongated galaxies in this class, with occasional intermediate values. Dwarf and compact varieties are preceded by a 'd' or 'c.' The supergiant elliptical NGC 4486 (Messier 87) in the Virgo cluster is distinguished by having a + sign following the E.

The lenticulars form a transition class between ellipticals and the commonly pictured pinwheel-shaped spirals. These have prominent smooth halos like the ellipticals, but also exhibit a thin disk as spirals do. Lenticulars whose form is closer to that of the ellipticals are classed S0⁻, while those more nearly like spirals are called S0⁺.

Spirals with the most tightly-wound arms are classed Sa; as the arms appear progressively more open and clumpy along their length, the classification proceeds through Sb, Sc and Sd (with intermediate two-letter combinations) to Sm, represented by the barely discernable spiral structure of the Magellanic Clouds. Unstructured galaxies are called irregulars, designated Im for patchy 'Magellanic' object, or I0 for diffuse objects whose appearance is more akin to lenticulars.

Spirals, lenticulars, and irregulars occur in ordinary and barred families, denoted with SA and SB, or IA or IB as appropriate. The Andromeda Galaxy is an ordinary spiral whose arms are wound moderately tightly, and thus classed SAb. The Large Magellanic Cloud shows a distinct bar, even if its spiral structure is not, and is classed SBm.

Most of the galaxies were chosen from the list provided by de Vaucouleurs in the 1989 *Astronomical Almanac*, and include all those with integrated V (visual) magnitudes equal to or brighter than 10.0. The *Almanac* list omits a number of relatively small objects brighter than this limit; these were added using information in the *Second Reference Catalogue of Bright Galaxies* (RC2). Objects of very low surface brightness were excluded. In a few cases where only an integrated B (blue) magnitude is given by de Vaucouleurs, more recently published aperture-photometry, collected in a catalogue of such measures by Longo and de Vaucouleurs, was used to infer an approximate integrated B-V color, and thence an integrated V magnitude. These cases are indicated with a colon (:); they are not likely to be in error more than 0.1 magnitude, consistent with the precision of the B magnitude given by de Vaucouleurs. Types and dimensions are also from the *Almanac* list or the RC2. The dimensions are rounded to two significant figures, consistent with the ±10% mean error quoted in the RC2. The types are on the revised morphological system of de Vaucouleurs, but many of the structural details coded in these types have been stripped out for simplicity, leaving only the basic class and stage de Vaucouleurs preserved in his elaboration of the more familiar Hubble classification system.

The Constellations Today

We have now come full circle and return to man's first attempt to order the universe. We started our journey with Jamieson's Atlas which was among the last extensive mythological atlases. Even in the 1820's, when this work was published we see that the fruits of the preceding two centuries of optically aided observing had caused new objects to be plotted. A mere two decades later (1843) Argelander produced *Uranometria Nova* with only the vaguest outlines of these mythological beings. In another 20 years (1863) he published his epochal *Bonner Durchmusterung* and a colorful era of star mapping essentially ended.

But yet, in a sense this mythology survives in our continued use of the constellations to indicate the general location in the sky where a celestial body can be found. Perhaps this is as it should be. Until the advent of the written record mankind preserved and passed on his wisdom, knowledge, and traditions to the next generation by word of mouth. To insure that the information passed correctly memory aids or "hooks" were used to successfully record and retain details of epic dimension. In the case of the starry scene, these "hooks" became those vivid visualizations (sometimes highly forced) that became today's constellations. Whether in ancient or modern times, they have enabled us to get to know the celestial canvas by breaking it up into "bite-size pieces" which

has also served as a link with our ancestors' culture. On the opposite page is a listing of the 88 constellations recognized today, their pronunciations, what they represent, the charts they can be found on, and their origins.

- In the listing, only those constellations officially recognized today are included, using their present names. For certain constellations, these have differed during previous times, as can be seen on the Jamieson charts (which also include a number of now-defunct star groups).

- The second column contains the most accepted phonetic pronunciations of each constellation's Latin name. These are not necessarily classical Latin; in some instances they are modified for English-speaking users. The syllables receiving the greatest stress are indicated with capital letters.

- In the columns that indicate on which Jamieson and Tirion charts each constellation appears, numbers refer to the maps which best show that particular group, either in its entirety or by inclusion of a significant portion.

- Generally speaking, a constellation is not referred to Jamieson's two circular hemispherical charts—Plates I and XXVIII—unless it is not found or well represented on any of his other plates. Invariably, these include only far-southerly groups near the south celestial pole that appear only on Plate XXVIII. A few constellations on this chart (such as Mensa, Musca, Telescopium, and Volans) are shown but not labeled.

- The constellations Carina, Puppis, Pyxis, and Vela were formerly part of the ancient constellation Argo Navis, the Ship, which only in this form dates from pre-Ptolemaic times. Also, constellations attributed to Bayer were actually created by the Dutchman Pieter Dirckszoon Keyser at the end of the 16th century and were introduced by Bayer in his classic *Uranometria* atlas of 1603.

- Users of the ten Tirion atlas charts will find it easy to scale off the positions of plotted objects or add new ones as desired with only a straightedge such as the edge of a sheet of paper. On the equatorial maps (Charts 3–8), it can be used to connect the right ascension scales at top-bottom of the declination calibrations in the margins. On the polar charts (1–2, 9–10), right ascension can be measured or plotted with this edge by connecting the peripheral calibrations with either pole. For declination, there are calibrations along the 6^h–18^h right ascension lines running horizontally across these polar maps; these can be copied along the edge of the paper which can then be pivoted around the poles. (The vertical declination scales on the equatorial charts can similarly be transferred to a paper edge to read or plot declination as the sheet moves horizontally.)

Constellation	Pronunciation	Meaning	Jamieson	Tirion	Origin (Century)
Andromeda	An-DROM-eh-da	Princess Andromeda	III	3,8	Pre-Ptolemaic
Antlia	ANT-lee-ah	Air Pump	XXVI	5	Lacaille, (18th)
Apus	AY-pus	Bird of Paradise	XXVIII	9,10	Bayer, (17th)
Aquarius	AK-WARE-ee-us	Water Carrier	XXI	8	Pre-Ptolemaic
Aquila	AK-will-ah	Eagle	X	7,8	Pre-Ptolemaic
Ara	A-ra, AY-rah	Altar	XXVIII	10	Pre-Ptolemaic
Aries	AY-ri-eez	Ram	XIII	3	Pre-Ptolemaic
Auriga	Aw-RYE-ga	Charioteer	IV	4	Pre-Ptolemaic
Bootes	Bo-OH-teez	Herdsman	VII	6	Pre-Ptolemaic
Caelum	SEE-lum	Graving Tool	XXIV, XXVIII	4,9	Lacaille, (18th)
Camelopardalis	Ka-MEL-oh-pard-al-iss	Giraffe	II,IV	1,2	Bartsch, (17th)
Cancer	KAN-ser	Crab	XVI	5	Pre-Ptolemaic
Canes Venatici	KAY-neez Ve-NAT-i-sy	Hunting Dogs	VII	1,2,5	Hevelius, (17th)
Canis Major	KAY-nis MAY-jer	Large Dog	XXV	4	Pre-Ptolemaic
Canis Minor	KAY-nis MY-ner	Small Dog	XXV	4	Pre-Ptolemaic
Capricornus	KAP-ri-kor-nus	Sea Goat	XXI	8	Pre-Ptolemaic
Carina	Ka-RYE-na, Ka-REE-na	Ship's Keel	XXVIII	9	Pre-Ptolemaic
Cassiopeia	Kass-ee-oh-PEE-ah	Queen Cassiopeia	II,III	1,2	Pre-Ptolemaic
Centaurus	Sen-TORE-us	Centaur	XXVIII	6,9,10	Pre-Ptolemaic
Cepheus	SEE-fuse, SEE-fuss	King Cepheus	II	1,2	Pre-Ptolemaic
Cetus	SEE-tus	Sea Monster	XXIII	3	Pre-Ptolemaic
Chamaeleon	Ka-MEE-leon	Chameleon	XXVIII	9,10	Bayer, (17th)
Circinus	SIR-si-nus	Drawing Compasses	XXVIII	10	Lacaille, (18th)
Columba	Kol-LUM-ba	Dove	XXIV, XXVIII	4	Bartsch, (17th)
Coma Berenices	KO-ma Beren-EYE-seez	Berenice's Hair	VII	6	Ulugh Beg, (15th)
Corona Australis	Kor-OH-na Os-TRAL-iss	Southern Crown	XX,XXVIII	7,10	Pre-Ptolemaic
Corona Borealis	Kor-OH-na Bor-ee-AL-is	Northern Crown	VII,VIII	6,7	Pre-Ptolemaic
Corvus	KOR-vus	Crow	XXVII	5,6	Pre-Ptolemaic
Crater	KRAY-ter	Cup	XXVI	5	Pre-Ptolemaic
Crux	Krucks	Southern Cross	XXVIII	9,10	Royer, (17th)
Cygnus	SIG-nus	Swan	XI	2,7,8	Pre-Ptolemaic
Delphinus	Del-FY-nus	Dolphin	X	8	Pre-Ptolemaic
Dorado	Do-RAH-do	Swordfish	XXVIII	9	Bayer, (17th)
Draco	DRAY-ko	Dragon	II	1,2	Pre-Ptolemaic
Equuleus	Ee-KWOO-lee-us	Colt	XIX	8	Pre-Ptolemaic
Eridanus	Eh-RID-an-us	River	XXIV, XXVIII	3,4,9	Pre-Ptolemaic
Fornax	FOR-naks	Furnace	XXIV	3	Lacaille, (18th)
Gemini	JEM-in-eye	Twins	XV	4	Pre-Ptolemaic
Grus	Grus	Crane	XXVIII	8,9,10	Bayer,(17th)
Hercules	HER-cue-leez	Strong Man Hercules	VIII	7	Pre-Ptolemaic
Horologium	Hor-oh-LOW-jee-um	Clock	XXVIII	3,4,9	Lacaille, (18th)
Hydra	HIGH-dra	Female Water Serpent	XXVI, XXVII	5,6	Pre-Ptolemaic
Hydrus	HIGH-drus	Male Water Serpent	XXVIII	9,10	Bayer, (17th)
Indus	IN-dus	American Indian	XXVIII	9,10	Bayer, (17th)
Lacerta	La-SIR-ta	Lizard	XI	1,2,8	Hevelius, (17th)
Leo	LEE-oh	Lion	XVII	5	Pre-Ptolemaic
Leo Minor	LEE-oh-MY-ner	Small Lion	V	5	Hevelius, (17th)
Lepus	LEE-pus	Hare	XXIV, XXV	4	Pre-Ptolemaic
Libra	LIE-bra, LEE-bra	Scales	XIX, XVIII	6	Pre-Ptolemaic
Lupus	LEW-puss	Wolf	XVIII	6,10	Pre-Ptolemaic
Lynx	Links	Lynx (Bobcat)	V	1,5	Hevelius, (17th)
Lyra	LIE-ra	Lyre	VIII, XI	7	Pre-Ptolemaic
Mensa	MEN-sa	Table Mountain	XXVIII	9,10	Lacaille, (18th)
Microscopium	Micro-SCOPE-ee-um	Microscope	XXI, XXVIII	8,10	Lacaille, (18th)
Monoceros	Mo-NOS-eros	Unicorn	XXV	4	Bartsch, (17th)
Musca	MUS-ka	Fly	XXVIII	9,10	Bayer, (17th)
Norma	NOR-ma	Carpenter's Square	XXVIII	7,10	Lacaille, (18th)
Octans	OK-tans	Octant	XXVIII	9,10	Lacaille, (18th)
Ophiuchus	Oh-fee-YOU-kus	Serpent Bearer	IX	7	Pre-Ptolemaic
Orion	Oh-RYE-an	Hunter Orion	XIV, XXIV	4	Pre-Ptolemaic
Pavo	PAY-vo	Peacock	XXVIII	10	Bayer, (17th)
Pegasus	PEG-a-sus	Flying Horse Pegasus	XII, XXII	8	Pre-Ptolemaic
Perseus	PUR-see-us	Hero Perseus	III	1,3	Pre-Ptolemaic
Phoenix	FEE-nicks	Phoenix	XXVIII	3,9,10	Bayer, (17th)
Pictor	PICK-tor	Painter's Easel	XXVIII	9	Lacaille, (18th)
Pisces	PIE-seez, PIS-eez	Fishes	XXII	3,8	Pre-Ptolemaic
Piscis Austrinus	PIE-sis Os-TRY-nus	Southern Fish	XXI	8	Pre-Ptolemaic
Puppis	PUP-is	Ship's Stern	XXV, XXVIII	4,9	Pre-Ptolemaic
Pyxis	PIK-sis	Mariner's Compass	XXV, XXVI	5	Lacaille, (18th)
Reticulum	Re-TICK-you-lum	Reticle	—	9	Lacaille, (18th)
Sagitta	Sa-JIH-ta	Arrow	X	7,8	Pre-Ptolemaic
Sagittarius	Sa-jih-TARE-ee-us	Archer	XX	7	Pre-Ptolemaic
Scorpius	SCORE-pee-us	Scorpion	XIX	7	Pre-Ptolemaic
Sculptor	SKULP-tor	Sculptor's Apparatus	XXIII	3,8	Lacaille, (18th)
Scutum	SKYOO-tum	Shield	XX	7	Hevelius, (17th)
Serpens (Caput & Cauda)	SIR-pens	Serpent (Head & Tail)	IX	7	Pre-Ptolemaic
Sextans	SEX-tans	Sextant	XVII XXVI	5	Hevelius, (17th)
Taurus	TORE-us	Bull	XIV	3,4	Pre-Ptolemaic
Telescopium	Te-le-SCOPE-ee-um	Telescope	XX, XVIII	7,10	Lacaille, (18th)
Triangulum	Tri-ANG-you-lum	Triangle	III	3	Pre-Ptolemaic
Triangulum Australe	Tri-ANG-you-lum Os-TRAY-lee	Southern Triangle	XXVIII	9	Bayer, (17th)
Tucana	Too-KAN-ah	Toucan	XXVIII	9,10	Bayer, (17th)
Ursa Major	ER-sa MAY-jer	Great Bear	VI	1,2,5	Pre-Ptolemaic
Ursa Minor	ER-sa MY-ner	Small Bear	II	1,2	Pre-Ptolemaic
Vela	VEE-la	Ship's Sails	XXVIII	5,9	Pre-Ptolemaic
Virgo	VER-go	Virgin	XVIII	6	Pre-Ptolemaic
Volans	VO-lanz	Flying Fish	XVIII	9	Bayer, (17th)
Vulpecula	Vul-PECK-you-la	Fox	X	7,8	Hevelius, (17th)

SEASONAL FINDING CHARTS

For Use Throughout The Populated World

Using the Seasonal Finding Charts

The six maps which start on the facing page serve two major purposes: to help the reader locate the more prominent and best-known stars and constellations in the real sky and as an index or gateway to the considerably more detailed Jamieson plates and Tirion's *Bright Star Atlas* charts.

For the second purpose there are green numerals scattered across these charts, the Roman numerals referring to Jamieson charts and Arabic ones to Tirions. In both cases these numbers are situated at the location against the starry background that falls approximately at the center of the corresponding Jamieson or Tirion map. The numbers are also oriented to correspond with the vertical direction of each chart; for the Jamiesons the book has to be turned 90° clockwise, while the Tirions are already vertical on their pages.

As star finding aids, these charts are destined for use in practically the entire populated world—from 60° north latitude to 40° south. Along the left and right margins are pairs of tick marks showing the positions of both the northern and southern horizons for each 10° of latitude. To better see how these horizons fall in relation to the stars, use a ruler or other straightedge to connect the appropriate left and right tick mark for your location. It is easy to estimate where the horizon falls at places intermediate to each 10° of latitude; for example, if you live at 35° north, your horizon runs halfway between the 30°N and 40°N tick marks at the top and bottom. If you are uncertain of your latitude, the map of the Earth, immediately below, will be of assistance.

These charts show a broad strip of sky centered on the observers meridian—the line running from the north point on the horizon through the overhead point (zenith) down to the south point on the opposite horizon. They extend some distance to the left and right: from beyond the northeast and northwest points in the north to beyond the southeast and southwest in the south. In order to accurately cover such a very large segment of sky on one chart which can be used over such a broad latitude range, we have adopted what cartographers call a transverse Mercator projection. On such a map the east and west points on the horizon cannot be shown since they are actually off at infinity beyond the left

and right margins. In fact, in the actual sky those are the places where the upper northern and lower southern horizons would meet, but on these maps they are parallel to each other.

This projection makes this "universal" multi-latitude feature possible, something that would be difficult to show with any other arrangement; in fact, we could easily have extended these charts' latitude range still farther north and south had we wished. This multiplicity of horizons offers much valuable information regarding from which parts of the world certain stars and constellations can or cannot be seen. For example, an often-asked question is how far south one must travel to see the famous Southern Cross, whose astronomical name is Crux. Look at Chart 3 and you'll see Crux about even with the 30°N southern horizon, which corresponds to, among other places, New Orleans and Cairo. However, using a ruler you'll see that Crux only partially rises above that horizon, and that you should go to 20°N or farther south to really see it well. By sliding your horizon ruler up and down along both the upper and lower portions of these charts, you can readily see how the visibility of stars changes as you travel north or south.

Your overhead point, or zenith, is always on the meridian (the chart's central vertical axis) and halfway between your northern and southern horizons. For example, if you're situated at 40°N, on Chart 1 the constellation Perseus will be overhead. Notice that over most of these maps the lettering is rightside up, except in the upper—or northern—portion where it's upside-down. This is to get you to invert the chart when you face north in order to see the stars properly in relation to that horizon. These labels are sort of "biased" for observers around 40°–50° north latitude, which is where most of the greatest population concentrations are located— United States, Europe, and elsewhere. However, we trust that observers in drastically different locales such as south of the Equator will not be seriously inconvenienced by some of this labeling being upside-down for them.

At the bottom of each map is an approximate time schedule indicating when each of these charts should be used. These refer to local time anywhere in the world; for daylight or summer time, add one hour.

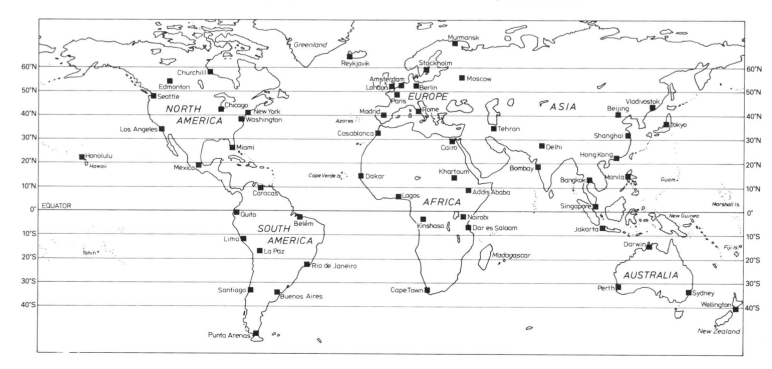

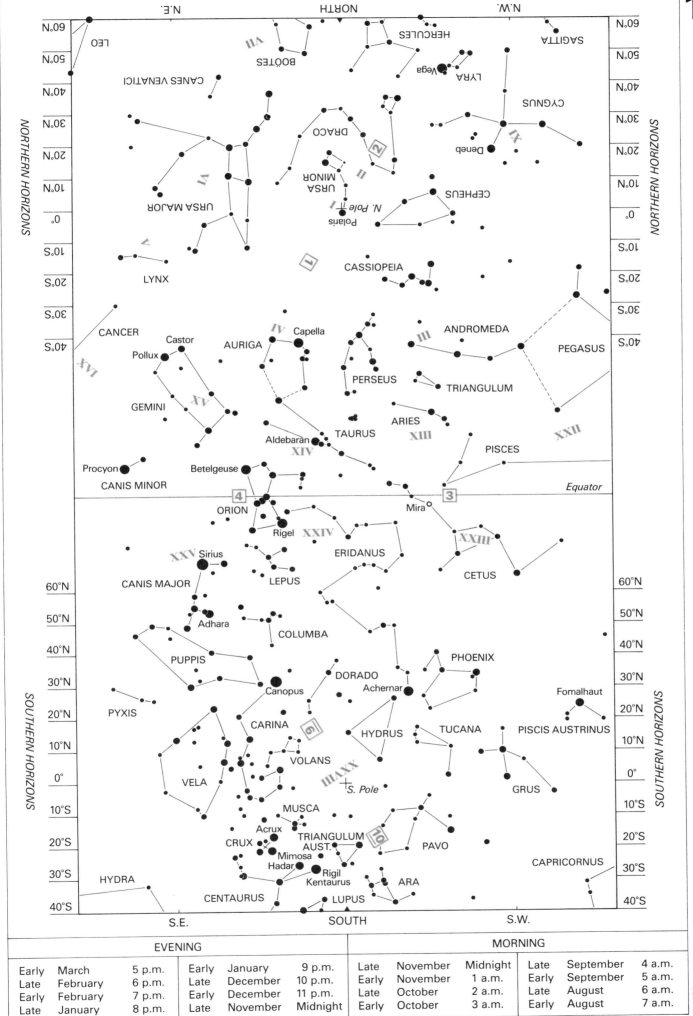

1

NORTHERN HORIZONS

NORTHERN HORIZONS

SOUTHERN HORIZONS

SOUTHERN HORIZONS

N.E.   NORTH   N.W.

N.E.   N.W.

60°N
50°N
40°N
30°N
20°N
10°N
0°
10°S
20°S
30°S
40°S

60°N
50°N
40°N
30°N
20°N
10°N
0°
10°S
20°S
30°S
40°S

60°N
50°N
40°N
30°N
20°N
10°N
0°
10°S
20°S
30°S
40°S

LEO

VII

BOÖTES

CANES VENATICI

HERCULES

Vega
LYRA

CYGNUS

SAGITTA

Deneb
XI

DRACO

2

URSA MINOR
II

N. Pole
Polaris
I

CEPHEUS

VI

URSA MAJOR

5

LYNX

1

CASSIOPEIA

ANDROMEDA

III

PEGASUS

CANCER

XVI

Castor
Pollux

AURIGA

IV   Capella

PERSEUS

TRIANGULUM

XXII

GEMINI

XV

ARIES

XIII

Aldebaran

TAURUS

XIV

PISCES

Procyon

Betelgeuse

CANIS MINOR

Equator

Mira

3

Equator

4

ORION

Rigel   XXIV

ERIDANUS

XXIII

CETUS

XXV   Sirius

CANIS MAJOR

LEPUS

Adhara

COLUMBA

PUPPIS

PHOENIX

PYXIS

Canopus

DORADO

Achernar

CARINA

6

HYDRUS

TUCANA

Fomalhaut

PISCIS AUSTRINUS

VOLANS

XXVIII

S. Pole

VELA

GRUS

MUSCA

Acrux

CRUX   TRIANGULUM AUST.   10

PAVO

CAPRICORNUS

Mimosa

Hadar

Rigil Kentaurus

ARA

HYDRA

CENTAURUS

LUPUS

S.E.   SOUTH   S.W.

EVENING				MORNING			
Early	March	5 p.m.	Early	January	9 p.m.	Late	November	Midnight	Late	September	4 a.m.

Wil Tirion

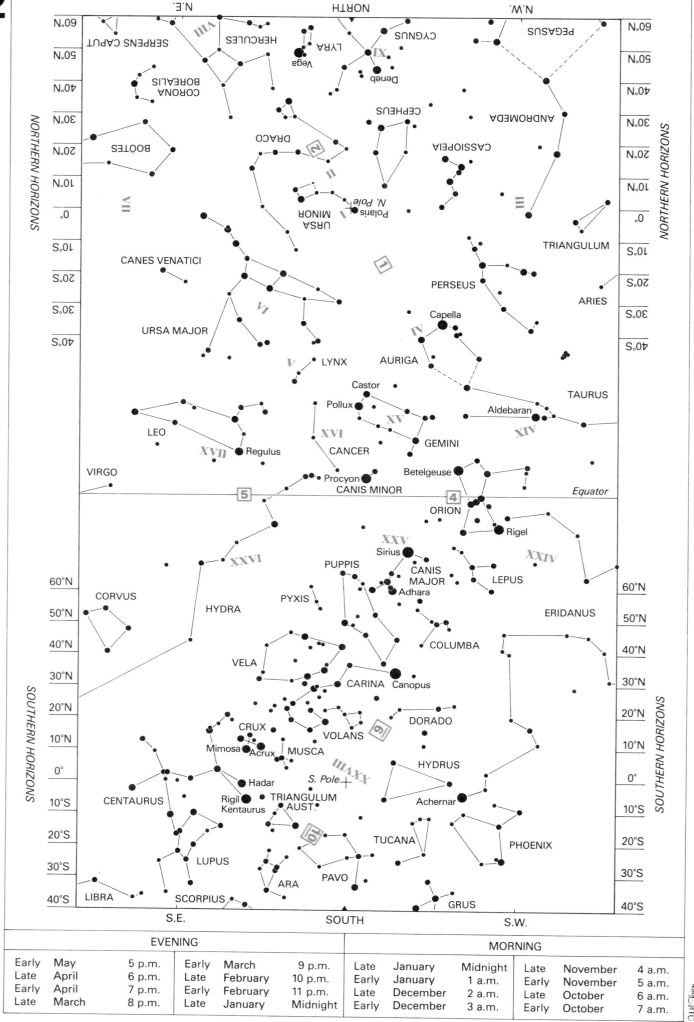

2

EVENING					
Early	May	5 p.m.	Early	March	9 p.m.
Late	April	6 p.m.	Late	February	10 p.m.
Early	April	7 p.m.	Early	February	11 p.m.
Late	March	8 p.m.	Late	January	Midnight

MORNING					
Late	January	Midnight	Late	November	4 a.m.
Early	January	1 a.m.	Early	November	5 a.m.
Late	December	2 a.m.	Late	October	6 a.m.
Early	December	3 a.m.	Early	October	7 a.m.

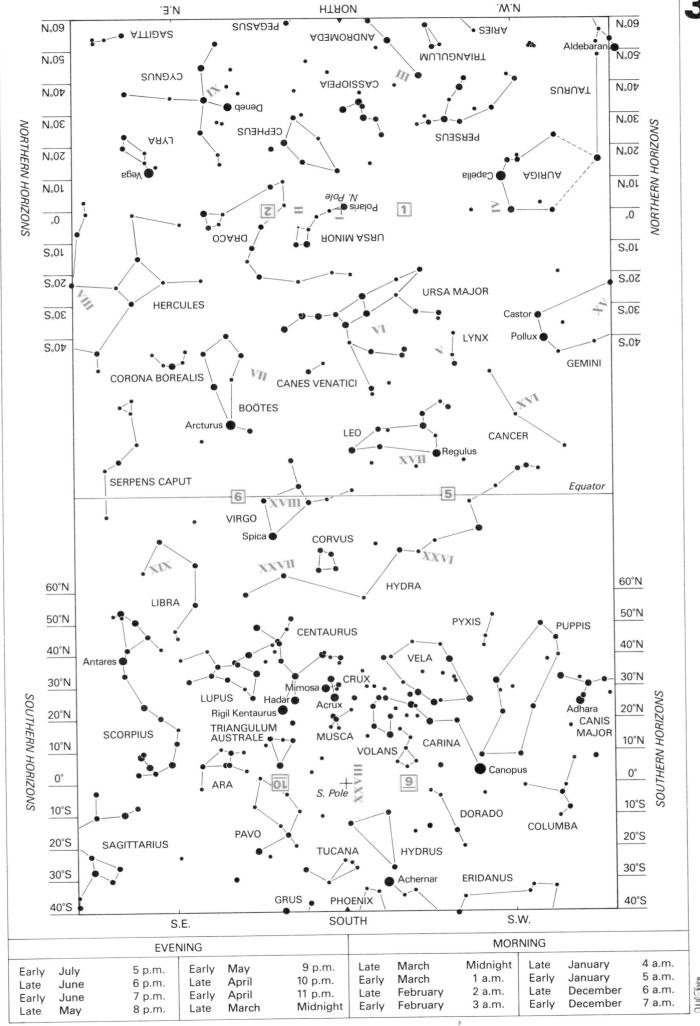

3

SAGITTA   PEGASUS   ANDROMEDA   ARIES   Aldebaran

60°N   50°N   40°N   30°N   20°N   10°N   0°

CYGNUS   XI   Deneb   CASSIOPEIA   III   TRIANGULUM   TAURUS

NORTHERN HORIZONS

CEPHEUS   PERSEUS

LYRA   Vega

AURIGA   Capella

N. Pole   Polaris   1   IV

DRACO   2   II   URSA MINOR

NORTHERN HORIZONS

S.10°   S.20°   S.30°   S.40°

VIII   HERCULES   URSA MAJOR   Castor   XV   Pollux   LYNX   GEMINI

CORONA BOREALIS   VII   CANES VENATICI   VI   V

BOÖTES   Arcturus   LEO   XVI   CANCER   Regulus

SERPENS CAPUT   XVII

Equator

6   XVIII   5

VIRGO   Spica   CORVUS   XXVI

XIX   XXXII   HYDRA

60°N   LIBRA   50°N   CENTAURUS   PYXIS   PUPPIS

40°N   VELA

30°N   Antares   Mimosa   CRUX

LUPUS   Hadar   Acrux   Adhara   CANIS MAJOR

20°N   Rigil Kentaurus   MUSCA   CARINA

SCORPIUS   TRIANGULUM AUSTRALE   VOLANS

10°N   ARA   10   XXXIII   9   Canopus

0°   S. Pole   DORADO

10°S   PAVO   COLUMBA

20°S   SAGITTARIUS   TUCANA   HYDRUS

30°S   GRUS   PHOENIX   Achernar   ERIDANUS

40°S

SOUTHERN HORIZONS

EVENING						MORNING					
Early	July	5 p.m.	Early	May	9 p.m.	Late	March	Midnight	Late	January	4 a.m.
Late	June	6 p.m.	Late	April	10 p.m.	Early	March	1 a.m.	Early	January	5 a.m.
Early	June	7 p.m.	Early	April	11 p.m.	Late	February	2 a.m.	Late	December	6 a.m.
Late	May	8 p.m.	Late	March	Midnight	Early	February	3 a.m.	Early	December	7 a.m.

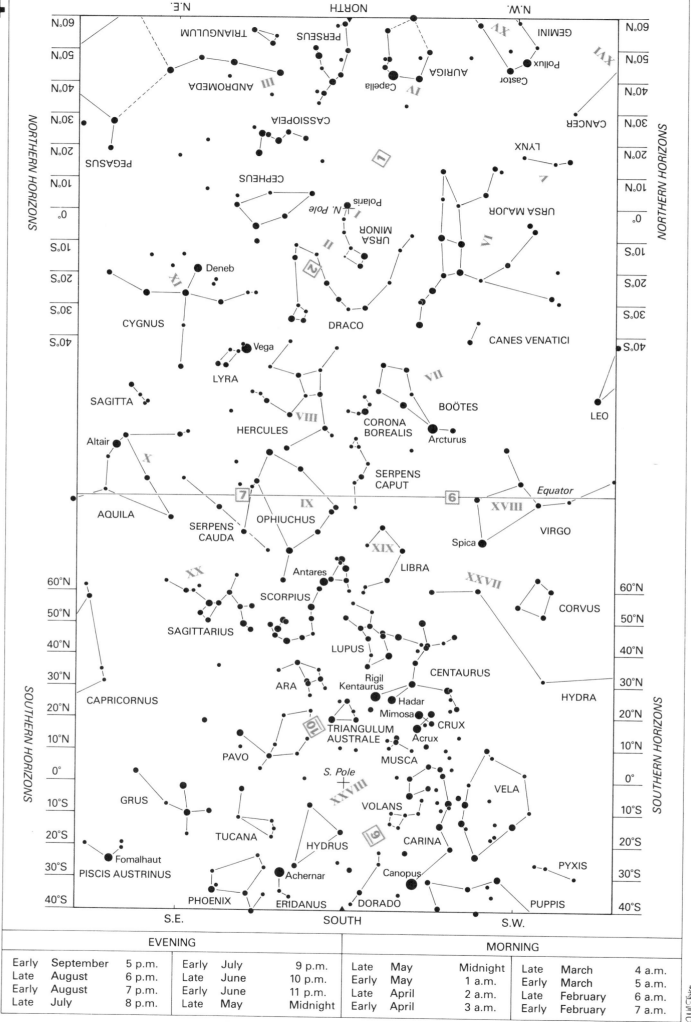

4

NORTHERN HORIZONS

SOUTHERN HORIZONS

EVENING						MORNING					
Early	September	5 p.m.	Early	July	9 p.m.	Late	May	Midnight	Late	March	4 a.m.
Late	August	6 p.m.	Late	June	10 p.m.	Early	May	1 a.m.	Early	March	5 a.m.
Early	August	7 p.m.	Early	June	11 p.m.	Late	April	2 a.m.	Late	February	6 a.m.
Late	July	8 p.m.	Late	May	Midnight	Early	April	3 a.m.	Early	February	7 a.m.

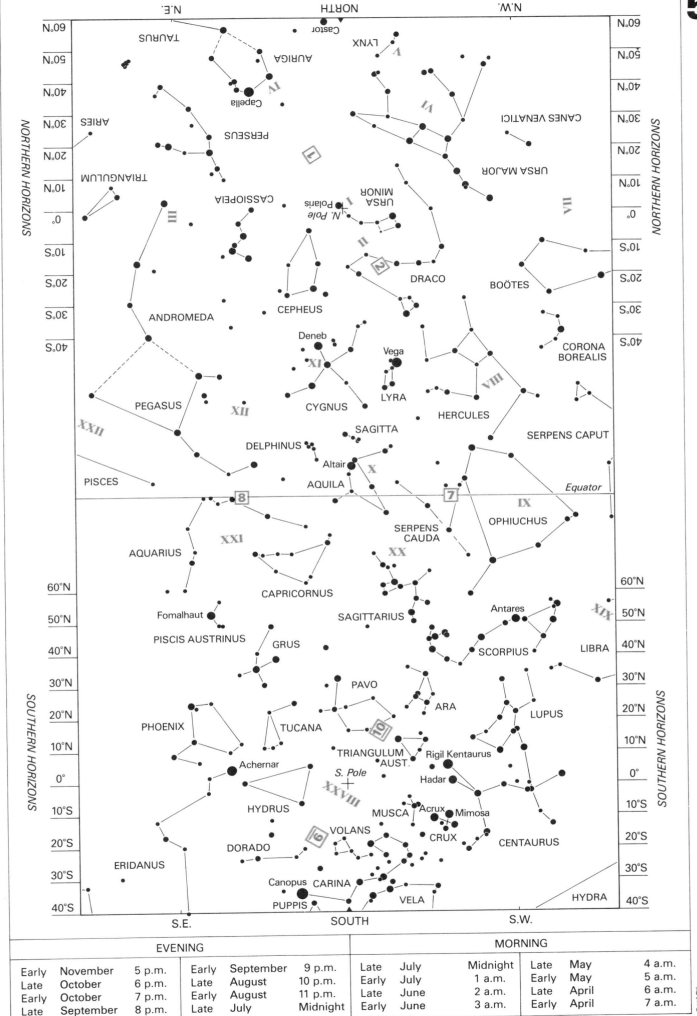

5

NORTHERN HORIZONS

N.E. — NORTH — N.W.

Castor
LYNX
TAURUS
AURIGA — V
Capella — IV
PERSEUS
1
ARIES
TRIANGULUM
CASSIOPEIA
CANES VENATICI
VI
URSA MAJOR
N. Pole — Polaris
URSA MINOR
I
VII
DRACO
2
III
ANDROMEDA
CEPHEUS
BOÖTES
Deneb
CORONA BOREALIS
Vega
XI
VIII
CYGNUS — LYRA
HERCULES
PEGASUS
XII
SERPENS CAPUT
XXII
SAGITTA
DELPHINUS
Altair — X
PISCES
AQUILA
Equator
8
7
IX
OPHIUCHUS
XXI
SERPENS CAUDA
AQUARIUS
XX
CAPRICORNUS
Fomalhaut
60°N
SAGITTARIUS
XIX
50°N
Antares
PISCIS AUSTRINUS
40°N
GRUS
SCORPIUS
LIBRA
30°N
PAVO
PHOENIX
20°N
ARA
LUPUS
TUCANA
10°N
TRIANGULUM AUST.
Rigil Kentaurus
Achernar
0°
S. Pole
Hadar
HYDRUS
10°S
MUSCA
Acrux — Mimosa
CRUX
CENTAURUS
VOLANS
20°S
DORADO
ERIDANUS
30°S
Canopus — CARINA
40°S
PUPPIS — VELA
HYDRA

S.E. — SOUTH — S.W.

NORTHERN HORIZONS

SOUTHERN HORIZONS

EVENING				MORNING		
Early	November	5 p.m.	Early September 9 p.m.	Late	July	Midnight	Late May 4 a.m.
Late	October	6 p.m.	Late August 10 p.m.	Early	July	1 a.m.	Early May 5 a.m.
Early	October	7 p.m.	Early August 11 p.m.	Late	June	2 a.m.	Late April 6 a.m.
Late	September	8 p.m.	Late July Midnight	Early	June	3 a.m.	Early April 7 a.m.

6

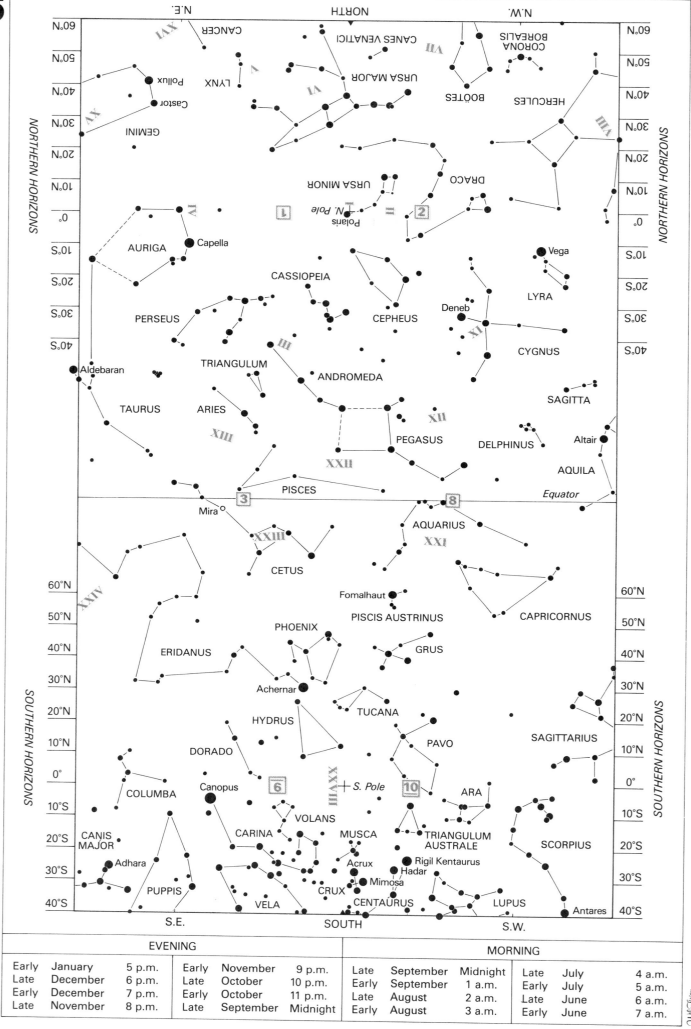

	EVENING						MORNING				
Early	January	5 p.m.	Early	November	9 p.m.	Late	September	Midnight	Late	July	4 a.m.
Late	December	6 p.m.	Late	October	10 p.m.	Early	September	1 a.m.	Early	July	5 a.m.
Early	December	7 p.m.	Early	October	11 p.m.	Late	August	2 a.m.	Late	June	6 a.m.
Late	November	8 p.m.	Late	September	Midnight	Early	August	3 a.m.	Early	June	7 a.m.

THE
BRIGHT STAR ATLAS
2000.0

Wil Tirion

Catalog of Selected Objects

Brian Skiff

DEEP-SKY OBJECTS

Name	R.A h m	Dec. ° ′	Con	Type	V	Dimensions	Notes
GALAXIES							
N 147	0 33.2	+48 30	Cas	dE5	9.3	13′ × 8′.1	
N 185	0 39.0	+48 20	Cas	dE3	9.1	11′ × 9′.8	
N 205	0 40.4	+41 41	And	dE5	8.0	17′ × 9′.8	M110
N 221	0 42.7	+40 52	And	cE2	8.2	7′.6 × 5′.8	M32
N 224	0 42.7	+41 16	And	SAb	3.5	180′ × 60′	M31, (1)
N 891	2 22.6	+42 21	And	SAb?	10.0	13′ × 2′.8	
N 925	2 27.3	+33 35	Tri	SAd	10.0	9′.8 × 6′.0	
N1023	2 40.4	+39 04	Per	SB0⁻	9.4	8′.7 × 3′.3	
I 342	3 46.8	+68 06	Cam	SAcd	8.1:	18′ × 17′	
N2403	7 36.9	+65 36	Cam	SAcd	8.4	18′ × 11′	
N2683	8 52.7	+33 25	Lyn	SAb	9.7	9′.3 × 2′.5	
N2768	9 11.6	+60 02	UMa	E6:	10.0	6′.3 × 2′.8	
N2841	9 22.0	+50 58	UMa	SAb	9.3	8′.1 × 3′.8	
N3031	9 55.6	+69 04	UMa	SAab	6.9	26′ × 14′	M81
N3034	9 55.8	+69 41	UMa	I0	8.4	11′ × 4′.6	M82
N3077	10 03.3	+68 44	UMa	I0	9.9	4′.6 × 3′.6	
N3184	10 18.3	+41 25	UMa	SAcd	9.8	6′.9 × 6′.8	
N3556	11 11.5	+55 40	UMa	SBcd	10.1	8′.3 × 2′.5	M108
N3992	11 57.6	+53 23	UMa	SBbc	9.8	7′.6 × 4′.9	M109
N4125	12 08.1	+65 11	Dra	E6	9.9	5′.1 × 3′.2	
N4258	12 19.0	+47 18	CVn	SAbc	8.3	18′ × 8′	M106
N4449	12 28.2	+44 06	CVn	IBm	9.5	5′.1 × 3′.7	
N4490	12 30.6	+41 38	CVn	SBd	9.8	5′.9 × 3′.1	
N4736	12 50.9	+41 07	CVn	SAab	8.2	11′ × 9′.1	M94
N5055	13 15.8	+42 02	CVn	SAbc	8.6	12′.3 × 7′.6	M63
N5194	13 29.9	+47 12	CVn	SAbc	8.4	11′ × 7′.8	M51, (8)
N5195	13 30.0	+47 16	CVn	I0	9.6	5′.4 × 4′.3	(9)
N5322	13 49.3	+60 12	UMa	E3-4	10.0	5′.5 × 3′.9	
N5457	14 03.2	+54 21	UMa	SAcd	7.7	27′ × 26′	M101
OPEN CLUSTERS							
N 457	1 19.1	+58 20	Cas	oc	6.4	12′	(2)
N 581	1 33.2	+60 42	Cas	oc	7.4	6′	M103
N 654	1 44.1	+61 53	Cas	oc	6.5	8′	
N 752	1 57.8	+37 41	And	oc	5.7	50′	
Stock 2	2 15.0	+59 16	Cas	oc	4.4	60′	
N 869	2 19.0	+57 09	Per	oc	3.5	30′	h Per
N 884	2 22.4	+57 07	Per	oc	3.6	30′	χ Per
I 1805	2 32.7	+61 27	Cas	oc-gn	6.5	22′	(3)
Trumpler 2	2 37.3	+55 59	Per	oc	5.9	17′	
N1039	2 42.0	+42 47	Per	oc	5.2	25′	M34
N1027	2 42.7	+61 33	Cas	oc	6.7	20′	
I 1848	2 51.2	+60 26	Cas	oc-gn	6.5	12′	(4)
Stock 23	3 16.3	+60 02	Cam	oc	∼6.5	18′	
Melotte 20	3 22	+49	Per	oc	1.2	2.8°	(5)
N1342	3 31.6	+37 20	Per	oc	6.7	17′	
N1502	4 07.7	+62 20	Cam	oc	5.7	8′	
N1528	4 15.4	+51 14	Per	oc	6.4	18′	
N1545	4 20.9	+50 15	Per	oc	6.2	12′	
N2281	6 49.3	+41 04	Aur	oc	5.4	15′	
N7160	21 53.7	+62 36	Cep	oc	6.1	7′	
N7654	23 24.2	+61 35	Cas	oc	6.9	13′	M52
N7789	23 57.0	+56 44	Cas	oc	6.7	16′	
PLANETARY NEBULAE							
N 650	1 42.4	+51 34	Per	pn	10.1	2′.7 × 1′.8	M76
N3587	11 14.8	+55 01	UMa	pn	9.9	3′.4 × 3′.3	M97 (7)
N7662	23 25.9	+42 33	And	pn	8.3	32″ × 28″	
DIFFUSE NEBULA							
N1499	4 00.7	+36 37	Per	gn	∼5	160′ × 40′	(6)

DOUBLE STARS

Name	R.A h m	Dec. ° ′	Con	V	Sep (Date)	Notes
ADS 1	0 02.6	+66 06	Cas	5.9,7.5	15″.2 (1969)	
ADS 671 = η Cas	0 49.1	+57 49	Cas	3.4,7.5	12″.9 (2000)	
ADS 824	1 00.1	+44 43	And	6.0,6.8	7″.8 (1967)	
ADS 1534 = 56 And	1 56.2	+37 15	And	5.7,5.9	3′.6 (2000)	(10)
ADS 1630 = γ And	2 03.9	+42 20	And	2.3,4.8	9″.7 (1983)	(11)
ADS 1683 = 59 And	2 10.9	+39 02	And	5.6,6.1	16″.7 (1972)	
ADS 1697 = 6 Tri	2 12.4	+30 18	Tri	5.2,6.7	3″.9 (1973)	(12)
ADS 1860 = ι Cas	2 29.1	+67 42	Cas	4.6,6.9	2″.5 (2000)	(13)
ADS 1477 = α UMi	2 31.8	+89 16	UMi	2.0,8.2	18″.4 (1973)	(14)
ADS 2270	3 00.9	+52 21	Per	5.3,6.7	12″.3 (1973)	
ADS 2582	3 31.3	+27 34	Tau	6.6,7.0	11″.3 (1973)	
ADS 3274 = 1 Cam	4 32.0	+53 55	Cam	5.8,6.9	10″.1 (1981)	
ADS 4773 = 41 Aur	6 11.6	+48 43	Aur	6.3,7.0	7″.7 (1973)	
ADS 5400 = 12 Lyn	6 46.2	+59 27	Lyn	5.4,6.0	1″.7 (2000)	(15)
ADS 6012 = 19 Lyn	7 22.9	+55 17	Lyn	5.6,6.5	15″.0 (1965)	
ADS 6988 = ι Cnc	8 46.7	+28 46	Cnc	4.0,6.6	30″.4 (1973)	
ADS 7137 = 66 Cnc	9 01.4	+32 15	Cnc	5.9,8.0	4″.5 (1973)	
h 4188	9 12.5	−43 37	Vel	6.0,6.8	2″.8 (1977)	(17)
ADS 7292 = 38 Lyn	9 18.8	+36 48	Lyn	3.9,6.6	2″.7 (1968)	
ADS 8682	12 49.2	+83 25	Cam	5.3,5.8	21″.6 (1958)	
ADS 8706 = α CVn	12 56.0	+38 19	CVn	2.9,5.6	19″.4 (1974)	(13)
ADS 8891 = ζ UMa	13 23.9	+54 56	UMa	2.3,4.0	14″.4 (1977)	(16)
ADS10759 = ψ Dra	17 41.9	+72 09	Dra	4.6,5.8	30″.3 (1977)	
ADS11061 = 41/40 Dra	18 00.2	+80 00	Dra	5.7,6.0	19″.1 (1975)	
ADS11870	18 53.6	+75 47	Dra	6.6,7.4	5″.6 (1968)	
ADS13007 = ε Dra	19 48.2	+70 16	Dra	3.8,7.4	3″.1 (1976)	
ADS15032 = β Cep	21 28.7	+70 34	Cep	3.2,7.8	13″.4 (1975)	(13)
ADS15600 = ξ Cep	22 03.8	+64 38	Cep	4.4,6.4	7″.8 (1982)	
ADS16666 = o Cep	23 18.6	+68 07	Cep	4.9,7.1	2″.8 (2000)	
ADS17140 = σ Cas	23 59.0	+55 45	Cas	5.0,7.1	3″.1 (1981)	

ECLIPSING VARIABLE STARS

Name	R.A h m	Dec. ° ′	Type	Mag.	Epoch (2400000+)	Period (days)
U Cep	1 02.3	+81 53	EA	6.75–9.24V	44541.603	2.493
β Per	3 08.2	+40 57	EA	2.12–3.40V	40953.465	2.867
ε Aur	5 02.0	+43 49	EA	2.92–3.83V	35629	9892
W UMa	9 43.8	+55 57	EW	7.9–8.63V	41004.397	0.333

PULSATING VARIABLE STARS

Name	R.A h m	Dec. ° ′	Type	Mag.	Epoch	Period
KK Per	2 10.3	+56 34	Lc	6.6–7.78V		
R Tri	2 37.0	+34 16	M	5.4–12.6v	42014	266.48
ρ Per	3 05.2	+38 50	SRb	3.30–4.0v		50:
VY UMa	10 45.1	+67 25	Lb	5.89–6.5 V		
VW UMa	10 59.0	+69 59	SR	6.85–7.71V		125
RY UMa	12 20.5	+61 19	SRb	6.68–8.5V	40810	311
V CVn	13 19.5	+45 32	SRa	6.52–8.56V	43929	191.89
UX Dra	19 21.6	+76 34	SRa	5.94–7.1v		168:
T Cep	21 09.5	+68 29	M	5.2–11.3v	44177	388.14
μ Cep	21 43.5	+58 47	SRc	3.43–5.1v		730
δ Cep	22 29.2	+58 25	δ Cep	3.48–4.37V	36075.445	5.366

OTHER VARIABLE STARS

Name	R.A h m	Dec. ° ′	Type	Mag.		
EG And	0 44.5	+40 41	Z And	7.08–7.8V		

NOTES

1. Andromeda Galaxy
2. Includes φ¹,² Cas
3. Nebula covers large area
4. Nebula 40′ in diameter
5. α Persei cluster
6. California Nebula
7. Owl Nebula
8. Whirlpool Galaxy
9. Companion to M51
10. Optical; binocular pair
11. Fainter star is close pair
12. Same as TZ Tri, brighter star slightly variable (not = ι Tri)
13. Brighter star slightly variable
14. Polaris, brighter star slightly variable
15. Third star: V=7.3; 8″.6 (1980)
16. Mizar; Alcor (V=4.0) is 11′.8 east-northeast
17. Brighter star is very close pair

1

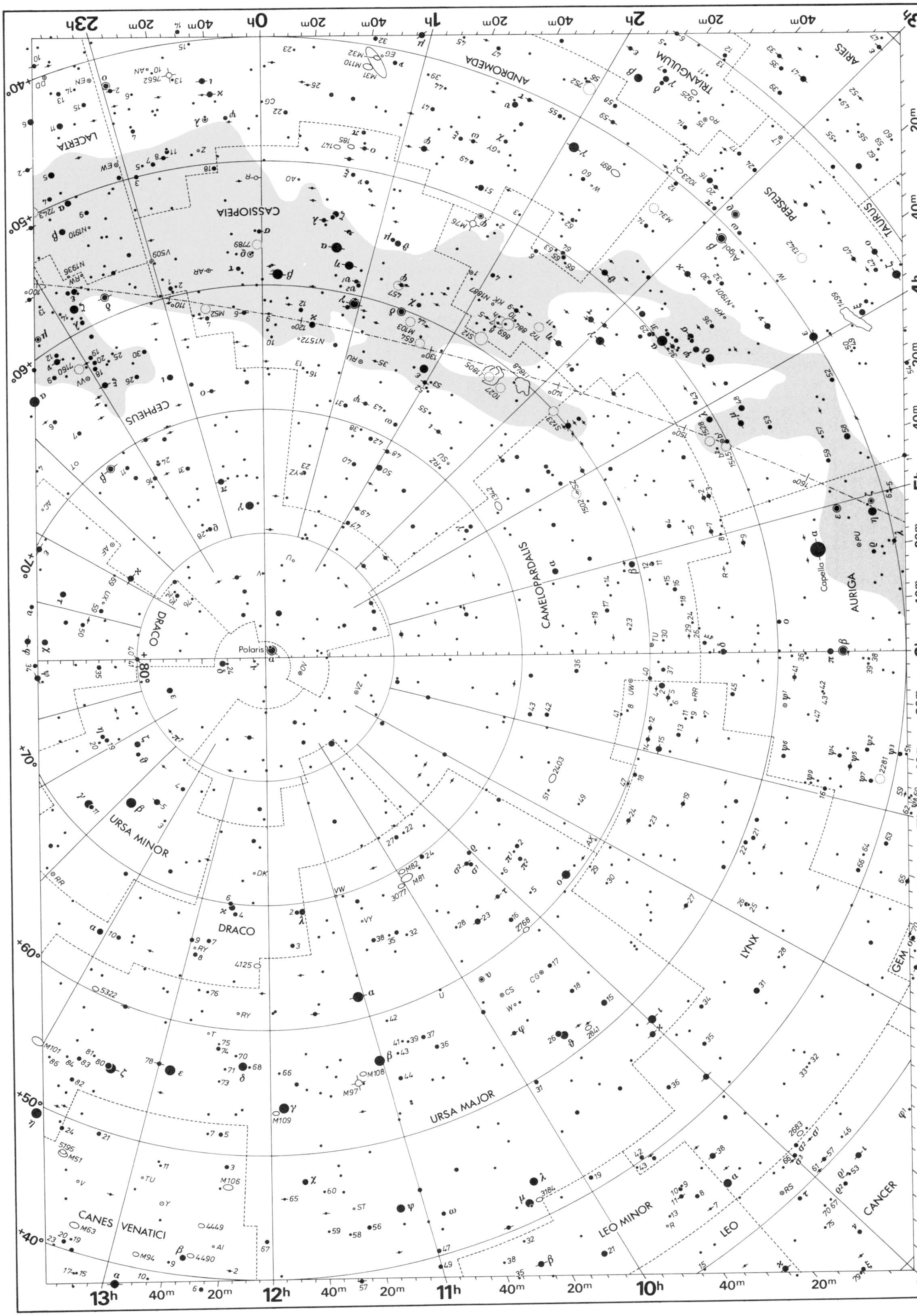
CASSIOPEIA
ANDROMEDA
TRIANGULUM
ARIES
PERSEUS
TAURUS
LACERTA
CEPHEUS
AURIGA
Capella
CAMELOPARDALIS
DRACO
Polaris
URSA MINOR
LYNX
GEM
URSA MAJOR
CANES VENATICI
LEO MINOR
LEO
CANCER
Algol
23h
0h
1h
2h
3h
4h
5h
6h
7h
8h
9h
10h
11h
12h
13h
+40°
+50°
+60°
+70°
+80°
M31
M32
M110
M76
M34
M81
M82
M101
M51
M63
M94
M106
M108
M97
M109
Wil Tirion

DEEP-SKY OBJECTS

Name	R.A h m	Dec. ° ′	Con	Type	V	Dimensions	Notes
GALAXIES							
N 147	0 33.2	+48 30	Cas	dE5	9.3	13′ × 8′.1	
N 185	0 39.0	+48 20	Cas	dE3	9.1	11′ × 9′.8	
N 205	0 40.4	+41 41	And	dE5	8.0	17′ × 9′.8	M110
N 221	0 42.7	+40 52	And	cE2	8.2	7′.6 × 5′.8	M32
N 224	0 42.7	+41 16	And	SAb	3.5	180′ × 60′	M31, (1)
N3031	9 55.6	+69 04	UMa	SAab	6.9	26′ × 14′	M81
N3034	9 55.8	+69 41	UMa	I0	8.4	11′ × 4′.6	M82
N3077	10 03.3	+68 44	UMa	I0	9.9	4′.6 × 3′.6	
N3556	11 11.5	+55 40	UMa	SBcd	10.1	8′.3 × 2′.5	M108
N3992	11 57.6	+53 23	UMa	SBbc	9.8	7′.6 × 4′.9	M109
N4125	12 08.1	+65 11	Dra	E6	9.9	5′.1 × 3′.2	
N4258	12 19.0	+47 18	CVn	SAbc	8.3	18′ × 8′	M106
N4449	12 28.2	+44 06	CVn	IBm	9.5	5′.1 × 3′.7	
N4490	12 30.6	+41 38	CVn	SBd	9.8	5′.9 × 3′.1	
N4736	12 50.9	+41 07	CVn	SAab	8.2	11′ × 9′.1	M94
N5055	13 15.8	+42 02	CVn	SAbc	8.6	12′.3 × 7′.6	M63
N5194	13 29.9	+47 12	CVn	SAbc	8.4	11′ × 7′.8	M51, (5)
N5195	13 30.0	+47 16	CVn	I0	9.6	5′.4 × 4′.3	(6)
N5322	13 49.3	+60 12	UMa	E3-4	10.0	5′.5 × 3′.9	
N5457	14 03.2	+54 21	UMa	SAcd	7.7	27′ × 26′	M101
N5866	15 06.5	+55 46	Dra	SA0+	10.1	5′.2 × 2′.3	(7)
N6946	20 34.8	+60 09	Cyg	SAcd	8.9	11′ × 9′.8	
OPEN CLUSTERS							
N 457	1 19.1	+58 20	Cas	oc	6.4	12′	(2)
N 581	1 33.2	+60 42	Cas	oc	7.4	6′	M103
N 654	1 44.1	+61 53	Cas	oc	6.5	8′	
Stock 2	2 15.0	+59 16	Cas	oc	4.4	60′	
I 1805	2 32.7	+61 27	Cas	oc-gn	6.5	22′	(3)
N6811	19 37.0	+46 24	Cyg	oc	6.8	13′	
N6871	20 05.9	+35 47	Cyg	oc	5.2	20′	(15)
N6910	20 23.1	+40 47	Cyg	oc	6.6	8′	
N6913	20 23.9	+38 32	Cyg	oc	6.6	7′	M29
N6940	20 34.6	+28 18	Vul	oc	6.3	25′	
N7092	21 32.2	+48 26	Cyg	oc	4.6	32′	M39
I 1396	21 39.1	+57 30	Cep	oc-gn	~4	170′ × 140′	
N7160	21 53.7	+62 36	Cep	oc	6.1	7′	
N7243	22 15.3	+49 53	Lac	oc	6.4	21′	
N7654	23 24.2	+61 35	Cas	oc	6.9	13′	M52
N7789	23 57.0	+56 44	Cas	oc	6.7	16′	
GLOBULAR CLUSTERS							
N6205	16 41.7	+36 28	Her	gc	5.7	17′	M13
N6341	17 17.1	+43 08	Her	gc	6.4	11′	M92
PLANETARY NEBULAE							
N 650	1 42.4	+51 34	Per	pn	10.1	2′.7 × 1′.8	M76
N3587	11 14.8	+55 01	UMa	pn	9.9	3′.4 × 3′.3	M97 (4)
N6543	17 58.6	+66 38	Dra	pn	8.1	23″ × 17″	
N6826	19 44.8	+50 31	Cyg	pn	8.8	27″ × 24″	(8)
N7027	21 07.1	+42 14	Cyg	pn	8.5	18″ × 10″	
N7662	23 25.9	+42 33	And	pn	8.3	32″ × 28″	
DIFFUSE NEBULAE							
N6960	20 50	+31	Cyg	gn	~7	3.5° × 2.7°	(16)
N7000	20 58.8	+44 20	Cyg	gn	~4	120′ × 100′	(17)

DOUBLE STARS

Name	R.A h m	Dec. ° ′	Con	V	Sep (Date)	Notes
ADS 1	0 02.6	+66 06	Cas	5.9,7.5	15″.2 (1969)	
ADS 671 = η Cas	0 49.1	+57 49	Cas	3.4,7.5	12″.9 (2000)	
ADS 824	1 00.1	+44 43	And	6.0,6.8	7″.8 (1967)	
ADS 1477 = α UMi	2 31.8	+89 16	UMi	2.0,8.2	18″.4 (1973)	(9)
ADS 8682	12 49.2	+83 25	Cam	5.3,5.8	21″.6 (1958)	
ADS 8706 = α CVn	12 56.0	+38 19	CVn	2.9,5.6	19″.4 (1974)	(14)
ADS 8891 = ζ UMa	13 23.9	+54 56	UMa	2.3,4.0	14″.4 (1977)	(18)
ADS 9173 = κ Boo	14 13.5	+51 47	Boo	4.5,6.7	13″.4 (1973)	
ADS 9406 = 39 Boo	14 49.7	+48 43	Boo	6.2,6.9	2″.9 (1981)	
ADS 9372 = ε Boo	14 45.0	+27 04	Boo	2.5,4.9	2″.8 (1977)	
ADS 9979 = σ CrB	16 14.7	+33 52	CrB	5.6,6.6	7″.1 (2000)	(20)
ADS10129 = 17 Dra	16 36.2	+52 55	Dra	5.4,6.4	3″.2 (1976)	(10)
ADS10345 = μ Dra	17 05.3	+54 28	Dra	5.7,5.7	1″.9 (2000)	
ADS10628 = ν Dra	17 32.2	+55 11	Dra	4.9,4.9	61″.9 (1967)	(11)
ADS10759 = ψ Dra	17 41.9	+72 09	Dra	4.6,5.8	30″.3 (1977)	
ADS11061 = 41/40 Dra	18 00.2	+80 00	Dra	5.7,6.0	19″.1 (1975)	
ADS11635 = ε¹ Lyr	18 44.3	+39 40	Lyr	5.0,6.1	2″.6 (2000)	(12)
ADS11635 = ε² Lyr	18 44.4	+39 37	Lyr	5.2,5.5	2″.3 (2000)	
ADS11870	18 53.6	+75 47	Dra	6.6,7.4	5″.6 (1968)	
ADS12169	19 12.1	+49 51	Cyg	6.6,6.8	7″.9 (1976)	
ADS12815 = 16 Cyg	19 41.8	+50 32	Cyg	6.0,6.2	39″.3 (1955)	(11)
ADS12880 = δ Cyg	19 45.0	+45 08	Cyg	2.9,6.3	2″.5 (2000)	
ADS12893	19 45.7	+36 05	Cyg	6.4,7.2	14″.9 (1967)	
ADS13007 = ε Dra	19 48.2	+70 16	Dra	3.8,7.4	3″.1 (1976)	
ADS13554 = o¹ 31 Cyg	20 13.6	+46 44	Cyg	3.8,6.7	1″.8 (1926)	(13)
ADS13692	20 18.4	+55 24	Cyg	6.1,7.5	3″.5 (1978)	
ADS14158 = 49 Cyg	20 41.0	+32 18	Cyg	5.7,7.8	2″.5 (1973)	
ADS14636 = 61 Cyg	21 06.9	+38 45	Cyg	5.2,6.0	30″.3 (2000)	
ADS14682	21 08.6	+30 12	Cyg	5.8,7.8	3″.4 (1980)	(19)
ADS15032 = β Cep	21 28.7	+70 34	Cep	3.2,7.8	13″.4 (1975)	(14)
ADS15600 = ξ Cep	22 03.8	+64 38	Cep	4.4,6.4	7″.8 (1982)	
ADS16095 = 8 Lac	22 35.9	+39 38	Lac	5.7,6.4	22″.4 (1969)	
ADS16666 = o Cep	23 18.6	+68 07	Cep	4.9,7.1	2″.8 (2000)	
ADS17140 = σ Cas	23 59.0	+55 45	Cas	5.0,7.1	3″.1 (1981)	

ECLIPSING VARIABLE STARS

Name	R.A h m	Dec. ° ′	Type	Mag.	Epoch (2400000+)	Period (days)
U Cep	1 02.3	+81 53	EA	6.75–9.24V	44541.603	2.493
i Boo	15 03.8	+47 39	EW	6.5–7.1v	39370.422	0.267
VV Cep	21 56.7	+63 38	EA	4.80–5.36V	43360	7430
AR Lac	22 08.7	+45 45	E	6.11–6.77V	39376.495	1.983

PULSATING VARIABLE STARS

Name	R.A h m	Dec. ° ′	Type	Mag.	Epoch (2400000+)	Period (days)
VY UMa	10 45.1	+67 25	Lb	5.89–6.5 V		
VW UMa	10 59.0	+69 59	SR	6.85–7.71V		125
RY UMa	12 20.5	+61 19	SRb	6.68–8.5V	40810	311
V CVn	13 19.5	+45 32	SRa	6.52–8.56V	43929	191.89
AT Dra	16 17.3	+59 45	Lb	6.8–7.5p		
g Her	16 28.6	+41 53	SRb	5.7–7.2p		70:
VW Dra	17 16.5	+60 40	SRd	6.0–6.5v		170:
OP Her	17 56.8	+45 21	Lb	7.7–8.3p		
R Lyr	18 55.3	+43 57	SRb	3.88–5.0V	35920	46.0
RR Lyr	19 25.5	+42 47	RRab	7.06–8.12V	42995.405	0.566
UX Dra	19 21.6	+76 34	SRa	5.94–7.1v		168:
X Cyg	20 43.4	+35 35	δ Cep	5.87–6.86V	35915.918	16.386
T Vul	20 51.5	+28 15	δ Cep	5.44–6.06V	35934.758	4.435
T Cep	21 09.5	+68 29	M	5.2–11.3v	44177	388.14
μ Cep	21 43.5	+58 47	SRc	3.43–5.1v		730
δ Cep	22 29.2	+58 25	δ Cep	3.48–4.37V	36075.445	5.366

ERUPTIVE VARIABLE STARS

Name	R.A h m	Dec. ° ′	Type	Mag.	Epoch (2400000+)	Period (days)
P Cyg	20 17.8	+38 02	S Dor	3.0–6.0v		
SS Cyg	21 42.7	+43 35	UG	8.2–12.4v		50.1:

OTHER VARIABLE STARS

Name	R.A h m	Dec. ° ′	Type	Mag.	Epoch (2400000+)	Period (days)
EG And	0 44.5	+40 41	Z And	7.08–7.8V		
AG Dra	16 01.7	+66 48	Z And	8.8–11.8p		
CH Cyg	19 24.5	+50 14	Z And	6.4–8.7 v		97

NOTES

1. Andromeda Galaxy
2. Includes φ¹,² Cas
3. Nebula covers large area
4. Owl Nebula
5. Whirlpool Galaxy
6. M51 companion
7. Not M102
8. Bright central star
9. Polaris, brighter star slightly variable
10. 16 Dra (V=5.5) is 1′.5 south
11. Binocular pair
12. "Double-Double"
13. Same as V695 Cyg, brighter star slightly variable; third star: V=7.0; 1′.8 (1926); fourth star: V=4.8; 5′.6 (1926)
14. Brighter star slightly variable
15. Includes 27 Cyg
16. Veil Nebula, supernova remnant
17. North America Nebula
18. Mizar. Alcor (V=4.0) is 11′.8 east-northeast
19. Same as V389 Cyg, brighter star slightly variable
20. Same as TZ CrB, brighter star slightly variable

Magnitudes
-1 0 1 2 3 4 5 6

Double stars   Variable stars   Nova   Open clusters   Globular clusters   Diffuse nebulae   Planetary nebulae   Galaxies

N 1975

Constellation boundaries

Ecliptic   170°

Galactic equator   90°

URSA MAJOR

CANES VENATICI

BOOTES

CORONA BOREALIS

SER

DRACO

URSA MINOR

HERCULES

CAMELOPARDALIS

Polaris

LYRA

Vega

CEPHEUS

CYGNUS

Deneb

PERSEUS

CASSIOPEIA

LACERTA

ANDROMEDA

PEGASUS

VULPECULA

DEL

LMI

M51

M63

M94

M106

M109

M108 M97

M81 M82

M31 M110 M32

M76

M52

M103

M39

M29

M92

M13

11ʰ 12ʰ 13ʰ 14ʰ 15ʰ

16ʰ 17ʰ 18ʰ 19ʰ 20ʰ 21ʰ

22ʰ 23ʰ 0ʰ 1ʰ

+40° +50° +60° +70° +80°

DEEP-SKY OBJECTS

Name	R.A h m	Dec. ° '	Con	Type	V	Dimensions	Notes
				GALAXIES			
N 55	0 14.9	−39 11	Scl	SBm	7.4:	32′ × 6′.5	
N 147	0 33.2	+48 30	Cas	dE5	9.3	13′ × 8′.1	
N 185	0 39.0	+48 20	Cas	dE3	9.1	11′ × 9′.8	
N 205	0 40.4	+41 41	And	dE5	8.0	17′ × 9′.8	M110
N 221	0 42.7	+40 52	And	cE2	8.2	7′.6 × 5′.8	M32
N 224	0 42.7	+41 16	And	SAb	3.5	180′ × 60′	M31, (1)
N 247	0 47.1	−20 46	Cet	SAd	8.9	20′ × 7′.4	
N 253	0 47.6	−25 17	Scl	SAc	7.2	25′ × 7′.4	(2)
N 300	0 54.9	−37 41	Scl	SAd	8.2:	20′ × 15′	
N 598	1 33.9	+30 39	Tri	SAcd	5.7	62′ × 39′	M33, (3)
N 613	1 34.3	−29 25	Scl	SBbc	10.0	5′.8 × 4′.6	
N 628	1 36.7	+15 47	Psc	SAc	9.2	10′ × 9′.5	M74
N 891	2 22.6	+42 21	And	SAb?	10.0	13′ × 2′.8	
N 925	2 27.3	+33 35	Tri	SAd	10.0	9′.8 × 6′.0	
N1023	2 40.4	+39 04	Per	SB0⁻	9.4	8′.7 × 3′.3	
N1068	2 42.7	− 0 01	Cet	SAb	8.9	6′.9 × 5′.9	M77, (4)
N1097	2 46.3	−30 17	For	SBb	9.2	9′.3 × 6′.6	
N1232	3 09.8	−20 35	Eri	SAc	9.9	7′.8 × 6′.9	
N1291	3 17.3	−41 08	Eri	SB0/a	8.5	10′ × 9′.1	
N1316	3 22.7	−37 12	For	SA0	8.9	7′.1 × 5′.5	
N1365	3 33.6	−36 08	For	SBb	9.6	9′.8 × 5′.5	
N1398	3 38.9	−26 20	For	SBab	9.7	6′.6 × 5′.2	
N1399	3 38.5	−35 27	For	E1	9.9	3′.2 × 3′.1	(7)
N1407	3 40.2	−18 35	Eri	E0	9.8	2′.5 × 2′.5	
N1433	3 42.0	−47 13	Hor	SBa	10.0	6′.8 × 6′.0	
N7793	23 57.8	−32 35	Scl	SAd	9.1	9′.1 × 6′.6	
				OPEN CLUSTERS			
N 752	1 57.8	+37 41	And	oc	5.7	50′	
N1039	2 42.0	+42 47	Per	oc	5.2	25′	M34
Melotte 20	3 22	+49	Per	oc	1.2	2.8°	(5)
N1342	3 31.6	+37 20	Per	oc	6.7	17′	
Pleiades	3 47.0	+24 07	Tau	oc-gn	1.2	120′	M45
Hyades	4 27	+16	Tau	oc	0.5	6°	
				GLOBULAR CLUSTER			
N 288	0 52.8	−26 35	Scl	gc	8.1	14′	
				PLANETARY NEBULAE			
N1360	3 33.3	−25 51	For	pn	9.4:	9′ × 5′	(6)
N1535	4 14.2	−12 44	Eri	pn	9.6	48″ × 42″	
				DIFFUSE NEBULA			
N1499	4 00.7	+36 37	Per	gn	∼5	160′ × 40′	(8)

DOUBLE STARS

Name	R.A h m	Dec. ° '	Con	V	Sep (Date)	Notes
ADS 191 = 35 Psc	0 15.0	+ 8 49	Psc	6.0,7.8	11″.5 (1972)	(9)
ADS 683 = 65 Psc	0 49.9	+27 43	Psc	6.3,6.3	4″.6 (1970)	
ADS 824	1 00.1	+44 43	And	6.0,6.8	7″.8 (1967)	
ADS 899 = ψ Psc	1 05.6	+21 28	Psc	5.3,5.6	30″.0 (1972)	
ADS 996 = ζ Psc	1 13.7	+ 7 35	Psc	5.2,6.3	23″.0 (1974)	
τ Scl	1 36.1	−29 54	Scl	6.0,7.1	2″.2 (2000)	
ADS 1457 = 1 Ari	1 50.1	+22 17	Ari	6.2,7.4	2″.9 (1981)	
ADS 1507 = γ Ari	1 53.5	+19 18	Ari	4.8,4.8	7″.8 (1969)	
ADS 1534 = 56 And	1 56.2	+37 15	And	5.7,5.9	3′.6 (2000)	(10)
ADS 1630 = γ And	2 03.9	+42 20	And	2.3,4.8	9″.7 (1983)	(11)
ADS 1683 = 59 And	2 10.9	+39 02	And	5.6,6.1	16″.7 (1972)	
ADS 1697 = 6 Tri	2 12.4	+30 18	Tri	5.2,6.7	3″.9 (1973)	(12)
ADS 1703 = 66 Cet	2 12.8	− 2 24	Cet	5.7,7.7	16″.5 (1975)	
ADS 1982 = 30 Ari	2 37.0	+24 39	Ari	6.5,7.1	38″.3 (1973)	(13)
θ Eri	2 58.3	−40 18	Eri	3.2,4.4	8″.3 (1975)	
ADS 2402 = α For	3 12.1	−28 59	For	3.9,7.1	5″.1 (2000)	
ADS 2582	3 31.3	+27 34	Tau	6.6,7.0	11″.3 (1973)	
Δ 16 = f Eri	3 48.6	−37 37	Eri	4.7,5.4	8″.0 (1975)	
ADS 2850 = 32 Eri	3 54.3	− 2 57	Eri	4.8,6.1	6″.8 (1966)	
θ¹,² Tau	4 28.7	+15 52	Tau	3.4,3.8	5′.6 (2000)	(14)
θ Phe	23 39.5	−46 38	Fhe	6.5,7.3	3″.9 (1975)	
ADS16979 = 107 Aqr	23 46.0	−18 41	Aqr	5.7,6.7	6″.6 (1975)	

ECLIPSING VARIABLE STARS

Name	R.A h m	Dec. ° '	Type	Mag.	Epoch (2400000+)	Period (days)
β Per	3 08.2	+40 57	EA	2.12–3.40V	40953.465	2.867
λ Tau	4 00.7	+12 29	EA	3.3–3.80p	35089.204	3.952
			PULSATING VARIABLE STARS			
S Scl	0 15.4	−32 03	M	5.5–13.6v	42343	365.32
T Cet	0 21.8	−20 03	SRc	5.0–6.9v	40562	158.9
R And	0 24.0	+38 35	M	5.8–14.9v	43135	409.33
TV Psc	0 28.0	+17 54	SR	4.65–5.42V		70
o Cet	2 19.3	− 2 59	M	2.0–10.1v	44839	331.96
U Cet	2 33.7	−13 09	M	6.8–13.4v	42137	234.76
R Tri	2 37.0	+34 16	M	5.4–12.6v	42014	266.48
R Hor	2 53.9	−49 53	M	4.7–14.3v	41490	403.97
ρ Per	3 05.2	+38 50	SRb	3.30–4.0v		50:
TX Psc	23 46.4	+ 3 29	Lb	6.9–7.7p		
			ERUPTIVE VARIABLE STAR			
WW Cet	0 11.4	−11 29	Z Cam	9.3–16.8p		31.2:
			OTHER VARIABLE STARS			
EG And	0 44.5	+40 41	Z And	7.08–7.8V		
Z And	23 33.7	+48 49	Z And	8.0–12.4p		
SX Phe	23 46.5	−41 35	δ Sct	6.78–7.51V	38636.617	0.054

NOTES

1. Andromeda Galaxy
2. Brightest in Sculptor galaxy group
3. Triangulum Galaxy
4. Seyfert galaxy
5. α Persei cluster
6. Bright central star
7. Brightest in Fornax galaxy cluster
8. California Nebula
9. Same as UU Psc, brighter star slightly variable
10. Optical; binocular pair
11. Fainter star is close pair
12. Same as TZ Tri, brighter star slightly variable (not = ι Tri)
13. Binocular pair
14. Naked-eye pair in Hyades; brighter star slightly variable

Magnitudes	Double stars	Variable stars	Nova	Open clusters	Globular clusters	Diffuse nebulae	Planetary nebulae	Galaxies
● ● ● ● ● · · −1 0 1 2 3 4 5 6	● ● ● ●	◉ ○ ⊙ ∘ ∘	∘ N 1975	◌ ○ ○ ○	⊕ ⊕ ⊕	⌇ □	✧ ✧ ✧	⬭ ∘ ∘ ∘
	Constellation boundaries				Ecliptic – – – 170°		Galactic equator – – – 90°	

3

CASSIOPEIA

PERSEUS

PERSEUS

ANDROMEDA

M31
M110
M32
EG

Algol
β

Hyades

Aldebaran
α

TAURUS

M45
PLEIADES
4 x enlarged

M45
See inset

ARIES

TRIANGULUM
M33

Mira

PISCES

PEGASUS

ERIDANUS

CETUS

AQUARIUS

M77

M74

FORNAX

SCULPTOR

SGP

CAELUM

HOROLOGIUM

DORADO

ERIDANUS

PHOENIX

DEEP-SKY OBJECTS

Name	R.A h m	Dec. ° '	Con	Type	V	Dimensions	Notes
GALAXIES							
N1399	3 38.5	−35 27	For	E1	9.9	3'.2 × 3'.1	(2)
N1407	3 40.2	−18 35	Eri	E0	9.8	2'.5 × 2'.5	
N1433	3 42.0	−47 13	Hor	SBa	10.0	6'.8 × 6'.0	
N1808	5 07.7	−37 31	Col	SAa	9.9	7'.2 × 4'.1	
OPEN CLUSTERS							
Pleiades	3 47.0	+24 07	Tau	oc-gn	1.2	120'	M45
Hyades	4 27	+16	Tau	oc	0.5	6°	
N1647	4 46.0	+19 04	Tau	oc	6.4	40'	
N1662	4 48.5	+10 56	Ori	oc	6.4	12'	
N1746	5 03.6	+23 49	Tau	oc	~6	40'	
N1912	5 28.7	+35 50	Aur	oc	6.4	21'	M38
N1981	5 35.2	− 4 26	Ori	oc	4.6	28'	(5)
N1976	5 35.4	− 5 23	Ori	oc-gn	3.7	45'	M42, (6)
N1980	5 35.4	− 5 54	Ori	oc	2.5	20'	(7)
N1977	5 35.5	− 4 52	Ori	oc-gn	4.2	20'	(5)
N1960	5 36.1	+34 08	Aur	oc	6.0	12'	M36
N2099	5 52.4	+32 33	Aur	oc	5.6	24'	M37
N2169	6 08.4	+13 57	Ori	oc	5.9	6'	
N2168	6 08.9	+24 20	Gem	oc	5.1	28'	M35
N2244	6 32.4	+ 4 52	Mon	oc-gn	4.8	27'	(9)
N2264	6 41.1	+ 9 53	Mon	oc-gn	3.9	20'	
N2281	6 49.3	+41 04	Aur	oc	5.4	15'	
N2287	6 46.0	−20 44	CMa	oc	4.5	38'	M41
N2301	6 51.8	+ 0 28	Mon	oc	6.0	15'	
N2323	7 03.2	− 8 20	Mon	oc	5.9	16'	M50
N2343	7 08.3	−10 39	Mon	oc	6.7	13'	
N2354	7 14.3	−25 44	CMa	oc	6.5	20'	
N2362	7 18.8	−24 57	CMa	oc	4.1	8'	(10)
N2422	7 36.6	−14 30	Pup	oc	4.4	25'	M47
N2423	7 37.1	−13 52	Pup	oc	6.7	12'	
N2439	7 40.8	−31 39	Pup	oc	6.9	9'	(12)
N2437	7 41.8	−14 49	Pup	oc	6.1	20'	M46
N2447	7 44.6	−23 52	Pup	oc	6.2:	10'	M93
N2451	7 45.4	−37 58	Pup	oc	2.8	50'	(13)
N2477	7 52.3	−38 33	Pup	oc	5.8	43'	
N2467	7 52.6	−26 23	Pup	oc-gn	~7	16'	
N2527	8 05.3	−28 10	Pup	oc	6.5	22'	
GLOBULAR CLUSTERS							
N1851	5 14.1	−40 03	Col	gc	7.2	11'	
N1904	5 24.5	−24 33	Lep	gc	7.8	8'.7	M79
PLANETARY NEBULAE							
N1360	3 33.3	−25 51	For	pn	9.4:	9' × 5'	(1)
N1535	4 14.2	−12 44	Eri	pn	9.6	48" × 42"	
I418	5 27.5	−12 42	Lep	pn	9.3	14" × 11"	
N2392	7 29.2	+20 55	Gem	pn	9.4:	47" × 43"	(11)
N2440	7 41.9	−18 12	Pup	pn	9.4	74" × 42"	
DIFFUSE NEBULAE							
N1499	4 00.7	+36 37	Per	gn	~5	160' × 40'	(3)
N1952	5 34.5	+22 01	Tau	gn	~8	6' × 4'	M1,(4)
N1982	5 35.6	− 5 16	Ori	gn	~7	20' × 15'	M43, (8)
N2068/71	5 46.7	+ 0 06	Ori	gn	~8	8' × 6'/7' × 5'	M78

DOUBLE STARS

Name	R.A h m	Dec. ° '	Con	V	Sep (Date)	Notes
ADS 2582	3 31.3	+27 34	Tau	6.6,7.0	11".3 (1973)	
Δ 16 = f Eri	3 48.6	−37 37	Eri	4.7,5.4	8".0 (1975)	
ADS 2850 = 32 Eri	3 54.3	− 2 57	Eri	4.8,6.1	6".8 (1966)	
θ¹,² Tau	4 28.7	+15 52	Tau	3.4,3.8	5'.6 (2000)	(14)
σ¹,² Tau	4 39.3	+15 55	Tau	4.7,5.1	7'.3 (2000)	(15)
ADS 3409 = 55 Eri	4 43.6	− 8 48	Eri	6.7,6.8	9".3 (1975)	(16)
ADS 3597	5 00.6	+ 3 37	Ori	6.7,7.0	21".3 (1973)	
ADS 3623	5 02.0	+ 1 37	Ori	6.5,7.7	14".6 (1973)	(17)
ADS 3823 = β Ori	5 14.5	− 8 12	Ori	0.1,6.8	9".5 (1974)	(18)
ADS 3824 = 14 Aur	5 15.4	+32 41	Aur	5.1,8.0	14".6 (1973)	(19)
ADS 3954	5 21.8	−24 46	Lep	5.4,6.6	3".5 (1983)	
ADS 3978	5 23.3	− 8 25	Ori	6.0,7.8	6".0 (1973)	
ADS 3991	5 23.9	− 0 52	Ori	6.1,7.1	2".7 (1975)	(20)
ADS 4068 = 118 Tau	5 29.3	+25 09	Tau	5.8,6.6	4".8 (1981)	
ADS 4131	5 32.2	+17 03	Tau	6.1,6.5	9".6 (1972)	
ADS 4179 = λ Ori	5 35.1	+ 9 56	Ori	3.6,5.6	4".4 (1978)	
ADS 4193 = ι Ori	5 35.4	− 5 55	Ori	2.8,6.9	11".4 (1973)	(21)
ADS 4241 = σ Ori	5 38.7	− 2 36	Ori	3.8,6.6	12".9 (1973)	(22)
ADS 4263 = ζ Ori	5 40.8	− 1 57	Ori	1.9,4.0	2".6 (1976)	
ADS 4749	6 09.0	+ 2 30	Ori	5.7,6.9	29".5 (1973)	
ADS 4773 = 41 Aur	6 11.6	+48 43	Aur	6.3,7.0	7".7 (1973)	
ADS 5012 = ε Mon	6 23.8	+ 4 36	Mon	4.4,6.7	12".9 (1961)	
ADS 5107 = β Mon	6 28.8	− 7 02	Mon	4.7,5.2	7".2 (1974)	(23)
ADS 5166 = 20 Gem	6 32.3	+17 47	Gem	6.3,7.0	20".0 (1973)	
Δ 32	6 42.3	−38 24	Pup	6.6,7.9	8".0 (1975)	
ADS 5559 = 38 Gem	6 54.6	+13 11	Gem	4.7,7.7	7".1 (2000)	
ADS 5654 = ε CMa	6 58.6	−28 58	CMa	1.5,7.4	7".5 (1951)	
Δ 38	7 04.0	−43 36	Pup	5.5,6.8	21".1 (1977)	
h 3928	7 05.5	−34 47	Pup	6.4,7.8	2".7 (1979)	
ADS 5951	7 16.6	−23 19	CMa	4.8,6.8	26".8 (1974)	
Δ 49	7 28.9	−31 51	Pup	6.4,7.1	8".9 (1968)	
ADS 6126	7 29.4	−15 00	Pup	6.4,7.5	2".0 (2000)	
ADS 6190	7 34.3	−23 28	Pup	5.8,5.9	9".6 (1965)	
ADS 6175 = α Gem	7 34.6	+31 53	Gem	1.9,2.9	3".9 (2000)	(24)
ADS 6255	7 38.8	−26 48	Pup	4.5,4.7	9".9 (1964)	
ADS 6381 = 5 Pup	7 47.9	−12 12	Pup	5.6,7.7	2".0 (1975)	
ADS 6348 = 2 Pup	7 45.5	−14 41	Pup	6.1,6.9	16".8 (1973)	(25)
Δ 59	7 59.2	−49 59	Pup	6.4,6.4	16".4 (1957)	

ECLIPSING VARIABLE STARS

Name	R.A h m	Dec. ° '	Type	Mag.	Epoch (2400000+)	Period (days)
λ Tau	4 00.7	+12 29	EA	3.3–3.80p	35089.204	3.952
HU Tau	4 38.3	+20 41	EA	5.92–6.7V	42412.456	2.056
ε Aur	5 02.0	+43 49	EA	2.92–3.83V	35629	9892
AR Aur	5 18.3	+33 46	EA	6.15–6.82V	38402.183	4.134
WW Aur	6 32.5	+32 27	EA	5.79–6.54V	41399.305	2.525
R CMa	7 19.5	−16 24	EA	5.70–6.34V	44289.361	1.135
V Pup	7 58.2	−49 15	EB	4.7–5.2p	28648.304	1.454

PULSATING VARIABLE STARS

Name	R.A h m	Dec. ° '	Type	Mag.	Epoch (2400000+)	Period (days)
R Lep	4 59.6	−14 48	M	5.5–11.7v	40800	432.13
RX Lep	5 11.4	−11 51	Lb	5.0–7.0v		
α Ori	5 55.2	+ 7 24	SRc	0.40–1.3v		2110
U Ori	5 55.8	+20 10	M	4.8–12.6v	42280	372.40
η Gem	6 14.9	+22 30	SRb	3.2–3.9v	37725	232.9
T Mon	6 25.2	+ 7 05	δ Cep	5.59–6.60V	36137.090	27.020
RT Aur	6 28.6	+30 30	δ Cep	5.00–5.82V	42361.155	3.728
ζ Gem	7 04.1	+20 34	δ Cep	3.66–4.16V	36791.922	10.150
L² Pup	7 13.5	−44 39	SRb	2.6–6.2v	40813	140.42

ERUPTIVE VARIABLE STAR

Name	R.A h m	Dec. ° '	Type	Mag.	Epoch (2400000+)	Period (days)
U Gem	7 55.1	+22 00	UG	8.2–14.9v		103:

OTHER VARIABLE STARS

Name	R.A h m	Dec. ° '	Type	Mag.	Epoch (2400000+)	Period (days)
U Mon	7 30.8	− 9 47	RVb	6.1–8.1p	37395	92.26
AI Vel	8 14.1	−44 34	δ Sct	6.4–7.1v		0.111

NOTES

1. Bright central star
2. Brightest in Fornax galaxy cluster
3. California Nebula
4. Crab Nebula, a supernova remnant
5. In Orion's Sword
6. Orion Nebula + Trapezium (θ¹ Ori)
7. Includes ι Ori (see ADS 4193) and in Orion's Sword
8. Appendage to Orion Nebula
9. Includes Rosette Nebula (90' diam)
10. Includes τ CMa
11. Eskimo Nebula, bright central star
12. Includes R Pup
13. Includes C Pup
14. Naked-eye pair in Hyades; brighter star slightly variable
15. Naked-eye/binocular pair in Hyades
16. Same as DW Eri, fainter star slightly variable
17. Fainter star is very close pair
18. Rigel
19. Same as KW Aur, brighter star slightly variable
20. Fainter star is very close pair
21. In cluster N1980
22. Same as V1030 Ori, fainter star slightly variable, several other components
23. Third star: V=6.1; 9".9 (1963), a remarkable triple!
24. Castor (Heintz 1988 orbit)
25. Same as PV Pup, fainter star slightly variable

4

LYNX

AURIGA

Capella

PERSEUS

Castor

Pollux

CANCER

GEMINI

TAURUS

Aldebaran

Hyades

CANIS MINOR

Procyon

ORION

Betelgeuse

HYDRA

MONOCEROS

Rigel

ERIDANUS

LEPUS

Sirius

CANIS MAJOR

Adhara

COLUMBA

FORNAX

CAELUM

PYXIS

PUPPIS

PICTOR

DORADO

HOROLOGIUM

VELA

See inset
chart 3

M45

M35

M36

M37

M38

M41

M42

M43

M47

M48

M50

M79

M93

M78

M1

DEEP-SKY OBJECTS

Name	R.A h m	Dec. ° '	Con	Type	V	Dimensions	Notes
GALAXIES							
N2683	8 52.7	+33 25	Lyn	SAb	9.7	9′.3 × 2′.5	
N2903	9 32.2	+21 30	Leo	SAbc	8.9	13′ × 6′.6	
N2997	9 45.6	−31 11	Ant	SAc	9.5	8′.1 × 6′.5	
N3115	10 05.2	− 7 43	Sex	SA0⁻	9.1	8′.3 × 3′.2	
N3184	10 18.3	+41 25	UMa	SAcd	9.8	6′.9 × 6′.8	
N3344	10 43.5	+24 55	LMi	SAbc	10.0	6′.9 × 6′.5	
N3351	10 44.0	+11 42	Leo	SBb	9.8	7′.4 × 5′.1	M95
N3368	10 46.8	+11 49	Leo	SAab	9.3	7′.1 × 5′.1	M96
N3379	10 47.8	+12 35	Leo	E1	9.3	4′.5 × 4′.0	M105
N3384	10 48.3	+12 38	Leo	SB0⁻:	10.0	5′.9 × 2′.6	
N3521	11 05.8	− 0 02	Leo	SAbc	9.2	9′.5 × 5′.0	
N3585	11 13.3	−26 45	Hya	E5	10.0	2′.9 × 1′.6	
N3621	11 18.3	−32 49	Hya	SAd	9.5:	10′ × 6′.5	
N3623	11 28.9	+13 05	Leo	SAa	9.3	10′ × 3′.3	M65
N3627	11 20.2	+12 59	Leo	SAb	9.0	8′.7 × 4′.4	M66
N3628	11 20.3	+13 36	Leo	SAb	9.5	15′ × 3′.6	
N4192	12 13.8	+14 54	Com	SAab	10.1	9′.5 × 3′.2	M98
N4214	12 15.6	+36 20	CVn	IAm	9.8	7′.9 × 6′.3	
N4216	12 15.9	+13 09	Vir	SAb	10.0	8′.3 × 2′.2	
N4254	12 18.8	+14 25	Com	SAc	9.9	5′.4 × 4′.8	M99
N4258	12 19.0	+47 18	CVn	SAbc	8.3	18′ × 8′	M106
N4303	12 21.9	+ 4 28	Vir	SAbc	9.6	6′.0 × 5′.5	M61
N4321	12 22.9	+15 49	Com	SAbc	9.4	6′.9 × 6′.2	M100
N4365	12 24.5	+ 7 19	Vir	E3	9.5:	6′.2 × 4′.6	
N4374	12 25.1	+12 53	Vir	E1	9.3	5′.0 × 4′.4	M84
N4382	12 25.4	+18 11	Com	SA0⁺	9.2	7′.2 × 5′.2	M85
N4406	12 26.2	+12 57	Vir	E3	9.1	7′.4 × 5′.5	M86
N4435	12 27.7	+13 05	Vir	SB0	10.0	3′.0 × 1′.9	(6)
N4438	12 27.8	+13 01	Vir	SA0/a	10.1	9′.3 × 3′.9	(7)
N4449	12 28.2	+44 06	CVn	IBm	9.5	5′.1 × 3′.7	
N4472	12 29.8	+ 8 00	Vir	E2	8.4	8′.9 × 7′.4	M49, (8)
OPEN CLUSTERS							
N2422	7 36.6	−14 30	Pup	oc	4.4	25′	M47
N2423	7 37.1	−13 52	Pup	oc	6.7	12′	
N2439	7 40.8	−31 39	Pup	oc	6.9	9′	(1)
N2437	7 41.8	−14 49	Pup	oc	6.1	20′	M46
N2447	7 44.6	−23 52	Pup	oc	6.2:	10′	M93
N2451	7 45.4	−37 58	Pup	oc	2.8	50′	(2)
N2477	7 52.3	−38 33	Pup	oc	5.8	43′	
N2467	7 52.6	−26 23	Pup	oc-gn	~7	16′	
N2527	8 05.3	−28 10	Pup	oc	6.5	22′	
N2539	8 10.7	−12 50	Pup	oc	6.5	22′	
N2547	8 10.7	−49 16	Vel	oc	4.7	74′	
N2546	8 12.4	−37 38	Pup	oc	6.3	70′	
N2548	8 13.8	− 5 48	Hya	oc	5.8	54′	M48
N2632	8 40.1	+19 59	Cnc	oc	3.1	95′	M44, (3)
I 2395	8 41.1	−48 12	Vel	oc	4.6	20′	
N2682	8 50.4	+11 49	Cnc	oc	6.9	30′	M67
Melotte 111	12 25	+26	Com	oc	1.8	4.6°	(5)
GLOBULAR CLUSTER							
N3201	10 17.6	−46 25	Vel	gc	6.7	18′	
PLANETARY NEBULAE							
N2392	7 29.2	+20 55	Gem	pn	9.4:	47″ × 43″	(15)
N2440	7 41.9	−18 12	Pup	pn	9.4	74″ × 42″	
N3132	10 07.7	−40 26	Vel	pn	9.4	84″ × 53″	(4)
N3242	10 24.8	−18 38	Hya	pn	7.8	45″ × 36″	

DOUBLE STARS

Name	R.A h m	Dec. ° '	Con	V	Sep (Date)	Notes
ADS 6190	7 34.3	−23 28	Pup	5.8,5.9	9″.6 (1965)	
ADS 6175 = α Gem	7 34.6	+31 53	Gem	1.9,2.9	3″.9 (2000)	(9)
ADS 6255	7 38.8	−26 48	Pup	4.5,4.7	9″.9 (1964)	
ADS 6348 = 2 Pup	7 45.5	−14 41	Pup	6.1,6.9	16″.8 (1973)	(10)
ADS 6381 = 5 Pup	7 47.9	−12 12	Pup	5.6,7.7	2″.0 (1975)	
Δ 59	7 59.2	−49 59	Pup	6.4,6.4	16″.4 (1957)	
γ Vel	8 09.5	−47 20	Vel	1.8,4.3	41″.2 (1951)	(16)
ADS 6650 = ζ¹,² Cnc	8 12.1	+17 39	Cnc	5.4,6.0	5″.6 (1981)	(11)
h 4093	8 26.3	−39 04	Pup	6.5,7.3	8″.1 (1975)	(12)
ADS 6815 = φ¹,² Cnc	8 26.8	+26 56	Cnc	6.3,6.4	5″.1 (1973)	
h 4104	8 29.1	−47 56	Vel	5.5,7.3	3″.6 (1979)	(13)
Δ 70	8 29.5	−44 44	Vel	5.2,7.1	4″.5 (1954)	
ADS 6977	8 45.3	− 2 36	Hya	6.4,7.4	4″.7 (1955)	
ADS 6988 = ι Cnc	8 46.7	+28 46	Cnc	4.0,6.6	30″.4 (1973)	
ADS 7137 = 66 Cnc	9 01.4	+32 15	Cnc	5.9,8.0	4″.5 (1973)	
h 4188	9 12.5	−43 37	Vel	6.0,6.8	2″.8 (1977)	(11)
ADS 7292 = 38 Lyn	9 18.8	+36 48	Lyn	3.9,6.6	2″.7 (1968)	
ζ Ant	9 30.8	−31 53	Ant	6.2,7.0	8″.0 (1977)	
ADS 7724 = γ Leo	10 20.0	+19 51	Leo	2.2,3.5	4″.4 (2000)	
ADS 7902 = 35 Sex	10 43.3	+ 4 45	Sex	6.1,7.2	6″.8 (1981)	
ADS 7979 = 54 Leo	10 55.6	+24 45	Leo	4.5,6.3	6″.5 (1973)	
ADS 8162 = 83 Leo	11 26.8	+ 3 01	Leo	6.5,7.6	28″.5 (1970)	
ADS 8202 = N Hya	11 32.3	−29 16	Hya	5.7,5.8	9″.3 (1967)	
ADS 8220 = 90 Leo	11 34.7	+16 48	Leo	6.0,7.3	3″.4 (1981)	
ADS 8406 = 2 Com	12 04.3	+21 28	Com	5.9,7.4	3″.7 (1978)	
Rmk 14	12 14.0	−45 43	Cen	5.6,6.8	2″.8 (1963)	
ADS 8505	12 18.2	− 3 57	Vir	6.5,7.0	20″.1 (1973)	

ECLIPSING VARIABLE STARS

Name	R.A h m	Dec. ° '	Type	Mag.	Epoch (2400000+)	Period (days)
TY Pyx	8 59.7	−27 49	E	6.87–7.47V	43187.230	3.198
S Ant	9 32.3	−28 38	EW	6.4–6.92V	35139.929	0.648

PULSATING VARIABLE STARS

AK Hya	8 39.9	−17 18	SRb	6.33–6.91V		112:
R Leo	9 47.6	+11 26	M	4.4–11.3v	41688	312.43
SS Vir	12 25.3	+ 0 48	M	6.0–9.6v	40653	354.66

ERUPTIVE VARIABLE STARS

| U Gem | 7 55.1 | +22 00 | UG | 8.2–14.9v | | 103: |
| T Pyx | 9 04.7 | −32 23 | Nr | 6.3–14.0v | 39501 | 7000: |

OTHER VARIABLE STARS

U Mon	7 30.8	− 9 47	RVb	6.1–8.1p	37395	92.26
AI Vel	8 14.1	−44 34	δ Sct	6.4–7.1v		0.111
VZ Cnc	8 40.9	+ 9 49	δ Sct	7.18–7.91V	41304.364	0.178
RU Cen	12 09.4	−45 25	RV	8.7–10.7p	28015.51	64.727

NOTES

1. Includes R Pup
2. Includes c Pup
3. Praesepe or Beehive cluster
4. Bright central star
5. Coma star cluster
6. Interacts with N4438
7. Interacts with N4435
8. Brightest in Virgo galaxy cluster
9. Castor (Heintz 1988 orbit)
10. Same as PV Pup, fainter star slightly variable
11. Brighter star is very close pair
12. Same as NO Pup, brighter star slightly variable
13. Brighter star is very close pair; third fainter star in group
14. Third star: V=4.9; 1′.5 (1973)
15. Eskimo Nebula, bright central star
16. Brighter star is brightest Wolf-Rayet star

Magnitudes	Double stars	Variable stars	Nova	Open clusters	Globular clusters	Diffuse nebulae	Planetary nebulae	Galaxies
● ● ● ● • · -1 0 1 2 3 4 5 6	● ● ●	⊙ ○ ○ ∘ ·	∘ N 1975	◌ ○ ○ ○	⊕ ⊕ ⊕	⬡ □	◇ ◇ ◇	◯ ◯ ○

Constellation boundaries ⋯⋯⋯   Ecliptic – – – 170° – – –   Galactic equator – – – 90°

5

URSA MAJOR

LYNX

AUR

LEO MINOR

CANES VENATICI

GEMINI

Castor α

Pollux β

CANCER

COMA BERENICES

LEO

Regulus α

CANIS MINOR

Procyon α

MONOCEROS

VIRGO

SEXTANS

HYDRA

CORVUS

CRATER

PUPPIS

HYDRA

ANTLIA

PYXIS

CENTAURUS

VELA

DEEP-SKY OBJECTS

Name	R.A h m	Dec. ° '	Con	Type	V	Dimensions	Notes
GALAXIES							
N4192	12 13.8	+14 54	Com	SAab	10.1	9.′5 × 3.′2	M98
N4214	12 15.6	+36 20	CVn	IAm	9.8	7.′9 × 6.′3	
N4216	12 15.9	+13 09	Vir	SAb	10.0	8.′3 × 2.′2	
N4254	12 18.8	+14 25	Com	SAc	9.9	5.′4 × 4.′8	M99
N4303	12 21.9	+ 4 28	Vir	SAbc	9.6	6.′0 × 5.′5	M61
N4321	12 22.9	+15 49	Com	SAbc	9.4	6.′9 × 6.′2	M100
N4365	12 24.5	+ 7 19	Vir	E3	9.5:	6.′2 × 4.′6	
N4374	12 25.1	+12 53	Vir	E1	9.3	5.′0 × 4.′4	M84
N4382	12 25.4	+18 11	Com	SA0+	9.2	7.′2 × 5.′2	M85
N4406	12 26.2	+12 57	Vir	E3	9.1	7.′4 × 5.′5	M86
N4435	12 27.7	+13 05	Vir	SB0	10.0	3.′0 × 1.′9	(2)
N4438	12 27.8	+13 01	Vir	SA0/a	10.1	9.′3 × 3.′9	(3)
N4472	12 29.8	+ 8 00	Vir	E2	8.4	8.′9 × 7.′4	M49, (4)
N4486	12 30.8	+12 24	Vir	E+0-1	8.6	7.′2 × 6.′8	M87
N4494	12 31.4	+25 47	Com	E1-2	9.8	4.′8 × 3.′8	
N4501	12 32.0	+14 25	Com	SAb	9.5	6.′9 × 3.′9	M88
N4526	12 34.0	+ 7 42	Vir	SA0	9.7	7.′2 × 2.′3	
N4535	12 34.3	+ 8 12	Vir	SAc	9.8	6.′8 × 5.′0	
N4548	12 35.4	+14 30	Com	SBb	10.2	5.′4 × 4.′4	M91
N4552	12 35.7	+12 33	Vir	E0	9.8	4.′2 × 4.′2	M89
N4559	12 36.0	+27 58	Com	SAcd	9.9	10′ × 4.′9	
N4565	12 36.3	+25 59	Com	SAb?	9.5	16′ × 2.′8	
N4569	12 36.8	+13 10	Vir	SAab	9.5	9.′5 × 4.′7	M90
N4579	12 37.7	+11 49	Vir	SAb	9.7	5.′4 × 4.′4	M58
N4594	12 40.0	−11 37	Vir	SAa	8.3	8.′9 × 4.′1	M104, (5)
N4621	12 42.0	+11 39	Vir	E5	9.8	5.′1 × 3.′4	M59
N4631	12 42.1	+32 32	CVn	SBd	9.3	15′ × 3.′3	
N4636	12 42.8	+ 2 41	Vir	E0-1	9.5	6.′2 × 5.′0	
N4649	12 43.7	+11 33	Vir	E2	8.8	7.′2 × 6.′2	M60
N4697	12 48.6	− 5 48	Vir	E6	9.3	6.′0 × 3.′8	
N4699	12 49.0	− 8 40	Vir	SAb	9.6	3.′5 × 2.′7	
N4725	12 50.4	+25 30	Com	SAab	9.3	11′ × 7.′9	
N4736	12 50.9	+41 07	CVn	SAab	8.2	11′ × 9.′1	M94
N4753	12 52.4	− 1 12	Vir	I0	9.9	5.′4 × 2.′9	
N4826	12 56.7	+21 41	Com	SAab	8.5	9.′3 × 5.′4	M64, (6)
N4945	13 05.4	−49 28	Cen	SBcd	8.3:	20′ × 4.′4	
N5005	13 10.9	+37 03	CVn	SAbc	9.9	5.′4 × 2.′7	
N5068	13 18.9	−21 02	Vir	SAcd	9.9:	6.′9 × 6.′3	
N5102	13 22.0	−36 38	Cen	SA0−	9.6	9.′3 × 3.′5	
N5128	13 25.5	−43 01	Cen	S0 pec	6.9	18′ × 14′	(7)
N5236	13 37.0	−29 52	Hya	SBc	7.5:	11′ × 10′	M83
N5248	13 37.5	+ 8 53	Boo	SAbc	10.0	6.′5 × 4.′9	
N5643	14 32.7	−44 10	Lup	SAc	9.8:	4.′6 × 4.′1	
OPEN CLUSTERS							
Melotte 111	12 25	+26	Com	oc	1.8	4.6°	(1)
N5460	14 07.6	−48 19	Cen	oc	5.6	25′	
N6124	16 25.6	−40 40	Sco	oc	5.8:	40′	
GLOBULAR CLUSTERS							
N4590	12 39.5	−26 45	Hya	gc	7.7	12′	M68
N5024	13 12.9	+18 10	Com	gc	7.5	13′	M53
N5139	13 26.8	−47 29	Cen	gc	3.7	36′	(8)
N5272	13 42.2	+28 23	CVn	gc	5.9	16′	M3
N5904	15 18.6	+ 2 05	Ser	gc	5.7	17′	M5
N6093	16 17.0	−22 59	Sco	gc	7.3	8.′9	M80
N6121	16 23.6	−26 32	Sco	gc	5.8	26′	M4
PLANETARY NEBULA							
N5882	15 16.8	−45 39	Lup	pn	9.4	7″ × 7″	

DOUBLE STARS

Name	R.A h m	Dec. ° '	Con	V	Sep (Date)	Notes
ADS 8202 = N Hya	11 32.3	−29 16	Hya	5.7,5.8	9.″3 (1967)	
ADS 8220 = 90 Leo	11 34.7	+16 48	Leo	6.0,7.3	3.″4 (1981)	
ADS 8406 = 2 Com	12 04.3	+21 28	Com	5.9,7.4	3.″7 (1978)	
Rmk 14	12 14.0	−45 43	Cen	5.6,6.8	2.″8 (1963)	
ADS 8505	12 18.2	− 3 57	Vir	6.5,7.0	20.″1 (1973)	
ADS 8600 = 24 Com	12 35.1	+18 23	Com	5.0,6.6	20.″3 (1973)	
ADS 8627	12 41.3	−13 01	Crv	6.0 6.1	5.″4 (1980)	
ADS 8630 = γ Vir	12 41.7	− 1 27	Vir	3.5,3.5	1.″8 (2000)	(9)
ADS 8706 = α CVn	12 56.0	+38 19	CVn	2.9,5.6	19.″4 (1974)	(10)
ADS 8966	13 36.8	−26 30	Hya	5.8,6.7	10.″1 (1968)	
k = 3 Cen	13 51.8	−33 00	Cen	4.6,6.1	7.″9 (1975)	
ADS 9053	13 55.0	− 8 04	Vir	6.5,7.7	3.″4 (1981)	
ADS 9247	14 23.4	+ 8 27	Boo	5.1,6.9	6.″2 (1973)	(11)
ADS 9338 = π Boo	14 40.7	+16 25	Boo	5.0,5.9	5.″6 (1977)	
ADS 9372 = ε Boo	14 45.0	+27 04	Boo	2.5,4.9	2.″8 (1977)	
ADS 9375 = 54 Hya	14 46.0	−25 27	Hya	5.1,7.1	8.″4 (1975)	
ADS 9406 = 39 Boo	14 49.7	+48 43	Boo	6.2,6.9	2.″9 (1981)	
α1,2 Lib	14 50.9	−16 02	Lib	2.8,5.2	3.′9 (1924)	(12)
ADS 9413 = ξ Boo	14 51.4	+19 06	Boo	4.7,7.0	6.″6 (2000)	(13)
h 4715	14 56.5	−47 53	Lup	6.1,6.9	2.″3 (1959)	
Δ 178	15 11.6	−45 17	Lup	6.4,7.4	32.″3 (1968)	
κ1,2 Lup	15 11.9	−48 44	Lup	3.9,5.7	26.″6 (1968)	
μ Lup	15 18.5	−47 53	Lup	5.0,5.1	1.″3 (1965)	(15)
ADS 9701 = δ Ser	15 34.8	+10 32	Ser	4.2,5.2	4.″4 (2000)	(14)
h 4788	15 35.9	−44 58	Lup	4.7,6.6	2.″1 (1975)	
ADS 9728	15 38.7	− 8 47	Lib	6.5,6.5	11.″9 (1965)	
ADS 9737 = ζ CrB	15 39.4	+36 38	CrB	5.1,6.0	6.″3 (1973)	
ξ Lup	15 56.9	−33 58	Lup	5.1,5.6	10.″4 (1968)	
η Lup	16 00.1	−38 24	Lup	3.4,7.8	15.″0 (1957)	
ADS 9909 = ξ Sco	16 04.4	−11 22	Sco	4.2,7.3	7.″6 (1975)	(16)
ADS 9913 = β Sco	16 05.4	−19 48	Sco	2.6,4.9	13.″6 (1976)	(17)
ADS 9933 = κ Her	16 08.1	+17 03	Her	5.0,6.3	28.″1 (1966)	
ADS 9951 = ν1,2 Sco	16 12.0	−19 28	Sco	4.0,6.3	41.″2 (1968)	(18)
ADS 9979 = σ CrB	16 14.7	+33 52	CrB	5.6O,6.6	7.″1 (2000)	(19)
BrsO 12	16 19.5	−30 54	Sco	5.5,7.1	23.″2 (1977)	
ADS10035	16 24.7	−29 42	Sco	5.8,6.6	5.″2 (1966)	
ADS10049 = ρ Oph	16 25.6	−23 27	Oph	5.3,6.0	3.″1 (1975)	
ε Nor	16 27.2	−47 33	Nor	4.5,7.2	22.″8 (1957)	

ECLIPSING VARIABLE STARS

Name	R.A h m	Dec. ° '	Type	Mag.	Epoch (2400000+)	Period (days)
δ Lib	15 01.0	− 8 31	EA	4.92−5.90V	42937.423	2.327
i Boo	15 03.8	+47 39	EW	6.5−7.1v	39370.422	0.267
GG Lup	15 18.9	−40 47	EB	5.4−6.0p	34532.325	2.164
PULSATING VARIABLE STARS						
SS Vir	12 25.3	+ 0 48	M	6.0−9.6v	40653	354.66
R Vir	12 38.5	+ 6 59	M	6.0−12.1v	42512	145.64
SW Vir	13 14.1	− 2 48	SRb	6.85−7.88V	40709	150:
FH Vir	13 16.4	+ 6 30	SRb	6.92−7.45V	40740	70:
V CVn	13 19.5	+45 32	SRa	6.52−8.56V	43929	191.89
R Hya	13 29.7	−23 17	M	4.5−9.5v	41676	389.61
T Cen	13 41.8	−33 36	SRa	5.5−9.0v	43242	90.44
τ4 Ser	15 36.5	+15 06	Lb	7.5−8.9p		
R Ser	15 50.7	+15 08	M	5.16−14.4v	42315	356.41
g Her	16 28.6	+41 53	SRb	5.7−7.2p		70:
α Sco	16 29.4	−26 26	SRc	0.88−1.80V	08600	1733
ERUPTIVE VARIABLE STARS						
T CrB	15 59.5	+25 55	Nr	2.0−10.8v	31860	9000:
U Sco	16 22.5	−17 53	Nr	8.8−19p	44048	3400:
OTHER VARIABLE STARS						
RU Cen	12 09.4	−45 25	RV	8.7−10.7p	28015.51	64.727
TX CVn	12 44.7	+36 46	Z And	9.2−11.8p		
R CrB	15 48.6	+28 09	RCB	5.71−14.8V		

NOTES

1. Coma star cluster
2. Interacts with N4438
3. Interacts with N4435
4. Brightest in Virgo galaxy cluster
5. Sombrero Galaxy
6. Blackeye Galaxy
7. Centaurus A
8. ω Centauri
9. Wider separation before 2000
10. Brighter star slightly variable
11. Fainter star is very close pair

12. Naked-eye/Binocular pair
13. Both stars slightly variable
14. Brighter star slightly variable
15. Third star: V=7.2; 24.″0 (1963)
16. Brighter star is close pair. ADS 9910 lies 5′ south
17. Brighter star is very close pair
18. Each component is a close double like ε1,2 Lyrae
20. Same as TZ CrB, brighter star slightly variable

Magnitudes
-1 0 1 2 3 4 5 6

Double stars Variable stars Nova Open clusters Globular clusters Diffuse nebulae Planetary nebulae Galaxies

Constellation boundaries ....

Ecliptic _ _ _ _ _ _ _ 170° + Galactic equator _ _ _ _ _ 90° +

6

UMA

CANES VENATICI

URSA MAJOR

BOÖTES

COMA BERENICES

LEO

CORONA BOREALIS

HERCULES

SERPENS CAPUT

VIRGO

OPHIUCHUS

CRATER

CORVUS

LIBRA

HYDRA

SCORPIUS

LUPUS

NORMA

CENTAURUS

Arcturus

Antares

Spica

NGP

16ʰ · 15ʰ · 14ʰ · 13ʰ · 12ʰ

+50° +45° +40° +35° +30° +25° +20° +15° +10° +5° 0° −5° −10° −15° −20° −25° −30° −35° −40° −45° −50°

DEEP-SKY OBJECTS

Name	R.A h m	Dec. ° '	Con	Type	V	Dimensions	Notes
GALAXY							
N6822	19 44.9	−14 48	Sgr	IBm	8.6:	$10' \times 9.'5$	
OPEN CLUSTERS							
N6124	16 25.6	−40 40	Sco	oc	5.8:	40'	
N6193	16 41.3	−48 46	Ara	oc	5.2	16'	
N6231	16 54.0	−41 48	Sco	oc	2.6	26'	
N6242	16 55.6	−39 30	Sco	oc	6.4	9'	
Trumpler 24	16 57.0	−40 40	Sco	oc-gn	∼5	60'	(1)
N6281	17 04.8	−37 54	Sco	oc	5.4	8'	
I4651	17 24.7	−49 57	Ara	oc	6.9	12'	
N6383	17 34.8	−32 34	Sco	oc	5.5	4.'0	
N6405	17 40.1	−32 13	Sco	oc	4.2	33'	M6, (3)
I4665	17 46.3	+ 5 43	Oph	oc	4.2	70'	
N6475	17 53.9	−34 49	Sco	oc	3.3	80'	M7
N6494	17 56.8	−19 01	Sgr	oc	5.5	30'	M23
N6514	18 02.5	−23 02	Sgr	oc-gn	6.3	13'	M20, (4)
N6531	18 04.6	−22 30	Sgr	oc	5.9	15'	M21
N6523/30	18 04.3	−24 20	Sgr	oc-gn	4.6	15'	M8, (5)
N6611	18 18.8	−13 47	Ser	oc-gn	6.0	21'	M16, (7)
N6613	18 19.9	−17 08	Sgr	oc	6.9	8'	M18
N6618	18 20.8	−16 11	Sgr	oc-gn	6.0	25'	M17, (8)
N6633	18 27.7	+ 6 34	Oph	oc	4.6	27'	
I4725	18 31.6	−19 15	Sgr	oc	4.6	30'	M25
I4756	18 39.0	+ 5 27	Ser	oc	4.6	52'	
N6694	18 45.2	− 9 24	Sct	oc	8.0	8'	M26
N6705	18 51.1	− 6 16	Sct	oc	5.8	25'	M11
N6709	18 51.5	+10 21	Aql	oc	6.7	13'	
Cr 394	18 53.5	−20 23	Sgr	oc	5.6	54'	
Stock 1	19 35.8	+25 13	Vul	oc	5.3:	80'	
N6811	19 37.0	+46 24	Cyg	oc	6.8	13'	
N6871	20 05.9	+35 47	Cyg	oc	5.2	20'	(11)
N6882/5	20 12.0	+26 29	Vul	oc	5.9	22'	(12)
N6910	20 23.1	+40 47	Cyg	oc	6.6	8'	
N6913	20 23.9	+38 32	Cyg	oc	6.6	7'	M29
GLOBULAR CLUSTERS							
N6093	16 17.0	−22 59	Sco	gc	7.3	8.'9	M80
N6121	16 23.6	−26 32	Sco	gc	5.8	26'	M4
N6171	16 32.5	−13 03	Oph	gc	8.1	10'	M107
N6205	16 41.7	+36 28	Her	gc	5.7	17'	M13
N6218	16 47.2	− 1 57	Oph	gc	6.8	15'	M12
N6254	16 57.1	− 4 06	Oph	gc	6.6	15'	M10
N6266	17 01.2	−30 07	Oph	gc	6.7	14'	M62
N6273	17 02.6	−26 16	Oph	gc	6.7	14'	M19
N6341	17 17.1	+43 08	Her	gc	6.4	11'	M92
N6333	17 19.2	−18 31	Oph	gc	7.6	9.'3	M9
N6388	17 36.3	−44 44	Sco	gc	6.7	8.'7	
N6402	17 37.6	− 3 15	Oph	gc	7.6	12'	M14
N6541	18 08.0	−43 42	CrA	gc	6.6	13'	
N6626	18 24.5	−24 52	Sgr	gc	6.8	11'	M28
N6637	18 31.4	−32 21	Sgr	gc	7.6	7.'1	M69
N6656	18 36.4	−23 54	Sgr	gc	5.1	24'	M22
N6681	18 43.2	−32 18	Sgr	gc	8.0	7.'8	M70
N6715	18 55.1	−30 29	Sgr	gc	7.6	9.'1	M54
N6779	19 16.6	+30 11	Lyr	gc	8.3	7.'1	M56
N6809	19 40.0	−30 58	Sgr	gc	6.4	19'	M55
N6838	19 53.8	+18 47	Sge	gc	8.0	7.'2	M71
N6864	20 06.1	−21 55	Sgr	gc	8.5	6.'0	M75
PLANETARY NEBULAE							
N6210	16 44.5	+23 49	Her	pn	8.8	$48'' \times 8''$	
N6572	18 12.1	+ 6 51	Oph	pn	8.1	$16'' \times 13''$	
N6720	18 53.6	+33 02	Lyr	pn	8.8	$86'' \times 62''$	M57, (9)
N6818	19 44.0	−14 09	Sgr	pn	9.3	$22'' \times 15''$	
N6853	19 59.6	+22 43	Vul	pn	7.3	$8.'0 \times 5.'7$	M27, (10)
DIFFUSE NEBULA							
N6302	17 13.7	−37 06	Sco	gn	9.6	$83'' \times 24''$	(2)
STAR CLOUD							
M24	18 16.4	−18 40	Sgr	✶cld	∼2	$2° \times 0.9°$	(6)

DOUBLE STARS

Name	R.A h m	Dec. ° '	Con	V	Sep (Date)	Notes
η Lup	16 00.1	−38 24	Lup	3.4,7.8	15.''0 (1957)	
ADS 9909 = ξ Sco	16 04.4	−11 22	Sco	4.2,7.3	7.''6 (1975)	(14)
ADS 9913 = β Sco	16 05.4	−19 48	Sco	2.6,4.9	13.''6 (1976)	(15)
ADS 9933 = κ Her	16 08.1	+17 03	Her	5.0,6.3	28.''1 (1966)	
ADS 9951 = ν^{1,2} Sco	16 12.0	−19 28	Sco	4.0,6.3	41.''2 (1968)	(17)
ADS 9979 = σ CrB	16 14.7	+33 52	CrB	5.6,6.6	7.''1 (2000)	(16)
BrsO 12	16 19.5	−30 54	Sco	5.5,7.1	23.''2 (1977)	
ADS10035	16 24.7	−29 42	Sco	5.8,6.6	5.''2 (1966)	
ADS10049 = ρ Oph	16 25.6	−23 27	Oph	5.3,6.0	3.''1 (1975)	
ε Nor	16 27.2	−47 33	Nor	4.5,7.2	22.''8 (1957)	
M1bO 8	16 41.3	−48 46	Ara	5.6,6.8	9.''6 (1956)	
ADS10418 = α Her	17 14.6	+14 23	Her	3.5,5.4	4.''6 (2000)	(13)
ADS10417 = 36 Oph	17 15.3	−26 36	Oph	5.1,5.1	4.''9 (2000)	
ADS10442 = ο Oph	17 18.0	−24 17	Oph	5.2,6.8	10.''2 (1962)	
ADS10526 = ρ Her	17 23.7	+37 09	Her	4.6,5.6	4.''1 (1979)	
h 4949	17 26.9	−45 51	Ara	5.7,6.5	2.''1 (1975)	
ADS10750 = 61 Oph	17 44.6	+ 2 35	Oph	6.2,6.6	20.''6 (1968)	
h 5003	17 59.1	−30 15	Sgr	5.2,7.0	5.''5 (1973)	

ECLIPSING VARIABLE STARS

Name	R.A h m	Dec. ° '	Type	Mag.	Epoch (2400000+)	Period (days)
V1010 Oph	16 49.5	−15 40	EB	6.1–7.0v	38937.771	0.661
V861 Sco	16 56.6	−40 49	EB	6.07–6.69V		7.848
U Oph	17 16.5	+ 1 13	EA	5.88–6.58V	36727.424	1.677
u Her	17 17.3	+33 06	EB	4.6–5.3p	44069.386	2.051
RS Sgr	18 17.6	−34 06	EA	6.0–6.9p	20586.387	2.415
β Lyr	18 50.1	+33 22	EB	3.34–4.34V	45342.39	12.935
RS Vul	19 17.7	+22 26	EA	6.9–7.6p	32808.257	4.477
U Sge	19 18.8	+19 37	EA	6.58–9.18V	40774.463	3.380

PULSATING VARIABLE STARS

Name	R.A h m	Dec. ° '	Type	Mag.	Epoch	Period
BM Sco	17 41.0	−32 13	SRd	6.8–8.7p		850:
X Sgr	17 47.6	−27 50	δ Cep	4.24–4.84V	36968.852	7.012
OP Her	17 56.8	+45 21	Lb	7.7–8.3p		
W Sgr	18 05.0	−29 35	δ Cep	4.30–5.08V	37678.578	7.594
VX Sgr	18 08.1	−22 13	SRc	6.5–12.5v	36493	732
Y Sgr	18 21.4	−18 52	δ Cep	5.40–6.10V	36230.180	5.773
T Lyr	18 32.3	+37 00	Lb	7.8–9.6v		
X Oph	18 38.3	+ 8 50	M	5.9–9.2v	41478	334.39
XY Lyr	18 38.1	+39 40	Lc	7.3–7.8p		
R Lyr	18 55.3	+43 57	SRb	3.88–5.0V	35920	46.0
FF Aql	18 58.2	+17 22	δ Cep	5.18–5.68V	41576.428	4.470
R Aql	19 06.4	+ 8 14	M	5.5–12.0v	43458	284.2
RR Lyr	19 25.5	+42 47	RRab	7.06–8.12V	42995.405	0.566

ERUPTIVE VARIABLE STAR

Name	R.A h m	Dec. ° '	Type	Mag.	Epoch	Period
RS Oph	17 50.2	− 6 43	Nr	5.3–12.3p	39791	

OTHER VARIABLE STARS

Name	R.A h m	Dec. ° '	Type	Mag.	Epoch	Period
RS Tel	18 18.9	−46 33	RCB	9.3–13.0p		
AC Her	18 30.3	+21 52	RVa	7.43–9.74R	35052	75.461
R Sct	18 47.5	− 5 42	RVa	4.45–8.20V	32078.3	140.05
RY Sgr	19 16.5	−33 31	RCB	6.0–15.0v		

NOTES

1. Includes gn I 4628
2. Bug Nebula, a planetary nebula?
3. Includes BM Sco
4. Trifid Nebula (30' diam)
5. Lagoon Nebula (90' diam)
6. A Milky Way starcloud
7. Includes I 4703 (35' diam)
8. Swan Nebula (40' diam)
9. Ring Nebula
10. Dumbbell Nebula
11. Includes 27 Cyg
12. Includes 20 Vul
13. Brighter star is a variable
14. Brighter star is close pair ADS 9910 lies 5' south
15. Brighter star is very close pair
16. Same as TZ CrB, brighter star slightly variable
17. Each component is a close double like $\epsilon^{1,2}$ Lyrae

REMARKS

Due to space limitations the double stars for this chart completed in list for Chart 8.

Magnitudes							Double stars	Variable stars	Nova	Open clusters	Globular clusters	Diffuse nebulae	Planetary nebulae	Galaxies
-1	0	1	2	3	4	5 6			∘ N1975					

Constellation boundaries

Ecliptic — — — 170° — — — Galactic equator — — — 90°

20ᵐ **20ʰ** 40ᵐ 20ᵐ **19ʰ** 40ᵐ 20ᵐ **18ʰ** 40ᵐ 20ᵐ **17ʰ** 40ᵐ 20ᵐ **16ʰ** 40ᵐ

+50° +45° +40° +35° +30° +25° +20° +15° +10° +5° 0° −5° −10° −15° −20° −25° −30° −35° −40° −45° −50°

DRACO

BOÖTES

CYGNUS

α Deneb

HERCULES

M92

M13

CORONA BOREALIS

LYRA

α Vega

M57

Vega

VULPECULA

SAGITTA

M27

DELPHINUS

SERPENS CAPUT

Altair

AQUILA

SCUTUM

M11

SERPENS CAUDA

OPHIUCHUS

LIBRA

M12

M10

M14

M107

M9

M23

CAPRICORNUS

M75

M16

M17

M18

M24

M25

M28

M22

M20

M8

M54

SAGITTARIUS

M70

M69

M55

MIC

Antares

M4

M19

M80

M62

SCORPIUS

M6

M7

M5

CORONA AUSTRALIS

LUPUS

NORMA

IND

TELESCOPIUM

ARA

20ᵐ **20ʰ** 40ᵐ 20ᵐ **19ʰ** 40ᵐ 20ᵐ **18ʰ** 40ᵐ 20ᵐ **17ʰ** 40ᵐ 20ᵐ **16ʰ** 40ᵐ

DEEP-SKY OBJECTS

GALAXIES

Name	R.A h m	Dec. ° '	Con	Type	V	Dimensions	Notes
N 55	0 14.9	−39 11	Scl	SBm	7.4:	32′ × 6.′5	
N6822	19 44.9	−14 48	Sgr	IBm	8.6:	10′ × 9.′5	
N7331	22 37.1	+34 25	Peg	SAbc	9.6	11′ × 4.′0	
I 1459	22 57.2	−36 28	Gru	E3	10.0	4.′5 × 3.′4	
N7793	23 57.8	−32 35	Scl	SAd	9.1	9.′1 × 6.′6	

OPEN CLUSTERS

Name	R.A h m	Dec. ° '	Con	Type	V	Dimensions	Notes
Stock 1	19 35.8	+25 13	Vul	oc	5.3:	80′	
N6811	19 38.2	+46 34	Cyg	oc	6.8	13′	
N6871	20 05.9	+35 47	Cyg	oc	5.2	20′	(2)
N6882/5	20 12.0	+26 29	Vul	oc	5.9	22′	(3)
N6910	20 23.1	+40 47	Cyg	oc	6.6	8′	
N6913	20 23.9	+38 32	Cyg	oc	6.6	7′	M29
N6940	20 34.6	+28 18	Vul	oc	6.3	25′	
N6994	20 59.0	−12 38	Aqr	oc	~9	2.′8	M73, (5)
N7092	21 32.2	+48 26	Cyg	oc	4.6	32′	M39
N7243	22 15.3	+49 53	Lac	oc	6.4	21′	

GLOBULAR CLUSTERS

Name	R.A h m	Dec. ° '	Con	Type	V	Dimensions	Notes
N6809	19 40.0	−30 58	Sgr	gc	6.4	19′	M55
N6838	19 53.8	+18 47	Sge	gc	8.0	7.′2	M71
N6864	20 06.1	−21 55	Sgr	gc	8.5	6.′0	M75
N6981	20 53.5	−12 32	Aqr	gc	9.3	6′	M72
N7078	21 30.0	+12 10	Peg	gc	6.0	12′	M15
N7089	21 33.5	− 0 49	Aqr	gc	6.5	13′	M2
N7099	21 40.4	−23 11	Cap	gc	7.3	11′	M30

PLANETARY NEBULAE

Name	R.A h m	Dec. ° '	Con	Type	V	Dimensions	Notes
N6818	19 44.0	−14 09	Sgr	pn	9.3	22″ × 15″	
N6853	19 59.6	+22 43	Vul	pn	7.3	8.′0 × 5.′7	M27, (1)
N7009	21 04.2	−11 22	Aqr	pn	8.0	44″ × 23″	(7)
N7027	21 07.1	+42 14	Cyg	pn	8.5	18″ × 10″	
N7293	22 29.6	−20 48	Aqr	pn	7.3:	12′ × 10′	(8)
N7662	23 25.9	+42 33	And	pn	8.3	32″ × 28″	

DIFFUSE NEBULAE

Name	R.A h m	Dec. ° '	Con	Type	V	Dimensions	Notes
N6960	20 50	+31	Cyg	gn	~7	3.5° × 2.7°	(4)
N7000	20 58.8	+44 20	Cyg	gn	~4	120′ × 100′	(6)

DOUBLE STARS

Name	R.A h m	Dec. ° '	Con	V	Sep (Date)	Notes
ADS 191 = 35 Psc	0 15.0	+ 8 49	Psc	6.0,7.8	11.″5 (1972)	(16)
ADS11061 = 41/40 Dra	18 00.2	+80 00	Dra	5.7,6.0	19.″1 (1975)	
ADS10993 = 95 Her	18 01.5	+21 36	Her	5.0,5.2	6.″3 (1974)	
ADS11046 = 70 Oph	18 05.5	+ 2 30	Oph	4.0,6.0	3.″8 (2000)	
ADS11089 = 100 Her	18 07.8	+26 06	Her	5.9,5.9	14.″2 (1970)	
$\kappa^{1,2}$ CrA	18 33.4	−38 44	CrA	5.6,6.3	21.″4 (1936)	
ADS11635 = ϵ^1 Lyr	18 44.3	+39 40	Lyr	5.0,6.1	2.″6 (2000)	(9)
ADS11635 = ϵ^2 Lyr	18 44.4	+39 37	Lyr	5.2,5.5	2.″3 (2000)	
ADS11639 = $\zeta^{1,2}$ Lyr	18 44.8	+37 36	Lyr	4.3,5.7	43.″7 (1982)	(10)
ADS11640	18 45.5	+ 5 30	Ser	6.2,7.2	2.″5 (1979)	(11)
ADS11667 = 5 Aql	18 46.5	− 0 58	Aql	5.9,7.5	12.″8 (1965)	
ADS11853 = θ Ser	18 56.2	+ 4 12	Ser	4.6,5.0	22.″3 (1973)	
BrsO 14	19 01.1	−37 04	CrA	6.4,6.7	12.″8 (1967)	
ADS12169	19 12.1	+49 51	Cyg	6.6,6.8	7.″9 (1976)	
ADS12540 = β Cyg	19 30.7	+27 58	Cyg	3.1,5.1	34.″4 (1982)	(12)
ADS12880 = δ Cyg	19 45.0	+45 08	Cyg	2.9,6.3	2.″5 (2000)	
ADS12893	19 45.7	+36 05	Cyg	6.4,7.2	14.″9 (1967)	
ADS13554 = o^1 31 Cyg	20 13.6	+46 44	Cyg	3.8,6.7	1.″8 (1926)	(17)
ADS13087 = 57 Aql	19 54.6	− 8 14	Aql	5.7,6.5	36.″0 (1968)	
ADS13645 = $\alpha^{1,2}$ Cap	20 18.1	−12 33	Cap	3.6,4.2	6.′3 (1924)	
$\beta^{1,2}$ Cap	20 21.0	−14 47	Cap	3.1,6.1	3.′4 (1922)	(10)
ADS13902 = o Cap	20 29.9	−18 35	Cap	5.9,6.7	18.″9 (1968)	
ADS14158 = 49 Cyg	20 41.0	+32 18	Cyg	5.7,7.8	2.″5 (1973)	
ADS14279 = γ Del	20 46.7	+16 07	Del	4.3,5.1	9.″6 (1976)	
ADS14592 = 12 Aqr	21 04.1	− 5 49	Aqr	5.9,7.3	2.″5 (1973)	
ADS14636 = 61 Cyg	21 06.9	+38 45	Cyg	5.2,6.0	30.″3 (2000)	
ADS14682	21 08.6	+30 12	Cyg	5.8,7.8	3.″4 (1980)	(13)
ADS15753 = 41 Aqr	22 14.3	−21 04	Aqr	5.6,7.1	5.″1 (1975)	
ADS15934 = 53 Aqr	22 26.6	−16 45	Aqr	6.4,6.6	2.″9 (1982)	(14)
ADS15971 = ζ Aqr	22 28.8	− 0 01	Aqr	4.3,4.5	2.″0 (2000)	(15)
ADS16095 = 8 Lac	22 35.9	+39 38	Lac	5.7,6.4	22.″4 (1969)	
ADS16519	23 07.5	+32 50	Peg	6.3,7.5	8.″4 (1969)	
ADS16672 = 94 Aqr	23 19.1	−13 28	Aqr	5.2,7.6	12.″6 (1981)	
θ Phe	23 39.5	−46 38	Phe	6.5,7.3	3.″9 (1975)	
ADS16979 = 107 Aqr	23 46.0	−18 41	Aqr	5.7,6.7	6.″6 (1975)	

NOTES

1. Dumbbell Nebula
2. Includes 27 Cyg
3. Includes 20 Vul
4. Veil Nebula, supernova remnant
5. Only four stars
6. North America Nebula
7. Saturn Nebula
8. Helix Nebula
9. "Double-Double"
10. Binocular pair
11. Each component an extremely close pair
12. Albireo, binocular pair
13. Same as V389 Cyg, brighter star slightly variable
14. Optical, closing at ~ 0.″45 per decade
15. Heintz 1984 orbit
16. Same as UU Psc, brighter star slightly variable
17. Same as V695 Cyg, brighter star slightly variable
   fourth star: V=4.8; 5.′6 (1926)
   third star : V=7.0; 1.′8 (1926);

ECLIPSING VARIABLE STARS

Name	R.A h m	Dec. ° '	Type	Mag.	Epoch (2400000+)	Period (days)
V505 Sgr	19 53.1	−14 36	EA	6.48−7.51V	40087.336	1.182
EE Peg	21 40.0	+ 9 11	EA	6.9−7.6v	40286.432	2.628
AR Lac	22 08.7	+45 45	E	6.11−6.77V	39376.495	1.983

PULSATING VARIABLE STARS

Name	R.A h m	Dec. ° '	Type	Mag.	Epoch (2400000+)	Period (days)
χ Cyg	19 50.6	+32 55	M	3.3−14.2v	42143	406.93
η Aql	19 52.5	+ 1 00	δ Cep	3.48−4.39V	36084.656	7.176
V449 Cyg	19 53.3	+33 57	Lb	7.4−9.0p		
RR Sgr	19 55.9	−29 11	M	5.6−14.0v	41133	334.58
S Sge	19 56.0	+16 38	δ Cep	5.28−6.04V	36082.168	8.382
EU Del	20 37.9	+18 16	SRb	5.8−6.9v	35794	59.5
X Cyg	20 43.4	+35 35	δ Cep	5.87−6.86V	35915.918	16.386
T Vul	20 51.5	+28 15	δ Cep	5.44−6.06V	35934.758	4.435
W Cyg	21 36.0	+45 22	SRb	6.8−8.9p	38659.73	126.26
V460 Cyg	21 42.0	+35 31	Lb	5.6−7.0v		
R Aqr	23 43.8	−15 17	M	5.8−12.4v	42398	386.96
TX Psc	23 46.4	+ 3 29	Lb	6.9−7.7p		

ERUPTIVE VARIABLE STARS

Name	R.A h m	Dec. ° '	Type	Mag.	Epoch (2400000+)	Period (days)
WW Cet	0 11.4	−11 29	Z Cam	9.3−16.8p		31.2:
WZ Sge	20 07.6	+17 42	Nr(E)	7.0−15.5p	32001	900:
P Cyg	20 17.8	+38 02	S Dor	3.0−6.0v		
V Sge	20 20.3	+21 06	NL	9.5−13.9v		
VY Aqr	21 12.2	− 8 50	UG	8.0−16.6p	45667	
SS Cyg	21 42.7	+43 35	UG	8.2−12.4v		50.1:
RU Peg	22 14.0	+12 42	UG	9.0−13.1v		67.8

OTHER VARIABLE STARS

Name	R.A h m	Dec. ° '	Type	Mag.	Epoch (2400000+)	Period (days)
AG Peg	21 51.0	+12 38	Z And	6.0−9.4v		830.14
Z And	23 33.7	+48 49	Z And	8.0−12.4p		
SX Phe	23 46.5	−41 35	δ Sct	6.78−7.51V	38636.617	0.054

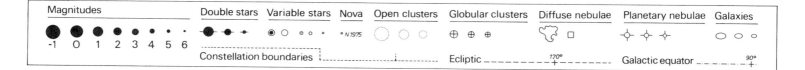

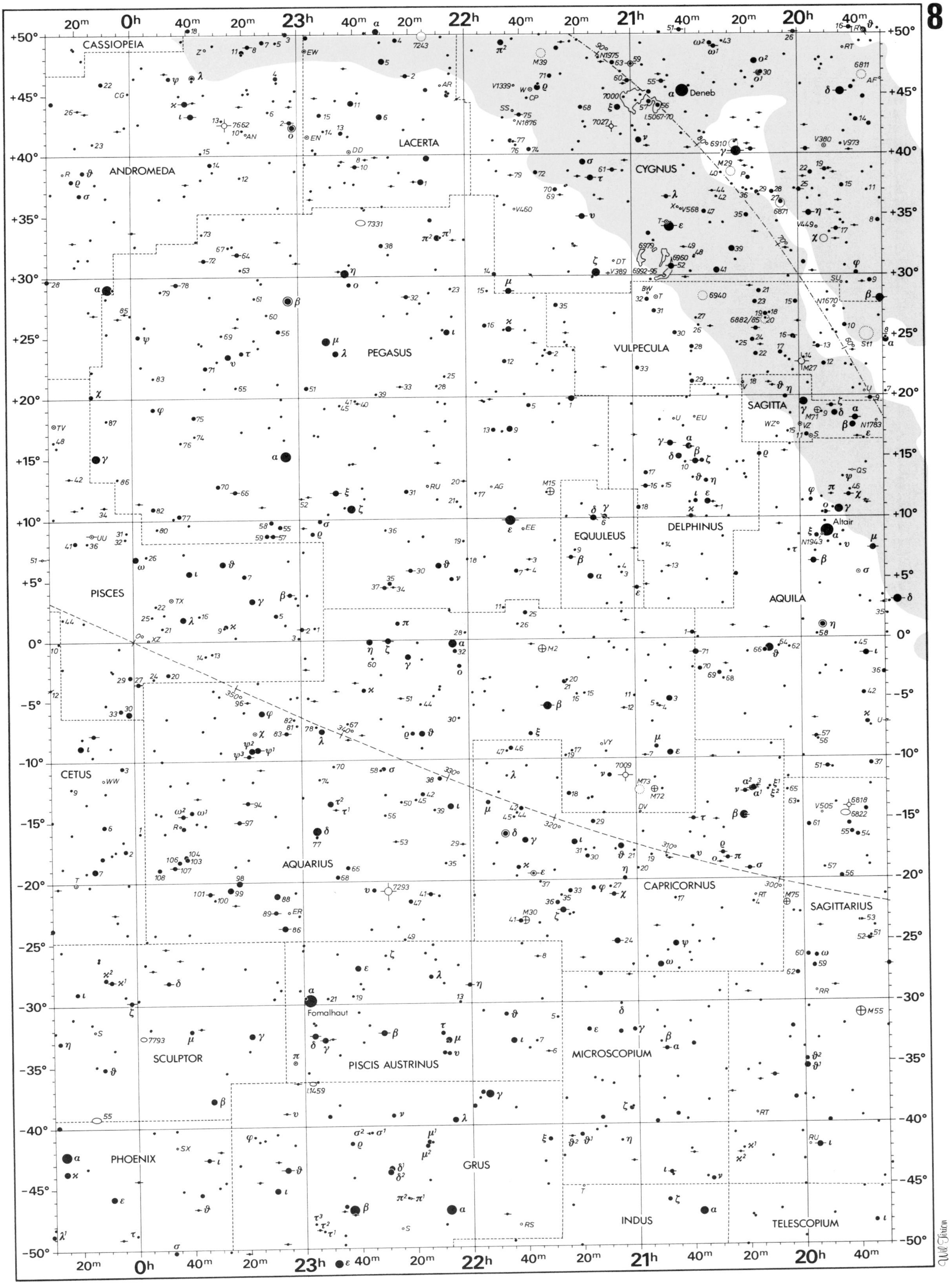
CASSIOPEIA
ANDROMEDA
LACERTA
CYGNUS
PEGASUS
VULPECULA
SAGITTA
PISCES
EQUULEUS
DELPHINUS
AQUILA
CETUS
AQUARIUS
CAPRICORNUS
SAGITTARIUS
SCULPTOR
PISCIS AUSTRINUS
MICROSCOPIUM
PHOENIX
GRUS
INDUS
TELESCOPIUM
Deneb
Altair
Fomalhaut
0h
23h
22h
21h
20h
+50°
+45°
+40°
+35°
+30°
+25°
+20°
+15°
+10°
+5°
0°
-5°
-10°
-15°
-20°
-25°
-30°
-35°
-40°
-45°
-50°
M39
M29
M27
M71
M15
M2
M73
M72
M30
M75
M55
Wil Tirion

DEEP-SKY OBJECTS

Name	R.A h m	Dec. ° ′	Con	Type	V	Dimensions	Notes
				GALAXIES			
N 292	0 52.7	−72 30	Tuc	SBm	2.3	4.7° × 2.6°	(2)
N1097	2 46.3	−30 17	For	SBb	9.2	9′.3 × 6′.6	
N1291	3 17.3	−41 08	Eri	SB0/a	8.5	10′ × 9′.1	
N1313	3 18.3	−66 30	Ret	SBbc	9.3	8′.5 × 6′.6	
N1316	3 22.7	−37 12	For	SA0	8.9	7′.1 × 5′.5	
N1365	3 33.6	−36 08	For	SBb	9.6	9′.8 × 5′.5	
N1399	3 38.5	−35 27	For	E1	9.9	3′.2 × 3′.1	(3)
N1433	3 42.0	−47 13	Hor	SBa	10.0	6′.8 × 6′.0	
N1566	4 20.0	−54 56	Dor	SAbc	9.4	7′.6 × 6′.2	
N1672	4 45.7	−59 15	Dor	SBb	9.9:	4′.8 × 3′.9	
LMC	5 23.6	−69 45	Dor	SBm	0.1	10.8° × 9.2°	(4)
N2997	9 45.6	−31 11	Ant	SAc	9.5	8′.1 × 6′.5	
N4945	13 05.4	−49 28	Cen	SBcd:	8.3:	20′ × 4′.4	
N5128	13 25.5	−43 01	Cen	S0 pec	6.9	18′ × 14′	(14)
				OPEN CLUSTERS			
N2070	5 38.7	−69 06	Dor	oc-gn	~3	40′ × 25′	(5)
N2451	7 45.4	−37 58	Pup	oc	2.8	50′	(6)
N2477	7 52.3	−38 33	Pup	oc	5.8	43′	
N2516	7 58.3	−60 52	Car	oc	3.8	30′	
N2547	8 10.7	−49 16	Vel	oc	4.7	74′	
N2546	8 12.4	−37 38	Pup	oc	6.3	70′	
I 2391	8 40.2	−53 04	Vel	oc	2.5	50′	(7)
I 2395	8 41.1	−48 12	Vel	oc	4.6	20′	
N3114	10 02.7	−60 07	Car	oc	4.2	35′	
I 2581	10 27.4	−57 38	Car	oc	4.3	8′	
N3293	10 35.8	−58 14	Car	oc	4.7	6′	
I 2602	10 43.2	−64 24	Car	oc	1.9	50′	(9)
N3372	10 43.8	−59 52	Car	oc-gn	~3	~ 2°	(10)
N3532	11 06.4	−58 40	Car	oc	3.0	55′	
N3766	11 36.3	−61 37	Cen	oc	5.3	12′	
N4609	12 42.3	−62 58	Cru	oc	5	5′	(12)
N4755	12 53.6	−60 20	Cru	oc	4.2	10′	(13)
N5281	13 46.6	−62 54	Cen	oc	5.9	5′	
N5316	13 53.9	−61 52	Cen	oc	6.0	14′	
N5617	14 29.8	−60 43	Cen	oc	6.3	10′	
				GLOBULAR CLUSTERS			
N 104	0 24.1	−72 05	Tuc	gc	3.8	31′	(1)
N 362	1 03.2	−70 51	Tuc	gc	6.6	13′	
N1851	5 14.1	−40 03	Col	gc	7.2	11′	
N2808	9 12.0	−64 52	Car	gc	6.3	14′	
N3201	10 17.6	−46 25	Vel	gc	6.7	18′	
N5139	13 26.8	−47 29	Cen	gc	3.7	36′	(20)
				PLANETARY NEBULAE			
N2867	9 21.4	−58 19	Car	pn	9.7	11″	
N3132	10 07.7	−40 26	Vel	pn	9.4	84″ × 53″	(8)
N3918	11 50.3	−57 11	Cen	pn	8.1	12″	
N5189	13 33.5	−65 59	Mus	pn	9.9	3′.1 × 1′.2	
N5315	13 53.9	−66 31	Cir	pn	9.8	5″ × 5″	
				DIFFUSE NEBULA			
I 2944	11 38.3	−63 22	Cen	gn	~7	75′ × 50′	(11)

DOUBLE STARS

Name	R.A h m	Dec. ° ′	Con	V	Sep (Date)	Notes
β[1,2] Tuc	0 31.5	−62 58	Tuc	4.4,4.5	27″.0 (1975)	
κ Tuc	1 15.8	−68 53	Tuc	5.0,7.6	5″.2 (1982)	
p Eri	1 39.8	−56 12	Eri	5.8,5.9	11″.5 (2000)	
θ Eri	2 58.3	−40 18	Eri	3.2,4.4	8″.3 (1975)	
ADS 2402 = α For	3 12.1	−28 59	For	3.9,7.1	5″.1 (2000)	
ι Pic	4 50.9	−53 28	Pic	5.6,6.4	12″.5 (1975)	
θ Pic	5 24.8	−52 19	Pic	6.3,6.8	38″.2 (1938)	(16)
ADS 5654 = ε CMa	6 58.6	−28 58	CMa	1.5,7.4	7″.5 (1951)	
Δ 38	7 04.0	−43 36	Pup	5.5,6.8	21″.1 (1977)	
γ Vol	7 08.8	−70 30	Vol	3.8,5.7	13″.6 (1977)	
Δ 59	7 59.2	−49 59	Pup	6.4,6.4	16″.4 (1957)	
ε Vol	8 07.9	−68 37	Vol	4.4,7.4	6″.1 (1968)	
γ Vel	8 09.5	−47 20	Vel	1.8,4.3	41″.2 (1951)	(17)
Rmk 8	8 15.3	−62 55	Car	5.3,7.8	3″.9 (1960)	
κ Vol	8 19.8	−71 31	Vol	5.4,5.7	65″.0 (1917)	(16)
h 4093	8 26.3	−39 04	Pup	6.5,7.3	8″.1 (1975)	(21)
h 4104	8 29.1	−47 56	Vel	5.5,7.3	3″.6 (1979)	(22)
Δ 70	8 29.5	−44 44	Vel	5.2,7.1	4″.5 (1954)	
δ Vel	8 44.7	−54 43	Vel	2.1,5.1	2″.2 (1953)	
h 4188	9 12.5	−43 37	Vel	6.0,6.8	2″.8 (1977)	(18)
ζ Ant	9 30.8	−31 53	Ant	6.2,7.0	8″.0 (1977)	
υ Car	9 47.1	−65 04	Car	3.0,6.3	5″.0 (1975)	
h 4432	11 23.4	−64 57	Mus	5.4,6.6	2″.4 (1976)	
Rmk 14	12 14.0	−45 43	Cen	5.6,6.8	2″.8 (1963)	
α Cru	12 26.6	−63 06	Cru	1.3,1.7	4″.2 (1979)	(19)
μ Cru	12 54.6	−57 11	Cru	4.0,5.2	34″.9 (1967)	
θ Mus	13 08.1	−65 18	Mus	5.7,7.7	5″.3 (1958)	
Δ 141	13 41.7	−54 34	Cen	5.3,6.6	5″.4 (1963)	
Rmk 18	13 52.0	−52 49	Cen	5.3,7.5	18″.1 (1959)	
α[1,2] Cen	14 39.6	−60 50	Cen	0.0,1.2	14″.1 (2000)	
Δ 249	23 23.9	−53 49	Gru	6.2,7.1	26″.5 (1951)	
θ Phe	23 39.5	−46 38	Phe	6.5,7.3	3″.9 (1975)	

ECLIPSING VARIABLE STARS

Name	R.A h m	Dec. ° ′	Type	Mag.	Epoch (2400000+)	Period (days)
ζ Phe	1 08.4	−55 15	EA	3.92–4.42V	41643.689	1.669
V Pup	7 58.2	−49 15	EB	4.7–5.2p	28648.304	1.454
TY Pyx	8 59.7	−27 49	E	6.87–7.47V	43187.230	3.198
CV Vel	9 00.6	−51 33	EA	6.5–7.3p	42048.668	6.889
S Ant	9 32.3	−28 38	EW	6.4–6.92V	35139.929	0.648

PULSATING VARIABLE STARS

Name	R.A h m	Dec. ° ′	Type	Mag.	Epoch (2400000+)	Period (days)
R Hor	2 53.9	−49 53	M	4.7–14.3v	41490	403.97
R Dor	4 36.8	−62 05	SRb	4.8–6.6v		338:
R Cae	4 40.5	−38 14	M	6.7–13.7v	40645	390.95
R Pic	4 46.2	−49 15	SRa	6.7–10.0v	38091	164.2
β Dor	5 33.6	−62 29	δ Cep	3.46–4.08V	35206.44	9.842
L² Pup	7 13.5	−44 39	SRb	2.6–6.2v	40813	140.42
R Car	9 32.2	−62 47	M	3.9–10.5v	42000	308.71
S Car	10 09.4	−61 33	M	4.5–9.9v	42112	149.49
U Car	10 57.8	−59 44	δ Cep	5.72–7.02V	37320.055	38.768
S Mus	12 12.8	−70 09	δ Cep	5.90–6.44V	35837.992	9.660
BO Mus	12 34.9	−67 45	Lb	6.0–6.7v		
R Mus	12 42.1	−69 24	δ Cep	5.93–6.73V	40896.13	7.476
V412 Cen	13 57.5	−57 43	Lb	7.1–9.6B		
θ Aps	14 05.3	−76 48	SRb	6.4–8.6p		119
R Cen	14 16.6	−59 55	M	5.3–11.8v	41942	546.2
π¹ Gru	22 22.7	−45 57	SRb	5.41–6.70V		150:

ERUPTIVE VARIABLE STAR

Name	R.A h m	Dec. ° ′	Type	Mag.	Epoch (2400000+)	Period (days)
VW Hyi	4 09.1	−71 18	UG	8.4–14.4v		27.8:

OTHER VARIABLE STARS

Name	R.A h m	Dec. ° ′	Type	Mag.	Epoch (2400000+)	Period (days)
AR Pup	8 03.0	−36 36	RVb	8.7–10.9p		75
AI Vel	8 14.1	−44 34	δ Sct	6.4–7.1v		0.111
WY Vel	9 22.0	−52 34	Z And	8.8–10.2p		
IW Car	9 26.9	−63 38	RVb	7.9–9.6p	29401	67.5
RU Cen	12 09.4	−45 25	RV	8.7–10.7p	28015.51	64.727
UW Cen	12 43.3	−54 32	RCB	9.1–14.5v		

NOTES

1. Same as 47 Tucanae
2. Small Magellanic Cloud
3. Brightest in Fornax galaxy cluster
4. Large Magellanic Cloud
5. Same as 30 Dor, Tarantula Nebula (in LMC)
6. Includes c Pup
7. Includes o Vel
8. Bright central star
9. Includes θ Car
10. η Carinae Nebula complex includes several bright open clusters
11. λ Centauri Nebula
12. In Coalsack
13. Same as Jewelbox. Includes κ Cru
14. Centaurus A
15. ω Centauri
16. Binocular pair
17. Brighter star is brightest Wolf-Rayet start
18. Brighter star is very close pair
19. Third star: V=4.9; 1′.5 (1973)
20. ω Centauri
21. Same as NO Pup, brighter star slightly variable
22. Brighter star is very close pair; third fainter star in group

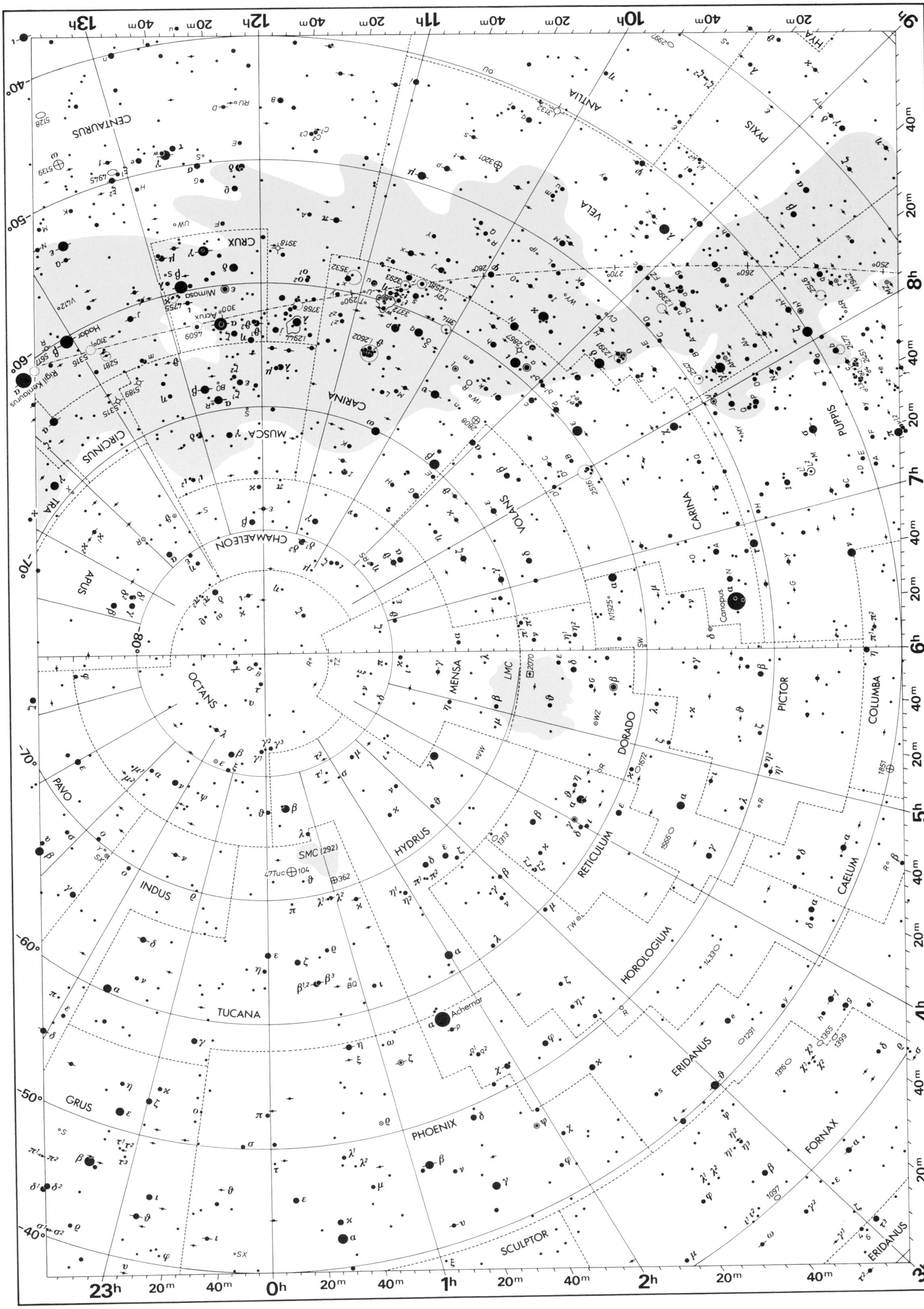

9
CENTAURUS
CRUX
Mimosa
Acrux
Hadar
Rigil Kentaurus
ANTLIA
PYXIS
VELA
PUPPIS
CARINA
Canopus
CIRCINUS
MUSCA
CHAMAELEON
VOLANS
APUS
OCTANS
MENSA
LMC
DORADO
PICTOR
COLUMBA
PAVO
HYDRUS
RETICULUM
CAELUM
SMC (292)
47Tuc
INDUS
HOROLOGIUM
TUCANA
Achernar
ERIDANUS
GRUS
PHOENIX
FORNAX
SCULPTOR
ERIDANUS
HYA
23h
0h
1h
2h
3h
4h
5h
6h
7h
8h
9h
10h
11h
12h
13h
-40°
-50°
-60°
-70°
-80°
Wil Tirion

DEEP-SKY OBJECTS

Name	R.A h m	Dec. ° '	Con	Type	V	Dimensions	Notes
GALAXIES							
N 292	0 52.7	−72 30	Tuc	SBm	2.3	4.7° × 2.6°	(2)
N4945	13 05.4	−49 28	Cen	SBcd:	8.3:	20′ × 4′.4	
N5128	13 25.5	−43 01	Cen	S0 pec	6.9	18′ × 14′	(8)
N5643	14 32.7	−44 10	Lup	SAc	9.8:	4′.6 × 4′.1	
N6744	19 09.8	−63 51	Pav	SBbc	8.5:	15′ × 10′	
OPEN CLUSTERS							
N3114	10 02.7	−60 07	Car	oc	4.2	35′	
I 2581	10 27.4	−57 38	Car	oc	4.3	8′	
N3293	10 35.8	−58 14	Car	oc	4.7	6′	
I 2602	10 43.2	−64 24	Car	oc	1.9	50′	(3)
N3372	10 43.8	−59 52	Car	oc-gn	∼3	∼ 2°	(4)
N3532	11 06.4	−58 40	Car	oc	3.0	55′	
N3766	11 36.3	−61 37	Cen	oc	5.3	12′	
N4609	12 42.3	−62 58	Cru	oc	6.9	5′	(6)
N4755	12 53.6	−60 20	Cru	oc	4.2	10′	(7)
N5281	13 46.6	−62 54	Cen	oc	5.9	5′	
N5316	13 53.9	−61 52	Cen	oc	6.0	14′	
N5460	14 07.6	−48 19	Cen	oc	5.6	25′	
N5617	14 29.8	−60 43	Cen	oc	6.3	10′	
N5662	14 35.2	−56 33	Cen	oc	5.5	12′	
N5822	15 05.2	−54 21	Lup	oc	6.5:	40′	
N6025	16 03.7	−60 30	TrA	oc	5.1	12′	
N6067	16 13.2	−54 13	Nor	oc	5.6	13′	
N6087	16 18.9	−57 54	Nor	oc	5.4	12′	
N6124	16 25.6	−40 40	Sco	oc	5.8:	40′	
N6193	16 41.3	−48 46	Ara	oc	5.2	16′	
N6231	16 54.0	−41 48	Sco	oc	2.6	26′	
N6242	16 55.6	−39 30	Sco	oc	6.4	9′	
Trumpler 24	16 57.0	−40 40	Sco	oc-gn	∼5	60′	(10)
I4651	17 24.7	−49 57	Ara	oc	6.9	12′	
GLOBULAR CLUSTERS							
N 104	0 24.1	−72 05	Tuc	gc	3.8	31′	(1)
N 362	1 03.2	−70 51	Tuc	gc	6.6	13′	
N2808	9 12.0	−64 52	Car	gc	6.3	14′	
N5139	13 26.8	−47 29	Cen	gc	3.7	36′	(9)
N6388	17 36.3	−44 44	Sco	gc	6.7	8′.7	
N6397	17 40.7	−53 40	Ara	gc	5.7	26′	
N6541	18 08.0	−43 42	Cra	gc	6.6	13′	
N6752	19 10.9	−59 59	Pav	gc	5.4	20′	
PLANETARY NEBULAE							
N3918	11 50.3	−57 11	Cen	pn	8.1	12″	
N5189	13 33.5	−65 59	Mus	pn	9.9	3′.1 × 1′.2	
N5315	13 53.9	−66 31	Cir	pn	9.8	5″ × 5″	
N5882	15 16.8	−45 39	Lup	pn	9.4	7″ × 7″	
DIFFUSE NEBULA							
I 2944	11 38.3	−63 22	Cen	gn	∼7	75′ × 50′	(5)

NOTES

1. Same as 47 Tucanae
2. Small Magellanic Cloud
3. Includes θ Car
4. η Carinae Nebula complex includes several bright open clusters
5. λ Centauri Nebula
6. In Coalsack
7. Same as Jewelbox; includes κ Cru
8. Centaurus A
9. ω Centauri
10. Includes diffuse nebulae I 4628
11. Binocular pair
12. Third star: V=4.9; 1′.5 (1973)
13. Third star: V=7.2; 24″.0 (1963)

DOUBLE STARS

Name	R.A h m	Dec. ° '	Con	V	Sep (Date)	Notes
β[1,2] Tuc	0 31.5	−62 58	Tuc	4.4,4.5	27″.0 (1975)	
κ Tuc	1 15.8	−68 53	Tuc	5.0,7.6	5″.2 (1982)	
p Eri	1 39.8	−56 12	Eri	5.8,5.9	11″.5 (2000)	
γ Vol	7 08.8	−70 30	Vol	3.8,5.7	13″.6 (1977)	
ε Vol	8 07.9	−68 37	Vol	4.4,7.4	6″.1 (1968)	
κ Vol	8 19.8	−71 31	Vol	5.4,5.7	65″.0 (1917)	(11)
υ Car	9 47.1	−65 04	Car	3.0,6.3	5″.0 (1975)	
h 4432	11 23.4	−64 57	Mus	5.4,6.6	2″.4 (1976)	
Rmk 14	12 14.0	−45 43	Cen	5.6,6.8	2″.8 (1963)	
α Cru	12 26.6	−63 06	Cru	1.3,1.7	4″.2 (1979)	(12)
μ Cru	12 54.6	−57 11	Cru	4.0,5.2	34″.9 (1967)	
θ Mus	13 08.1	−65 18	Mus	5.7,7.7	5″.3 (1958)	
Δ 141	13 41.7	−54 34	Cen	5.3,6.6	5″.4 (1963)	
k = 3 Cen	13 51.8	−33 00	Cen	4.6,6.1	7″.9 (1975)	
Rmk 18	13 52.0	−52 49	Cen	5.3,7.5	18″.1 (1959)	
Δ 159	14 22.6	−58 28	Cen	4.9,7.1	9″.2 (1958)	
α[1,2] Cen	14 39.6	−60 50	Cen	0.0,1.2	14″.1 (2000)	
ADS 9375 = 54 Hya	14 46.0	−25 27	Hya	5.1,7.1	8″.4 (1975)	
h 4715	14 56.5	−47 53	Lup	6.1,6.9	2″.3 (1959)	
Δ 178	15 11.6	−45 17	Lup	6.4,7.4	32″.3 (1968)	
κ[1,2] Lup	15 11.9	−48 44	Lup	3.9,5.7	26″.6 (1968)	
μ Lup	15 18.5	−47 53	Lup	5.0,5.1	1″.3 (1965)	(13)
h 4788	15 35.9	−44 58	Lup	4.7,6.6	2″.1 (1975)	
ξ Lup	15 56.9	−33 58	Lup	5.1,5.6	10″.4 (1968)	
η Lup	16 00.1	−38 24	Lup	3.4,7.8	15″.0 (1957)	
ε Nor	16 27.2	−47 33	Nor	4.5,7.2	22″.8 (1957)	
MlbO 8	16 41.3	−48 46	Ara	5.6,6.8	9″.6 (1956)	
h 4949	17 26.9	−45 51	Ara	5.6,7.1	2″.1 (1975)	
Δ 227	19 52.6	−54 58	Tel	5.8,6.5	22″.9 (1967)	
θ Ind	21 19.9	−53 27	Ind	4.5,7.1	6″.3 (1975)	
Δ 246	23 07.2	−50 41	Gru	6.3,7.0	8″.7 (1975)	
Δ 249	23 23.9	−53 49	Gru	6.2,7.1	26″.5 (1951)	
θ Phe	23 39.5	−46 38	Phe	6.5,7.3	3″.9 (1975)	

ECLIPSING VARIABLE STARS

Name	R.A h m	Dec. ° '	Type	Mag.	Epoch (2400000+)	Period (days)
ζ Phe	1 08.4	−55 15	EA	3.92−4.42V	41643.689	1.669
GG Lup	15 18.9	−40 47	EB	5.4−6.0p	34532.325	2.164
R Ara	16 39.7	−57 00	EA	6.0−6.9p	25818.028	4.425
V861 Sco	16 56.6	−40 49	EB	6.07−6.69V		7.848
V539 Ara	17 50.5	−53 37	EA	5.66−6.18V	39314.342	3.169

PULSATING VARIABLE STARS

Name	R.A h m	Dec. ° '	Type	Mag.	Epoch (2400000+)	Period (days)
R Car	9 32.2	−62 47	M	3.9−10.5v	42000	308.71
S Car	10 09.4	−61 33	M	4.5−9.9v	42112	149.49
U Car	10 57.8	−59 44	δ Cep	5.72−7.02V	37320.055	38.768
S Mus	12 12.8	−70 09	δ Cep	5.90−6.44V	35837.992	9.660
BO Mus	12 34.9	−67 45	Lb	6.0−6.7v		
R Mus	12 42.1	−69 24	δ Cep	5.93−6.73V	40896.13	7.476
V412 Cen	13 57.5	−57 43	Lb	7.1−9.6B		
θ Aps	14 05.3	−76 48	SRb	6.4−8.6p		119

ERUPTIVE VARIABLE STARS

Name	R.A h m	Dec. ° '	Type	Mag.	Epoch (2400000+)	Period (days)
VW Hyi	4 09.1	−71 18	UG	8.4−14.4v		27.8:

OTHER VARIABLE STARS

Name	R.A h m	Dec. ° '	Type	Mag.	Epoch (2400000+)	Period (days)
RU Cen	12 09.4	−45 25	RV	8.7−10.7p	28015.51	64.727
UW Cen	12 43.3	−54 32	RCB	9.1−14.5v		
RY Ara	17 21.1	−51 07	RV	9.2−12.1p	30220	143.5
RS Tel	18 18.9	−46 33	RCB	9.3−13.0p		
RR Tel	20 04.2	−55 43	Z And	6.5−16.5p		
RS Gru	21 43.1	−48 11	δ Sct	7.93−8.49V	41599.999	0.147
SX Phe	23 46.5	−41 35	δ Sct	6.78−7.51V	38636.617	0.054

Magnitudes
−1 0 1 2 3 4 5 6

Double stars   Variable stars   Nova   Open clusters   Globular clusters   Diffuse nebulae   Planetary nebulae   Galaxies

° N 1975

Constellation boundaries

Ecliptic ———— 170°   Galactic equator ———— 90°

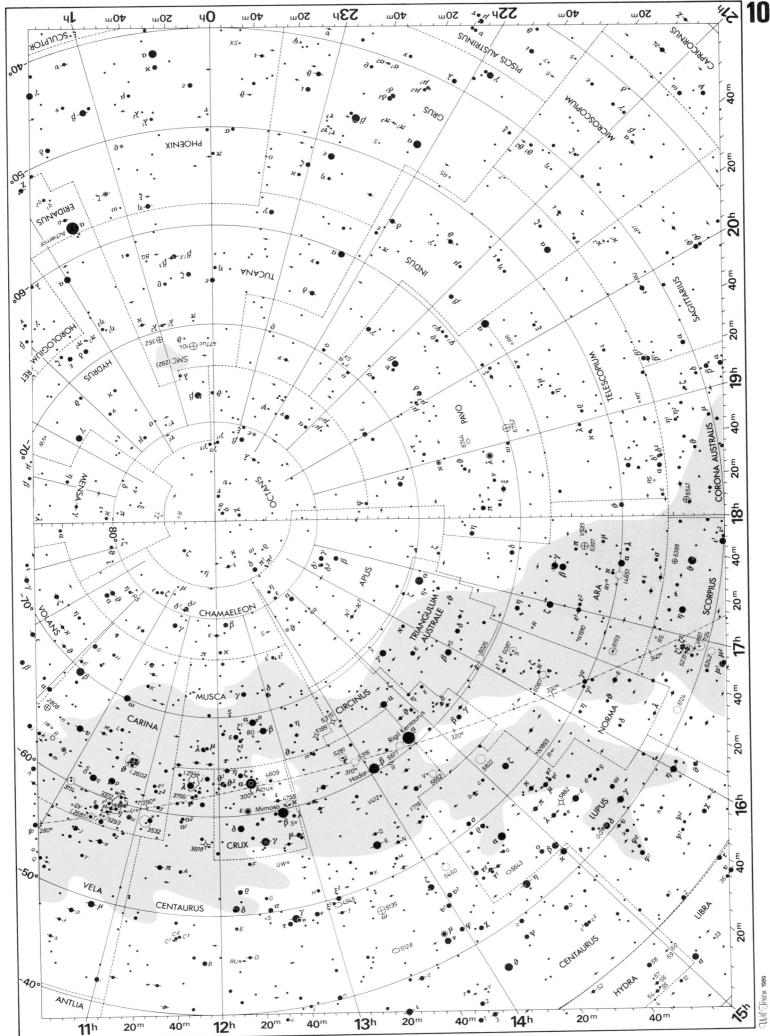

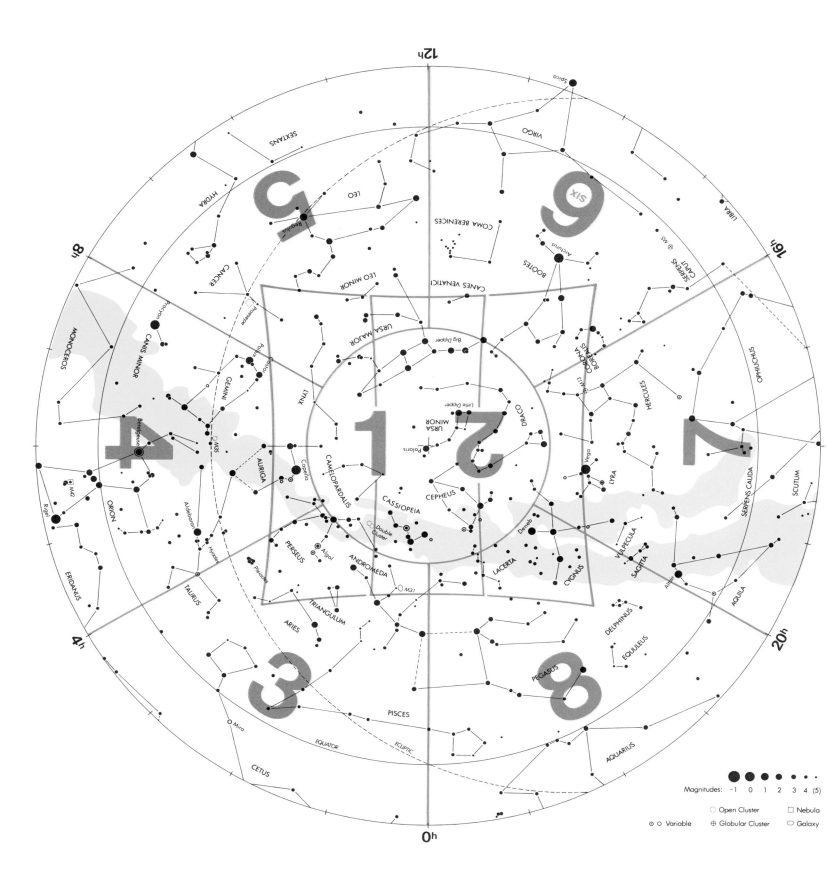

Magnitudes: -1 0 1 2 3 4 (5)

⬭ Open Cluster ▢ Nebula
⊙ ○ Variable ⊕ Globular Cluster ○ Galaxy

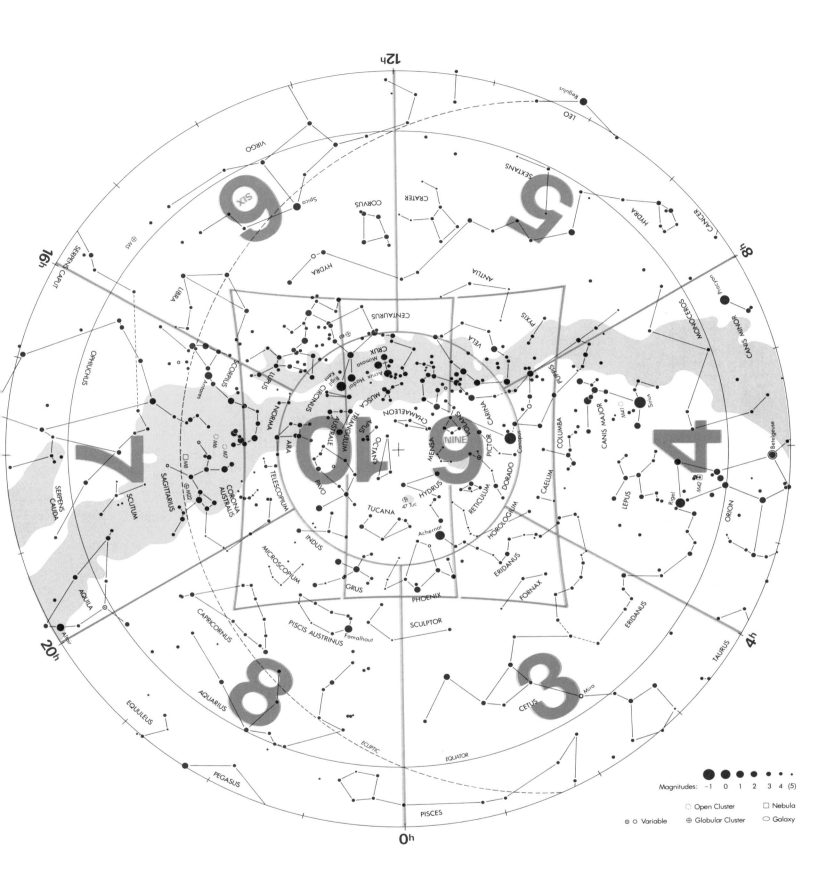

INDEX TO MESSIER OBJECTS

Object	Map	Type	Object	Map	Type
M 1 = N1952	4	gn	M56 = N6779	7	gc
M 2 = N7089	8	gc	M57 = N6720	7	pn
M 3 = N5272	6	gc	M58 = N4579	6	SAb
M 4 = N6121	6,7	gc	M59 = N4621	6	E5
M 5 = N5904	6	gc	M60 = N4649	6	E2
M 6 = N6405	7	oc	M61 = N4303	5,6	SAbc
M 7 = N6475	7	oc	M62 = N6266	7	gc
M 8 = N6523/30	7	oc-gn	M63 = N5055	1,2	SAbc
M 9 = N6333	7	gc	M64 = N4826	6	SAab
M10 = N6254	7	gc	M65 = N3623	5	SAa
M11 = N6705	7	oc	M66 = N3627	5	SAb
M12 = N6218	7	gc	M67 = N2682	5	oc
M13 = N6205	2,7	gc	M68 = N4590	6	gc
M14 = N6402	7	gc	M69 = N6637	7	gc
M15 = N7078	8	gc	M70 = N6681	7	gc
M16 = N6611	7	oc-gn	M71 = N6838	7,8	gc
M17 = N6618	7	oc-gn	M72 = N6981	8	gc
M18 = N6613	7	oc	M73 = N6994	8	oc
M19 = N6273	7	gc	M74 = N 628	3	SAc
M20 = N6514	7	oc-gn	M75 = N6864	7,8	gc
M21 = N6531	7	oc	M76 = N 650	1,2	pn
M22 = N6656	7	gc	M77 = N1068	3	SAb
M23 = N6494	7	oc	M78 = N2068/71	4	gn
M24	7	⋆cld	M79 = N1904	4	gc
M25 = I 4725	7	oc	M80 = N6093	6,7	gc
M26 = N6694	7	oc	M81 = N3031	1,2	SAab
M27 = N6853	7,8	pn	M82 = N3034	1,2	I0
M28 = N6626	7	gc	M83 = N5236	6	SBc
M29 = N6913	2,7,8	oc	M84 = N4374	5,6	E1
M30 = N7099	8	gc	M85 = N4382	5,6	SA0+
M31 = N 224	1,2,3	SAb	M86 = N4406	5,6	E3
M32 N 221	1,2,3	cE2	M87 = N4486	6	E+0-1
M33 = N 598	3	SAcd	M88 = N4501	6	SAb
M34 = N1039	1,3	oc	M89 = N4552	6	E0
M35 = N2168	4	oc	M90 = N4569	6	SAab
M36 = N1960	4	oc	M91 = N4548	6	SBb
M37 = N2099	4	oc	M92 = N6341	2,7	gc
M38 = N1912	4	oc	M93 = N2447	4,5	oc
M39 = N7092	2,8	oc	M94 = N4736	1,2,6	SAab
M40 None			M95 = N3351	5	SBb
M41 = N2287	4	oc	M96 = N3368	5	SAab
M42 = N1976	4	oc-gn	M97 = N3587	1,2	pn
M43 = N1982	4	gn	M98 = N4192	5,6	SAab
M44 = N2632	5	oc	M99 = N4254	5,6	SAc
M45 Pleiades	3,4	oc-gn	M100 = N4321	5,6	SAbc
M46 = N2437	4,5	oc	M101 = N5457	1,2	SAcd
M47 = N2422	4,5	oc	M102 None		
M48 = N2548	5	oc	M103 = N 581	1,2	oc
M49 = N4472	5,6	E2	M104 = N4594	6	SAa
M50 = N2323	4	oc	M105 = N3379	5	E1
M51 = N5194	1,2	SAbc	M106 = N4258	1,2,5	SAbc
M52 = N7654	1,2	oc	M107 = N6171	7	gc
M53 = N5024	6	gc	M108 = N3556	1,2	SBcd
M54 = N6715	7	gc	M109 = N3992	1,2	SBbc
M55 = N6809	7,8	gc	M110 = N 205	1,2,3	dE5

Variable Star Classification

δ Cep	cepheid, classical type
δ Sct	δ Sct type, pulsating stars of spectral class A and F
CWa	cepheid, W Vir type
EA	eclipsing, Algol type
EB	eclipsing, β Lyr type
EW	eclipsing, W UMa type
E	eclipsing, type unknown
Lb	slow irregular type
Lc	irregular supergiants of late spectral type
M	Mira, long period variable
NL	nova like stars
Nr(E)	recurrent novae and eclipsing variable
Nr	recurrent novae
RCB	R CrB type, high luminosity stars with non-periodic drops in brightness
RRab	RR Lyr with sharp asymmetric light curves
RRc	RR Lyr with symmetric sinusoidal light curves
RVa	RV Tauri type with constant mean brightness
RVb	RV Tauri type with varying mean brightness
RV	unspecified RV Tauri type
S Dor	high luminosity stars of spectral classes Bpeq-Fpeq, irregular variations
SRa	semi-regular, late spectral class, strong periodicities
SRb	semi-regular, late spectral class, weak periodicities
SRc	semi-regular, late spectral class, disk component stars
SRd	semi-regular, spectrum F, G, or K
SR	semi-regular, unknown type
UG	U Gem, SS Cyg type, outbursts
Z And	Z And type (symbiotic stars)
Z Cam	Z Cam type, UG type variations with standstills

THE GREEK ALPHABET

Name	Capital	Small	Name	Capital	Small
Alpha	A	α	Nu	N	ν
Beta	B	β	Xi	Ξ	ξ
Gamma	Γ	γ	Omicron	O	o
Delta	Δ	δ	Pi	Π	π
Epsilon	E	ε	Rho	P	ϱ
Zeta	Z	ζ	Sigma	Σ	σ
Eta	H	η	Tau	T	τ
Theta	Θ	ϑ	Upsilon	Υ	υ
Iota	I	ι	Phi	Φ	φ
Kappa	K	κ	Chi	X	χ
Lambda	Λ	λ	Psi	Ψ	ψ
Mu	M	μ	Omega	Ω	ω

MAGNITUDE CLASSIFICATION

p	photographic-blue
v	visual
V	photoelectric visual
B	photoelectric blue